ACCOUNTING
RESEARCH
STUDY NO. 6

REPORTING THE

FINANCIAL EFFECTS

OF PRICE-LEVEL CHANGES

By the Staff of the Accounting
Research Division of the American
Institute of Certified Public Accountants

Published by the
American Institute of Certified Public Accountants, Inc.
666 Fifth Avenue   New York, New York   10019

This study is financed by funds from the AICPA Foundation and sets forth
the views of the authors. Its publication by the American Institute of CPAs
does not in any way constitute official endorsement or approval of the conclusions reached or the opinions expressed.

REPORTING THE

FINANCIAL EFFECTS

OF PRICE-LEVEL CHANGES

0197700-4

Table of Contents

Lists *a number of studies of actual situations which
have been carried out even though the results were not
incorporated in the financial reports of the companies
involved. The methods used and the findings of these
studies are summarized.*

Acknowledgments

The entire staff of the Accounting Research Division had an active part in this study. Each member contributed something more than routine assistance to a major part of the whole—Harold Arnett (now at the University of Michigan), Leonard Lorensen, Perry Mason, Alexander Russ, Reed Storey and Cecilia Tierney. Perry Mason had participated in the American Accounting Association's study of price-level changes under the direction of Ralph C. Jones (a member of the advisory committee on this project) and was accordingly already conversant with the technical difficulties involved. I am especially grateful to Cecilia Tierney for her patient conquest of the index number problem. Her major contribution (Appendix A, page 121) is far more comprehensive, definitive and leading than any similar work on index numbers directed to the accounting problem.

Professor Dorothy S. Brady of the University of Pennsylvania reviewed the index number material for technical accuracy. A leading statistician, she had previously served on the committee of the National Bureau of Economic Research that analyzed the statistical procedures of the U. S. Bureau of Labor Statistics. Both her considerable technical competence and her practical experience were placed at our disposal and our study is the beneficiary.

Carman Blough acted as chairman of a project advisory committee that took an active interest in the study at all stages and contributed much in the way of suggestions and criticisms. The other members of the committee are Solomon Fabricant, Ralph C. Jones, Mark Massel, Herbert E. Miller, Russell Morrison, Alexander L. Stott, Robert C. Tyson, and William W. Werntz. The comments of Herbert E. Miller, Russell Morrison, and Robert C. Tyson will be found on pages 250 to 253. The fact that their comments may be restricted to specific parts of our study does not necessarily mean that they agree with all the other parts. Similarly, the absence of comment by the other members does not imply agreement. The obligation imposed on the members of an advisory committee is not to agree or disagree with the conclusions or recommendations of a research study but rather to make the milder judgment as to the suitability of the study for publication for purposes of education and discussion.

New York, N. Y., July 1963   MAURICE MOONITZ
                                     Director of Accounting Research

The Accounting Research Study on price levels was completed prior to my appointment as director of accounting research. The time required for printing has afforded me the opportunity of commending the quality of this research work and endorsing its publication.

October 1963   PAUL GRADY

Highlights

1. The annotated bibliography of actual cases where price-level adjustments have been carried out (Appendix E, page 221) together with the volume of literature on the subject give clear evidence of the widespread concern of businessmen and accountants with the need for changes in financial reporting to reflect the effects of inflation and deflation.

2. The examples quoted from financial statements around the world are sufficient to demonstrate that recognition of price-level changes in financial statements is practical, and not misleading or dangerous to investors.

3. The study of the index number problem indicates that at least one index of the general price level is available in the United States and is reliable enough for use in financial statements.

4. The effects of price-level changes should be disclosed as a supplement to the conventional statements. This disclosure may take the form of physically separate statements, or of parallel columns in a combined statement, or of detailed supporting schedules (including charts and graphs), or some combination of these.

5. In the supplementary data, all elements of the financial statements (e.g., balance sheet, income statement, analysis of retained earnings) should be restated by means of a single index of the general price level as of the balance-sheet date so that all the financial data will be expressed in terms of dollars of the same purchasing power.

6. Restatement by means of a single index of the general price level is not a means of introducing replacement costs into the financial statements. To introduce replacement costs requires the use of current

market prices, or appraisals, or a series of highly specific indexes, one for each account or group of accounts in the financial statements. For the sake of simplicity and precision in analysis, this study assumes that replacement costs are *not* to be introduced into the financial statements. With or without replacement costs, the measurement and disclosure of the effects of changes in the purchasing power of the dollar (as measured by an index of the movement in *all* prices) is still desirable.

7. Gains or losses do not arise from recognizing the effect of a changing price level on the nonmonetary items (principally the inventories, the fixed assets, and the equity of the common shareholders). The recognition of the effect of a changing price level on these items is merely a restatement of acquisition cost or of owners' equity in terms of the purchasing power of the dollar at the balance-sheet date.

8. Gains or losses do arise from recognizing the effect of a changing price level on the monetary items (principally the cash balance and the contracts to receive or pay money). The recognition of the effect of a changing price level on these items results in a gain or loss from inflation which should be separately disclosed.

9. This study neither expresses nor implies any recommendations on questions of social policy (e.g., Who is injured by inflation or deflation? Who benefits from it? Who should pay for it? How can it be controlled?) or on the impact on rate regulation in the case of public utilities or on the tax definition of income. The study is centered on the proposition that the major accounting issue created by a changing price level is the accuracy of the *measurements* of the results of operations and of financial position, and that more accurate measures will be beneficial to all who use or are influenced by financial statements.

10. Because so many of the goods and services currently available resulted from wartime (World War II) and postwar technology, the precision of comparisons of current price levels with those prevailing in periods prior to World War II are unreliable. For this reason, a 1945 cut-off date is proposed in preference to using prewar or even wartime index numbers for the adjustment of the applicable data in financial statements.

1

The Problem in Perspective

A. BACKGROUND OF THIS PROJECT

On November 4, 1960, the Accounting Principles Board of the American Institute of Certified Public Accountants discussed whether a consideration of the effects on accounting of price-level changes should be incorporated in the study of the basic postulates and broad principles of accounting or in a separate research project. By the time of the meeting on April 28, 1961 it became clear that the price-level problem was too complex for adequate treatment in the postulates and principles studies. As a result the Board took the action summarized in the following excerpt from its minutes:

> . . . the Board . . . agreed that the assumption in accounting that fluctuations in the value of the dollar may be ignored is unrealistic, and that therefore the Director of Accounting Research should be instructed to set up a research project to study the problem and to prepare a report in which recommendations are made for the disclosure of the effect of price-level changes upon the financial statements. In this study, special attention should be paid to the use of supplementary statements as a means of disclosure.

One aspect of the Board's preliminary discussion of the price-level problem is noteworthy. A general feeling was expressed that if price-level changes were to be introduced into financial reporting, the effects on all elements of the financial statements should be disclosed. A piecemeal or partial approach, for example, which would adjust one item and leave all others unadjusted was not viewed with favor. It is to the credit of the accounting profession in this country that it has resisted strong pressures to back partial adjustments which have little or nothing to do with improved reporting of the financial position or results of operations, but instead are designed to buttress a campaign for tax relief or other nonaccounting objectives. These other objectives are frequently worthy of support in their own right and on their merits but they do not supply a sufficient basis for a change in accounting principles.

The study actually got under way in the fall of 1961. At the time of the first meeting of the project advisory committee on October 13, 1961, the Director of Accounting Research pointed out that the problem of price-level changes had been discussed for many years, both here and abroad, and that techniques to deal with the problem in accounting had been developed and demonstrated without resolving the question as to what should be done at the reporting level. In view of the work done by others (see Selected Bibliography, page 254, for specific examples), the Director thought that the Institute's project could be simplified by concentrating on

2

1. A clarification of the meaning of "price-level adjustments" of accounting data by the use of an index of the general price level

2. A study of the indexes currently available and

3. An exploration of the forms that disclosure of price-level changes has taken or could take.

The study of "The Basic Postulates of Accounting"[1] did include some discussion of the price-level problem in a passage on "the monetary unit" and the formulation of a postulate that "accounting reports should be based on a stable measuring unit."[2]

By way of comment on this postulate, the study pointed out that:

> Stated in this fashion, the proposition leaves open certain factual (statistical) questions, for example, (1) has the U. S. dollar been so unstable as to warrant the use of some other basis (e.g., another currency; index numbers); (2) are the methods of measur-

---

[1] Maurice Moonitz, "The Basic Postulates of Accounting," *Accounting Research Study No. 1.* American Institute of Certified Public Accountants. 1961. Accounting research studies are prepared to stimulate discussion, and are not official statements of policy.

[2] *Ibid.,* pp. 44-46. Postulate C-4, p. 50.

ing instability reliable enough to warrant the introduction of a new basis of measurement?

＊　　＊　　＊　　＊　　＊

The evidence of the instability of the monetary unit in recent decades is overwhelming; the probability that the instability will prevail into the foreseeable future is high. Accountants should move quickly therefore to implement modest proposals such as those of the Study Group and the American Accounting Association Committee.

The Division of Accounting Research is setting up a research project to study the problem of price-level changes. This project is based on the premise that it is no longer realistic to ignore fluctuations in the value of the dollar. The study will pay special attention to the use of supplementary statements, but other methods of disclosure will be explored.

The later study of accounting principles did recommend the disclosure of the effects of price-level changes but did not support the recommendation with detailed analysis:

> We observe that it is technically feasible to reflect changes in some assets in a more timely fashion, and thereby give more current information in the balance sheet. In this connection we propose to use a classification that distinguishes among (a) the amount attributable to changes in the dollar (price-level changes). . . .

＊　　＊　　＊　　＊　　＊

> As the preceding discussion indicates, we are in agreement with the Board that "the assumption in accounting that fluctuations in the value of the dollar may be ignored is unrealistic. . . ." Furthermore, because a separate study is under way to explore the price-level problem, we have not, in this study, given any detailed attention to its impact on accounting. That detailed attention is given in the study now under way, the results of which should be published in the near future.[3]

The passages quoted do not indicate whether the "classification" proposed is to be incorporated into the primary (official, conventional) statements or in supplementary statements because the effects of price-level changes will be the same in nature and in magnitude whichever method of disclosure is adopted. Other parts of the "Principles" study

3

---

[3] Robert T. Sprouse and Maurice Moonitz, "A Tentative Set of Broad Accounting Principles for Business Enterprises," *Accounting Research Study No. 3.* American Institute of Certified Public Accountants. 1962, pp. 17-18.

do make reference to "primary or supplementary statements." One example is given here, with emphasis supplied:

> All items of plant and equipment in service, or held in stand-by status, should be recorded at cost of acquisition or construction, with appropriate modification for the effect of the changing dollar *either in the primary statements or in supplementary statements. . . .*[4]

Primarily because supplementary statements (including schedules, charts, graphs, and notes) have marked advantages in a period of education, experimentation, and transition, the present study assumes that they will be used to disclose price-level effects. The consequence of this procedure is that the effects of price-level changes are reported as additional information and interpretation for the benefit of investors and others interested in what has been going on in the business concern.

As part of this same conception, the present study does not discuss the impact of price-level changes on rate regulation (public utilities) or on tax policies. These and other similar questions of social policy (e.g., what should be done about inflation, by whom, and by what means) are beyond the scope of this inquiry. Instead the position is taken that the major *accounting* issue created by a changing price level is the accuracy of the *measurements* of the results of operations and of financial position.

B. CHANGING PRICES AND CHANGING DOLLARS

The investigation of the problem had not proceeded very far before it became evident that "price-level adjustment" means different things to different people. In some discussions, for example, the term refers to an approximation of current replacement cost by the use of index numbers that measure the changes in prices of specific commodities. This usage probably arose because the term "replacement cost" came into disfavor in the early 30's when it became clear that the writeup of asset values during the 20's, which were supposedly based on re-placement costs as determined by appraisals, had often resulted in flagrant overvaluations. Because many accountants today still associate the term with its former abuse, there is a tendency to avoid it. Adjust-

---

[4] *Ibid. p. 57.*

ment for "price-level" change, on the other hand, does not carry over-tones from the past. As a result, the objective measure of changes in either the price-level or the prices of specific commodities by use of index numbers has been referred to as a "price-level adjustment." The label, however, is properly applied to the former, but not the latter.

In this study, use of the term "price-level change" is limited to the change in the general purchasing power of the dollar that occurs during a period of inflation or deflation. Accordingly, this study views the purpose of "price-level adjustments" to be the expression of each item in the financial statements in terms of a "common" dollar, that is, in terms of dollars of the same general purchasing power.

This approach appears to be in accord with most discussions of price-level changes. Of the published financial statements analyzed in which the "price-level effect" had been disclosed, however, few companies actually followed a procedure which adjusted for the decline in the value of the monetary unit during inflation. Most made adjustments for changes in the prices of individual items of inventory, plant, or equipment. In other words, the accounts were adjusted to a current cost basis without separate disclosure of the extent to which the in-creased cost was attributable to an elastic dollar and how much to changes in the relative market position of the individual item. Index numbers were used to make the adjustment from historical (acquisi-tion) cost to current replacement cost, but the use of index numbers does not necessarily result in adjustment for price-level changes. The index numbers used in these cases were indexes of highly specific com-modities or groups of commodities and not measures of the movements of the general price level. (Examples of disclosure in financial state-ments are given in Appendix D, page 169, of the study.) The use of index numbers merely expedited the objective approximation of cur-rent replacement costs.

This confusion as to the meaning of "price level," "common dollar," and "purchasing power of the dollar" has to be reckoned with. This research study on "price-level changes" is not aimed at resolving the relative merits of historical (acquisition) cost for inventories and fixed assets, with or without correction for general price-level effects, as compared with the systematic use of current replacement costs, whether calculated on the basis of direct quotations of market prices or by the use of special index numbers. The study is aimed at explor-ing the problems to be encountered if, as a matter of practice, financial statements are to disclose the effects of general price-level changes. The evidence accumulated thus far, however, indicates that the study

5

should spell out in detail the distinction between the accounting effects of changes in the market prices of goods and services when the dollar is stable and the accounting effects of the same changes when the dollar is unstable.

Changing Prices and a Stable Dollar

As measured by the index derived from the calculations of Gross National Product, the general level of prices in the U. S. moved less than 5 per cent in the four-year period, 1959-62, inclusive.[5] For all practical purposes, then, this period was one of stable prices *in general;* in other words, the dollar did not change very much in its function as a standard of exchange-value or as a measure of purchasing power. Nevertheless, individual prices and groups of prices did move. With respect to the year 1961, for example, the "Survey of Current Business" makes comments like the following in a section titled "Stable Prices During Year":[6]

... there were price declines of some importance during the year in the fuel, rubber and chemical product groups. ...

... Price reductions were marked in electrical machinery. There was some evidence of a strengthening in equipment prices toward the end of the year mainly under the influence of the rising prices of agricultural machinery.

✿ ✿ ✿ ✿ ✿

... Used car prices increased substantially through most of 1961. ...

Even in a period of over-all price stability some individual prices move up, some down. But in every case they move because the supply and demand factors that determine their market behavior are different from the supply and demand factors affecting money and "the dollar." Since the dollar was stable, for all practical purposes, in this 1959-62 period, the monetary factors (e.g., a change in the quantity of money

6

---

[5] U. S. Dept. of Commerce, *Survey of Current Business,* Feb. 1962 and 1963. The data are as follows, with 1954 = 100:

1959	112.7
1960	114.4
1961	115.8
1962	117.4

[6] Feb. 1962, pp. 23-24.

and credit) that bring about inflation or deflation were in equilibrium. The changes in the prices of individual goods and services then had to be the result of factors other than the monetary ones.

In terms of traditional accounting standards, these individual price changes give rise to profits and losses. To buy at a lower price and sell at a higher one in these circumstances is to make a profit; to buy at a higher price and sell at a lower one is to suffer a loss. This relationship is true in a direct fashion in the case of dealings in merchandise or other stock in trade. It is also true in the case of plant and equipment, but less directly. A rise in the market price (replacement cost) of equipment, for example, is not recorded in the accounts under conventional accounting standards. The benefit from having bought at the lower price is reflected in a lower depreciation cost, lower than that on equipment acquired more recently by the business entity itself or by one of its competitors.

Even if the higher replacement cost is recorded, the increase is in the nature of an unrealized profit (e.g., appraisal surplus). Its recording does not change the total *amount* of profit earned by the business over its lifetime; it may change the *accounting period* in which the profit is reported. To sum up, whether the changed market price is reflected before or at time of sale or other conversion does not alter the nature of the change itself. The change is in the nature of profit or loss. The mere fact of variations in individual prices is therefore no evidence at all as to the existence of inflation or deflation; these variations reflect the ordinary normal functioning of a market economy.

Changing Prices and an Unstable Dollar

As measured by the index derived from the calculations of Gross National Product, the general level of prices in the U. S. increased more than 70 per cent in the 18-year period, 1945-62, inclusive.[7] On the average, if the size of the dollar is measured by its purchasing power in 1945, it had shrunk from 100 per cent to 58 per cent by 1962.

---

[7] The indexes for selected years are listed below, as published by the U. S. Department of Commerce. (1954 = 100)

1945	68.0
1950	89.5
1955	101.2
1960	114.4
1962	117.4

7

Meanwhile, the individual prices of some goods and services moved upward and some moved downward. These changes in individual prices occurred partly as the result of the same type of market factors referred to in the preceding discussion of "changing prices and a stable dollar," and partly as the result of the factors that caused the value of the dollar to shrink about 40 per cent in 18 years. These new factors are merely of passing interest if the only prices involved are those which prevail on a given date. They are of critical interest, however, if prices at two or more points of time are to be compared for any reason whatsoever. The dollar of 1962 is a different size in its command over goods and services from the one of 1960 or 1955 or 1950 or 1945. To make comparisons that are logical and meaningful, the differences must be allowed for in some manner or other. The bulk of this study is, in essence, a study of the most sophisticated technique thus far devised for making this allowance, namely, the use of a measure of the general level of prices.

The problems created for accounting by a changing dollar remain whether the accounts are kept on a conventional basis of historical cost or on a market price (replacement-cost) basis. As pointed out in the preceding section, the essential difference between historical cost and current (replacement) cost is in the *timing* of the recognition of profit or loss, and this difference between the two kinds of cost is not affected by the presence of a changing dollar. What *is* changed is the validity of the measure of the *amount* of profit or loss as reported on either basis, historical cost or replacement cost. If an investment is made in assets in 1945 and recovered in 1962, the resultant amount of gain or loss is not measurable in any meaningful sense by a comparison of dollars received (recovered) with dollars paid out (invested). As in all types of accounting analysis, the problem at hand is not solved solely by a satisfactory determination of the *size* of a business event. Its solution requires a further determination as to the nature of the change, e.g., whether it represents a "return of capital," a "return on capital," or a mere transfer or substitution of one item for another without effect on capital.

The Value of Money

The price (i.e., the value in exchange) of a unit of any good or service is an expression of the "bundle of things in general" which can be obtained in exchange for it. If the unit-price is $100, then the good or service can be exchanged for $100 in money which, in turn, can be spent on a unit of any other good or service or any combination of goods or services with a value in exchange (i.e., a price) of $100. Similarly, the value of a unit of money is an expression of things in general which can be obtained in exchange for it, and that value can vary, just as the value of any good or service can vary for the same kinds of reasons. Finally, the variation in the value of a unit of money can be measured in the same way that the variation in the value of a unit of any good or service can be measured, namely, by measuring the change in the "bundle of things in general" which can be obtained in exchange for it. This change can be measured by observing the behavior of an index of the level of prices in general.[8]

Index Numbers to Measure an Unstable Dollar

To measure the changes in the dollar from time to time in a *direct* fashion would require a market place or other equivalent device where the dollars of different years were in fact bought and sold in arms'-length exchange transactions. Such a market place does not exist, certainly not within the domestic economy of the U. S. If it did, ten "1962 dollars," for example, would have exchanged for approximately six "1945 dollars," based on the evidence of the index numbers already cited. These explicit "exchange rates" for dollars of different years would then provide the basis for an objective translation of accounting data to a common basis.

9

A market place that is "direct" with respect to money is the foreign exchange market in which the money of one country is exchanged for the money of another country, both moneys representing debt-paying media. In some cases and under certain circumstances, the quotations in the foreign exchange market can, in effect, be used for the purpose of recording business events in terms of a more stable unit of measurement. Apparently this was done to some extent in Central Europe during the great inflations of the early 1920's when transactions were recorded as though they had been effectuated in Swiss gold francs rather than in the local currencies actually used.

This "solution" to the "price-level problem" merely shifts the basic problem from the instability of one kind of money (e.g., marks) to the instability of another kind of money (e.g., Swiss gold francs) between

---

[8] See D. H. Robertson, *Money*. Chicago, 1957, espec. chapter 2. This booklet is one of the *Cambridge Economic Handbooks*, originally published by the Cambridge (Eng.) University Press.

two or more points of time. It undoubtedly resulted in better financial reports at the time, but even the improved reports were based on an inherently unstable unit of measurement.

A somewhat more satisfactory measure can be obtained if an indirect measure is accepted in place of a direct measure. This indirect measure is the exchange-ratio between the domestic currency (e.g., the dollar) in its capacity as "free capital" and all the goods and services it is capable of acquiring. This indirect measure is made by the use of index numbers representing the movement in the prices of all the goods and services in the country at specified points of time. More accurately, it is the *reciprocal* of the price index that measures the movement in the dollar. A doubling in an all-commodity index or index of the general price level, e.g., from 100 to 200, is the same thing as a reduction by one-half in the size (the purchasing power) of the dollar over the same period of time.

The technical problems of index number construction, with a discussion of the weaknesses and strengths of available indexes, together with some tentative conclusions and recommendations, will be found in Appendix A, page 61. In addition, the Supplement to this chapter, page 17, contains material that is pertinent to this problem.

10

Impact on Financial Reports

A detailed exposition of the impact of price-level changes on financial reports is presented in Appendix B, page 121. At this point a summary statement is given to provide perspective.

With respect to "invested costs" or "nonmonetary items" (e.g., assets that are not in the form of money or claims to money), and with all technical details aside, the dollar amounts ascribed to the item at one point of time may be restated in terms of the dollar at any other point of time by the use of a suitable index of the general price level. Thus, $10,000 invested at a time when the general index stands at 125 becomes $14,000 when the same index rises to 175, and becomes $8,000 when the index drops to 100. This kind of change logically has nothing whatever to do with gain or loss, realized or unrealized. It is a simple restatement of invested cost to compensate for a "yardstick" that contains thirty-six "inches" of different length at different points of time. No profit or loss emerges because the adjustment of "basis" for profit determination is not the result of an actual or potential sale, a shift in the market price of the item, the performance of any economic activity by the business, a using-up of an asset in whole or in part, or any other real event that would give rise to a gain or loss. The adjustment simply recasts or restates precisely the same information as before (e.g., invested cost) in terms of the "new" situation with respect to the dollar.

With respect to the "monetary items" (e.g., claims to money such as bank deposits, receivables, and payables) the dollar amounts ascribed to the item at óne point of time may also be restated in terms of the dollar at some other point of time. But, unlike the "nonmonetary" case, the restatement cannot stop there. A gain or loss on the monetary item occurs as the purchasing power of the dollar decreases or increases because the dollar as legal tender does not change and has not changed in this country since the Gold Standard Act of 1900 made all U. S. moneys interchangeable at face amount. Accordingly the monetary items are worth their face amount at maturity, no more and no less, and a gain or loss on holding a balance of "net monetary items" emerges as the result of restating the accounting data. To illustrate, consider the following simple example in which a monetary and a nonmonetary item are held while the general price-level index rises from 100 to 200. The accounts are to be restated in terms of the situation at the end of the period.

11

	Index = 100	Restate			Index = 200
Cash	$1,000	(1) $1,000	1,000 (2)		$1,000
Land, at cost	1,000	(1) 1,000			2,000
	$2,000				$3,000
Capital	$2,000			$2,000 (1)	$4,000
Loss from hold-ing cash		(2) 1,000			(1,000)
	$2,000	$3,000	$3,000		$3,000

Entry (1) under "Restate" converts each element into the dollar (in the economic or business sense) at the end of the year by multiplying the initial amount by $\frac{200}{100}$. Entry (2) under "Restate" reduces the cash balance to its face amount which is its debt paying ability as determined by law. As a short cut, these two entries can be combined in any case where the accounts are to be restated in terms of the dollar current at the balance-sheet date. In the preceding example, a single restatement could have been made, increasing Land, $1,000, and Capital, $2,000, and recording a loss on monetary items of $1,000.

This short-cut technique is used in the examples and discussion of Chapter 2, page 23, and Appendixes B and C, pages 121 and 137. The result is consistent with a common sense interpretation—an invested cost of 1,000 "date-of-acquisition" dollars is restated as the equivalent of 2,000 "end-of-period" dollars, with no gain or loss recorded, while cash held through a doubling of the price level loses half its value, or $1,000, measured in "end-of-period" dollars. The technical details are elaborated further in Appendix C.

One striking feature of the gain or loss on monetary items is that it has no counterpart in conventional accounting (with the possible exception of gains or losses on foreign exchange transactions). In the case of the nonmonetary items, by contrast, every element does have a counterpart. For example, inventories, cost of goods sold, equipment, and depreciation on equipment are found in the balance sheets and operating reports whether the financial statements are adjusted for the effects of price-level changes or not. With respect to these nonmonetary items, "price-level adjustments" introduce new measures (i.e., in terms of "new" dollars) of old categories, but do not introduce new categories. With respect to the monetary items, however, the reverse is true — the $1,000 cash balance in the example just given was $1,000 in terms of both "date-of-acquisition" and "end-of-period" dollars, so that no change in the amount of cash was introduced. But the "loss" of 1,000 "end-of-year" dollars is a new category, with no counterpart in conventional (unadjusted) statements.

Reporting the Gain or Loss on Monetary Items

The principal problem at this point is to determine an appropriate method of reporting this new category of gain or loss on net monetary balances. In order to pinpoint clearly the relationship of this gain or loss to financial position as a whole, a brief analysis is presented,[9] using the following five symbols:

$$M = \text{total amount of monetary assets}$$
$$N = \text{total amount of nonmonetary assets}$$
$$L = \text{total amount of liabilities, all}$$
$$\text{assumed to be monetary}$$

---

[9] Adapted from R. J. Chambers, "Towards a General Theory of Accounting," Australian Society of Accountants Annual Lecture, 1961, University of Adelaide

R = total amount of residual equity
p = proportionate rise in price level

Assume that a business engages in no transactions during a period in which the price level rises from 1 to $(1 + p)$.

Position at beginning of period:

$$M + N = L + R \tag{1}$$

Recognize the rise in the price level by multiplying all terms by $(1 + p)$:

$$M(1 + p) + N(1 + p) = L(1 + p) + R(1 + p) \tag{2}$$

But by assumption the business has the same monetary assets and liabilities at the end of the period; by law these monetary items have the same magnitude at the end as at the beginning of the period. The financial position of the business is therefore more correctly stated by the following equation (balance sheet):

$$M + N(1 + p) = L + [R(1 + p) + (Lp - Mp)] \tag{3}$$ 13

The last term, $Lp - Mp$, is the net gain (loss) on holding monetary items. Examination of [3] indicates that if monetary items are not adjusted for price-level changes, but nonmonetary assets (N) and beginning balance of owners equity (R) are so adjusted, the gain (loss) on holding monetary items (M, L) will be equal to the amount necessary to "balance" the equation (the balance sheet).

The net gain or loss on monetary items would then be reported (1) in the statement of changes in owners' equity, (2) as a component part of the calculation of net income for the period, or (3) in a statement of net income and inflation gain or loss. Because it is a new category in accounting, with no counterpart in conventional (unadjusted) statements, we feel that it should not be "buried" in owners' equity, but instead should be shown either as the last element in or immediately following the calculation of net income. It should be distinctly labeled and separately set forth.

Since there is considerable disagreement as to the proper handling of these items, other viewpoints are presented in Appendix C in the section titled "Reporting Purchasing-Power Gains and Losses," page 149, and in an addendum to Appendix C by Marvin Deupree titled "Accounting for Gains and Losses in Purchasing Power of Monetary Items," page 153.

Restatement of Prior Years' Financial Statements

Assume that price-level adjusted financial statements are included in annual reports to stockholders as supplementary statements. If the price level continues to change, should all prior years' data included for comparative purposes be restated in terms of the price level used in the current year's statements? If the comparisons are to reflect real differences and not represent an optical illusion, prior years' data will have to be restated in subsequent reports for comparative purposes. Technically this restatement is not difficult to do, as illustrated in Appendix B, but psychologically it may pose substantial problems. If the price level is changing, however, and current year's statements are stated in terms of the current price level, the restatement of the significant data from prior years is unavoidable. It is the price level that is changing and not the accounting "principles" involved. The very heart of the "money illusion" has always been the belief that the unit of measure (the "dollar") is stable and that "prices" (i.e., values in exchange) are in motion when in fact the exchange-values may be reasonably stable and the unit of measure itself in flux.

14

In the midst of all this flux, some stabilizing elements are present. Take, for example, the case of a set of supplementary financial statements that have been completely restated in terms of the price level prevailing at the end of 1960, with the relevant index assumed to be at 100. If the index is at 120 in 1965, those same financial statements are restated in terms of the price level at that time merely by multiplying every figure by 1.2. As a result none of the relationships among the elements of the financial statements are disturbed by this type of translation. For example, the ratios of current assets to current liabilities, of liabilities to stockholders' equity, of net profit to sales, etc., are not changed by a rolling forward (or backward, for that matter) of the data contained in a set of financial statements already stated in terms of the price level prevailing at any given point of time.

C. WHAT DIFFERENCE DOES IT MAKE?

The preceding discussion demonstrates that if price-level changes can be measured in some satisfactory manner, and if the effects of those changes can be properly disclosed, the inferences that can be drawn from accounting data will be statistically more reliable. Specifically, for example, all the revenues and expenses in the earnings statement for any one year will be expressed in dollars of the same size and not in a mixture of dollars from different years. Similarly, the various balance-sheet items will all be expressed in terms of a common dollar. Since both the results of operations and financial position will be stated in terms of the same "common dollar," a calculation of a rate of return on invested capital can be made in which both numerator and denominator are expressed in the same units.

Some inferences can be drawn in terms of the various groups interested in business activity. Investors and their representatives (e.g., management, including the board of directors) can tell whether the capital invested in the business has been increased or decreased as the result of all the policies followed and all the financial events that have taken place bearing on the business entity. More specifically, management and owners can tell if the dividend policy actually followed in the past has resulted in distributions out of economic or business capital, and, if not, what proportion of the earnings (adjusted for price-level changes) has in fact been distributed. With price-level adjusted data before them, the directors can tell if a proposed dividend will equal, exceed, or fall short of current earnings, or any other norm or standard they wish to use.

15

Owners, management, and government can tell if taxes levied on income were less than pretax earnings, and if so, to what extent, and, if not, how much they exceeded pretax earnings. Creditors will be better informed as to the buffer or cushion behind their claims. In addition, employees, as well as investors, and management will have a more reliable gauge of the rate of return to date on the capital employed, and will be able to use the information more intelligently to decide if the business entity has been profitable or not.

Financial statements fully adjusted for the effect of price-level changes will also reveal the losses or gains from holding or owing monetary items. All interested groups then have one important measure of the effect of a changing dollar on their position as debtors or creditors.

The advantages of price-level adjusted financial data should not be exaggerated. That is why the preceding discussion has leaned so heavily on the *comparative* improvement potentially available from the use of "common-dollar" accounting, instead of trying to determine which procedure is "right" and which is "wrong." The case has been well put by George O. May who wrote:

It has been said that the proposal here put forward contemplates a departure from the accepted manner of using the monetary unit as the unit of accounting. It has even been suggested ... that the proposal involves the *adoption* of an elastic yardstick. But the yardstick used has always been elastic and its usefulness has been impaired (though not destroyed) by that fact. Today a natural elasticity has been supplanted by an artificial and purposive elasticity which goes much further towards destroying the appropriateness of the monetary unit for secondary employment in accounting in the same way as in the past.

The proposal does not contemplate discontinuance of the use of the yardstick. It is intended only to use the yardstick intelligently with a frank recognition of its defects, rather than to close one's eyes to its shortcomings.[10]

In a nutshell, financial data adjusted for price-level effects provide a basis for a more intelligent, better informed allocation of resources, whether those resources are in the hands of individuals, of business entities, or of government.

16

---

[10] *Business Income and Price Levels—An Accounting Study,* a monograph prepared for The Study Group on Business Income, July 1, 1949. pp. 72-73.

Exchange Value, Money, Price, and the Price-level Problem

In order to visualize the essence of the price-level problem as it affects accounting measurements and financial statements, assume a situation in which three commodities, g, s, and m, are the only ones available. Assume further the following relationship among the three: **17**

	Relative Importance
1 unit of g =	10
1 unit of s =	4
1 unit of m =	2

In other words, the following "ratios of exchange" prevail:

g/s $=$ $^{10}/_4$, or 1 unit of g $=$ 2½ units of s
s/g $=$ $^4/_{10}$, or 1 unit of s $=$ ⅖ units of g
g/m $=$ $^{10}/_2$, or 1 unit of g $=$ 5 units of m
m/g $=$ $^2/_{10}$, or 1 unit of m $=$ ⅕ units of g
s/m $=$ $^4/_2$, or 1 unit of s $=$ 2 units of m
m/s $=$ $^2/_4$, or 1 unit of m $=$ ½ units of s

Under the conditions assumed, exchanges could actually be effected by the use of these ratios because any one interested in making an exchange would have to consider just six ratios in order to decide what he wanted to do. If, however, the number of commodities is increased to four, the number of ratios to be kept in mind rise to 12, if the number of commodities is increased to six, the number of ratios becomes 30, and so on.

This difficulty (the rapid rise in the number of ratios to be kept in mind) can be met if one commodity is selected in terms of which to express the others. If m is selected, the following results emerge in the situation described above:

1.   1 unit of g = 5 units of m

                  1 unit of s = 2 units of m

1 unit of g + 1 unit of s = 7 units of m

The preceding discussion introduces the following ideas:

a. Ratio of exchange among goods and services. Fundamentally, "value in exchange" is a ratio, e.g.: How many yards of cloth equals one ton of steel? How many tons of steel equals one automobile? How many units of commodity A equals one unit of commodity B? To say that there has been an increase or decrease in "exchange value" of any one commodity is the same thing as saying that there has been a change in its *ratios* of exchange. Similarly, if there has been no change in these ratios, there has been no shift in the exchange values of the commodities involved.

18

b. Use of one commodity as "money." As soon as commodity "m" was used to express the other commodities, "m" assumed the function of money as a "common denominator" or "standard of value" or "money of account." The ratios of exchange now represent "prices," that is, value in exchange expressed in terms of money. Money itself is a commodity whose exchange value changes for the same reasons as the exchange values of other commodities, and, in addition, changes for some special reasons of its own, e.g., the control of the money supply by central banks or government treasuries, and the relative unimportance of consumption and production of the money medium under modern conditions.

c. Money facilitates calculation and exchange. Instead of six "ratios," as before, two "prices" are all that are necessary. Each commodity (other than money) has a single price which is stated in absolute terms (e.g., $5, or $200), without the explicit intervention of an awkward ratio. As a result, the number of "prices" in any given situation is much less than the number of exchange ratios.

The evident simplification introduced by the use of money, however, introduces a new difficulty, namely, that no *direct* expression of ratios of exchange is available.

This difficulty is minimal *at any given point of time* because the ratios of exchange among commodities in that case are the same as the ratios of their prices. Thus, in the example above, the "price" of g is 5m, and of s, 2m. The ratios of the two prices are $\frac{5}{2}$ (i.e., g/s), and $\frac{2}{5}$ (i.e., s/g), which are the same as the ratios initially set forth. The difficulty is greater *as between two points of time*, but can be readily met if all prices move proportionally. Consider the following situation, at a date later than the one assumed above:

2.
$$1 \text{ unit of } g = 10 \text{ units of } m$$
$$1 \text{ unit of } s = \underline{\ \ 4} \text{ units of } m$$
$$1 \text{ unit of } g + 1 \text{ unit of } s = \underline{\underline{14}} \text{ units of } m$$

In this situation, the prices of g and of s have doubled, but the ratio of exchange of g to s is unchanged at $1\frac{9}{4}$, or $\frac{5}{2}$, and the ratio of s to g is still $\frac{4}{10}$, or $\frac{2}{5}$. Each unit of m now has a ratio of exchange exactly one-half the magnitude it had before. The value (i.e., ratio in exchange) of m has changed, but not the value of g or of s, although the price of each (g and s) has doubled. In making comparisons between (1) and (2), above, then, the change in the value of money can be readily allowed for.

The difficulty becomes greater under circumstances such as the following, at a date still later than (2), above:

3.
$$1 \text{ unit of } g = 16 \text{ units of } m$$
$$1 \text{ unit of } s = \underline{\ \ 5} \text{ units of } m$$
$$1 \text{ unit of } g + 1 \text{ unit of } s = \underline{\underline{21}} \text{ units of } m$$

The prices of g and of s have clearly increased, but, unlike case (2), above, their ratios of exchange (i.e., their values) have also changed. The values of g, of s, and of m have all changed.

The situations prevailing at the three points of time are summarized below. All ratios are expressed as decimals in order to facilitate comparisons.

	Point of Time		
Ratios of Exchange (Values)	*(1)*	*(2)*	*(3)*
g/s	2.5	2.50	3.2000
s/g	0.4	0.40	0.3125
*g/m	5.0	10.00	16.0000
m/g	0.2	0.10	0.0625
*s/m	2.0	4.00	5.0000
m/s	0.5	0.25	0.2000

* Prices, i.e., values in exchange, expressed in terms of money.

This table shows that between points of time (1) and (2), only the ratios involving m (money) changed; as between points (2) and (3), all the ratios changed, with the "terms of trade" continuing to worsen for m, and now also for s, whereas the "terms of trade" have improved for g.

How can the effects of the changes in the value of money be disentangled from the effects of the changes in the other items? One way was illustrated above, namely, to calculate the ratios of exchange among all the pairs of items. In simple cases of the type used above for illustrative purposes, this method is workable. In more complex situations a different approach is both desirable and possible.

Observe the following relationship in the three situations:

Point of Time	Amount of m Required to Purchase 1 Unit of g Plus 1 Unit of s	Ratio
1	7 units	1.00
2	14 units	2.00
3	21 units	3.00

The amount of money necessary to finance the exchange of one unit of all commodities, other than money, has increased three-fold from points of time (1) to (3). Each unit of money at (3) has on the average, decreased to one-third its value in exchange at (1). From (2) to (3) the exchange-value of money has declined by one-third. At point (2), 14 units of m would buy one combined unit of g and of s; at point (3), the same amount of money (14 units) would buy only two-thirds of a combined unit of g and s. This relationship can be used to restate (2) and (3), as follows, in order to compare g and s, free of the influence of the change in m:

	Commodity	
	g	s
a. Price at point of time (2)	10m	4m
b. Multiply by $2\frac{1}{14}$	15m	6m
c. Price at point of time (3)	16m	5m
	+1m	−1m

This tabulation restates (2) in terms of the situation prevailing at (3). The tabulation below restates (3) in terms of the situation in (2).

20

	Commodity	
	g	s
a. Price at point of time (3)	16 m	5 m
b. Multiply by 14/21	10⅔ m	3⅓ m
c. Price at point of time (2)	10 m	4 m
	−⅔ m	+⅔ m

Either restatement will serve the purpose; both reveal clearly the shift in the "terms of trade" as between g and s by indicating the relationship between the restated prices on line (b) and the actual prices on line (c).

The preceding paragraphs have demonstrated the essence of the "price-level" problem and its resolution by the use of "index numbers" (ratios). The following comments are pertinent.

1. The essence of any adjustment for "price-level changes" is the measurement of the changes, if any, in the "value in exchange" of money. It is a measurement designed to separate any movements in the exchange value of money from those in any or all other goods and services. Any attempt, then, to express economic or business data in "common dollars" is an attempt simply to express exchange values in a way to eliminate the effects of fluctuations in the "exchange value" of money itself. Incidentally, one fault of the stress on index numbers is that it reverses the proper emphasis—instead of saying that "prices have doubled," it is more enlightening to say that "the exchange value of money has fallen by one-half."

2. The measurement of the change in the value of money makes it possible to treat money as thought it were "neutral" in the economic process, as though it were merely a catalytic agent, enabling the process to take place but not becoming an integral part of that process.

3. The adjusted data are still in financial terms, not in physical or in welfare terms. The adjusted prices are still financial magnitudes, expressed in terms of a "neutral" dollar. These financial magnitudes are useful in accounting where one of the central issues is to determine if a given commitment of capital has been maintained or not. For other purposes, a real or a physical measurement may be more appropriate. For example, if the problem is to determine the change in physical quantities between two points of time, a procedure which adjusts each commodity by its own price change is called for. But a change in

physical quantities will not measure changes in values or in prices. These latter are financial magnitudes.

4. The price-level problem in accounting is a problem in the relationship of money to all goods and services in the aggregate, not of its relationship to a specific good or service. The price of an individual good or service changes in response to factors other than money, as illustrated above.

5. The technical problems in the compilation and use of an acceptable index number to measure changes in "the price level" are discussed in Appendix A. For example, the preceding discussion did not touch on the technical problems created by a change in the number or types of goods and services in the economy at different points of time.

2

What is Meant by Price-level Adjustments?

The amount of goods and services in general that can be purchased with any given amount of money changes from day to day, month to month, and year to year. When prices in general or "on the average" are rising, we say that the value of the dollar is falling and characterize the situation as a period of inflation; when prices are falling, the value of the dollar rises and we have a period of deflation.

Dollars Are Not Comparable

This means that the dollar, as a measuring device, is unstable or elastic. In terms of its command over goods and services, it represents something different at each point of time. It is proper, therefore, to distinguish between the 1940 dollar, the 1950 dollar, and the 1960 dollar, and so on, in that each one represents a different amount of general purchasing power, different quantities of goods and services. These dollars at different dates are no more comparable than if each one were a different foreign monetary unit. If the change is material, the dollar at two points of time cannot, for most purposes, be added, subtracted, or otherwise compared with any expectation of getting meaningful or useful results.

Effect Upon Accounting Data

The figures which emerge from the conventional accounting records at the present time suffer from this lack of comparability of the dollar at different points of time. "Monetary" items such as cash, receivables and payables will automatically be stated in current dollars, but there will be no indication of the loss or gain in purchasing power from holding or maintaining such items during a period of price-level changes.[1] Such "nonmonetary" items as inventories, plant, and equipment, if carried at unadjusted original cost, will be stated in a conglomeration of dollars of the various dates of acquisition. Sales, and expenses such as labor, will be recorded at various values of the dollar during the current period; it can be said that they are stated in terms of the average dollar for the period. Depreciation is usually the most drastically affected item on the operating statement, since it typically reflects the value of the dollar at many different points of time, depending upon when the various depreciable assets were acquired. Cost of goods sold will be affected in similar fashion but to a lesser degree because the turnover period of inventories is shorter than that of plant and equipment.

The figure conventionally shown as net income, therefore, cannot at all measure the gain or loss resulting from the units of purchasing power received as revenues and the units of purchasing power consumed in obtaining such revenues. Since the difference between the two figures is often large, use of the conventional figure as a basis for income tax may lead to unintended results. It may equally thwart a main objective of dividend restrictions, both statutory and contractual — that is, the preservation of a buffer for creditors — and it may mislead investors not only as to the nature of dividends received but also as to the profitability of the enterprise. Similarly, the various amounts within a set of financial statements may not be comparable, and a comparative statement covering several years is apt to become useless as an indication of the changes that have taken place, if the changes in the price level have been at all significant.

Price-level Adjustments as Restatements

The purpose of price-level adjustments, which might more accurately be characterized as corrections for changes in the price level, is to express or restate each item on the financial statements in terms of a

---

[1] See Appendix C, "Gains and Losses Attributable to the Holding of Monetary Items When Prices Change," for a discussion of the treatment of monetary items in making price-level adjustments.

"common" dollar,[2] that is, in terms of a dollar of the same general purchasing power.[3] Such figures can logically be compared and more meaningful conclusions can be drawn than from the original unadjusted cost figures.[4]

The meaning and significance of the restatement in common dollars can be demonstrated with the use of physical measurements. Assume that a man weighs 75 kilograms, and that his weight is to be restated in pounds. Since a kilogram equals 2.2 pounds (approximately), his weight can be restated as 75 × 2.2, or 165 pounds. It is now equally proper to state that he weighs 75 "units of the measure of weight called a kilogram" or that he weighs 165 "units of the measure of weight called a pound." The "change" of his weight from 75 "units" to 165 "units" is not an "increase" in weight since a comparison of the two figures, 75 and 165, has merely an abstract and not a real meaning. The "increase" of 90 (165 −75) is an optical illusion, as it were. For precisely the same reason, a kind of optical illusion is present when the $75 cost of an asset acquired when the index of the general price level was 100 is restated as $165 at a later point of time when the index is 220. The two figures ($75 and $165) are not comparable in the sense that one can be subtracted from or divided by the other. Their difference is the result of a mere restatement in terms of a different unit of measure of the "value in exchange" represented by the cost of $75 when the index of general prices stood at 100.

Now suppose that five years later the man who weighed 75 kilograms is weighed again, and his weight at the end of the fifth year is 220 pounds. Does the difference between 220 and 75, the "increase" of 145, have any real significance? To answer the question, either the 75 kilograms will have to be restated in pounds, or the 220 pounds will have to be restated in kilograms:

25

---

[2] The term "constant" dollar is sometimes used, but it is an inappropriate term because for accounting purposes the adjustments are usually made at successive statement dates so as to convert the amounts to the then current dollar and not to a constant base, such as the base year of an index series.

[3] For a somewhat simplified but reasonably complete demonstration of the conversion of a set of financial statements to a common-dollar basis, see *Price-Level Changes and Financial Statements—Basic Concepts and Methods,* by Perry Mason. American Accounting Association. 1956. Also see Appendix B of this report.

[4] There are, of course, some situations in which unadjusted dollars must be used in order to meet legal or contractual requirements.

| | Weight in | |
	Kilograms	Pounds
Beginning of first year	$75 = 100\%$	$165 = 100\%$
End of fifth year	$100 = 133\%$	$220 = 133\%$
Increase	$25 = 33\%$	$55 = 33\%$

The difference of 145 (220 −75) is a difference in abstract numerals and is not of significance in and of itself. The numerals may be grouped in two sets, one of which (165 −75 = 90) is purely abstract and is the result of a mere restatement of the units in which the man's weight is expressed while the other (220 −165 = 55) is the result of a real change in his weight expressed in pounds.

· This real increase corresponds to the portion of the change in the specific price of a unit of a given asset from $75 (price level at 100) to $220, five years later, (price level at 133). In terms of the price level at the beginning of the first year, the "value in exchange" has risen from $75 to $100, a real increase of $25 or one-third. In terms of the price level at the end of the fifth year, the "value in exchange" has risen from $165 to $220, a real increase of $55 or one-third.

The variation can be measured in terms of the dollar existing at either point of time, or for that matter at any other point of time. If the general price level has changed, dollars at different points of time are no more comparable than are kilograms and pounds. One essential condition for the logical, accurate measurement of real changes is that all of the magnitudes involved be expressed in terms of some one unit. In accounting and in business affairs generally, this means the dollar in being at some one point of time.

As another example, assume that a piece of land[5] was acquired for $10,000 at the starting point of an index of the general price level — the "base period," when the price index would be expressed as 100. Another piece of similar land was acquired for $10,000 at a later time after prices had risen 25 per cent, so that the index was then 125. A third parcel was purchased for $10,000 still later after a period of falling prices when the index was 75. Unless the figures are adjusted, the balance sheet will show land at a cost of $30,000, but with each $10,000 segment being expressed in dollars of significantly different meaning.

---

[5] Land is chosen for illustrative purposes to avoid the complicating effects of depreciation.

The correction or adjustment, to eliminate the effect of the unstable dollar, involves stating each $10,000 purchase in terms of a uniform or common dollar. This could be done, for example, in terms of the base-period dollar.

Purchase	Unadjusted Cost	Index No.	Multiplier	Adjusted Cost
First	$10,000	100	100/100	$10,000
Second	10,000	125	100/125	8,000
Third	10,000	75	100/75	13,333
	$30,000			$31,333

Another and more commonly used possibility is to express each purchase in terms of the current dollar. It will be assumed that prices have risen substantially since the third purchase took place and that the current index now stands at 200.

Purchase	Unadjusted Cost	Multiplier	Adjusted Cost
First	$10,000	200/100	$20,000
Second	10,000	200/125	16,000
Third	10,000	200/75	26,667
	$30,000		$62,667

Either of these calculations shows the cost of each parcel of land in proper relation to the cost of the others, that is, the adjusted amounts indicate the relative sacrifice which the purchaser made in acquiring each parcel, and the relative significance to the seller of the amounts received. The totals of $31,333 and $62,667 represent the same amount of general purchasing power and either will be comparable to other similarly adjusted items on the financial statements.

Adjusted Cost and Replacement Cost

Replacement costs (fair market value) and costs adjusted for the change in the price level are two different types of "current costs" which will be the same only by coincidence. In the previous illustration nothing was said about the quantity of land that was acquired in each purchase or about the comparative market values of the three parcels at the time of each purchase. To deal with these factors requires a knowledge of the changes in the price of the *specific* type of property, which might or might not correspond to the degree of change or even to the trend in the *general* price level. The facts could have been as follows:

(The three parcels of land are of equal market value at each of the four points in time.)

Purchase	Acres	Price Per Acre	General Price Index
First	10	$1,000	100
Second	15	667	125
Third	5	2,000	75
	30		
Current price		3,000	200

The unadjusted average cost is $1,000 an acre ($30,000 ÷ 30), the current-dollar adjusted average cost is $2,089 an acre ($62,677 ÷ 30), and the replacement cost is $3,000 an acre, or the total current appraised value is $90,000. The adjustment technique, therefore, is merely an expression of the original cost of the land in current dollars and cannot properly be characterized as an adoption of current appraisal value or replacement cost. If the value of the land has gone down instead of up, say to $400 an acre so that the replacement cost was $12,000, the adjusted cost would still have been shown as $62,667 in current dollars (if the general price index remained at 200).

Appreciation and Price-level Adjustments

If the cost basis of asset valuation is abandoned, and the assets are shown at their appraisal value or replacement cost, a different type of problem is presented. For example, if the land in the previous illustration were written up on the books from $30,000 to $90,000, we should ordinarily show an appraisal surplus of $60,000. The $90,000 would necessarily be expressed in current dollars and would require no adjustment. The original cost, however, when expressed in current dollars, was $62,667, so the appreciation in value on this basis was only $27,333 instead of $60,000. In other words, the writeup of $60,000 is a combination of an adjustment of the cost to a current common-dollar basis, $32,667, plus appreciation in value of $27,333.

If the appraisal value of the land had fallen to $12,000, the recorded writedown of $18,000 ($30,000–$12,000) would have been $50,667 in terms of current dollars ($62,667–$12,000).

Replacement Cost a Separate Problem

We stress this distinction between replacement costs and price-level adjustments because much of what has been said and written on the subject displays a failure to recognize the difference. The calculation and recording of depreciation on replacement cost is frequently said to be a type of price-level adjustment when actually it is not. Only by coincidence would the results be the same, and the underlying valuation philosophy is entirely different. The conversion of asset costs to a common-dollar basis is a natural extension rather than an abandonment of the "cost principle" or the original cost basis of asset valuation.

It is often said that technological developments have made price-level adjustments open to question. Technological developments are widespread and comparatively few items are literally replaced. The new item will almost invariably have innovations which will affect the unit cost of production or operation. The cost of a new machine may be more than the cost of the old one, but the unit cost of production may be less. These are valid points in connection with the construction of an index (see Appendix A) and with a consideration of the use of replacement costs. Since the new item is not the same as the old, there is no replacement and "replacement costs" are not relevant. An attempt to compute the replacement cost of an item that is not to be replaced can easily lead to absurd results. But all of this has nothing to do with the restatement of original cost to a common-dollar basis because the restatement is with respect to dollars invested in the item and not with respect to the dollars needed to replace (if replacement is, indeed, to take place).

Arguments are often carried on as to the relative merits of an index of the general price level and "specific" price indexes in adjusting the financial statements for the effects of inflation. It is only the general price-level index that measures the effect of inflation or deflation. The use of specific price indexes involves the adoption of the replacement cost or "fair market value" principle of valuation, the results of which may be either higher or lower than those obtained with the use of a general price-level index.

Each number in a price index is a weighted average of the prices of many products. The prices of many of the individual products move in the opposite direction from the general trend. For example, the 1962 preliminary monthly average of the all commodity Wholesale Price Index was reported at 100.6 [1957-59=100], but the indexes of the

29

Chart I

SELECTED DURABLES

SELECTED NONDURABLES

(1957-59=100)

30

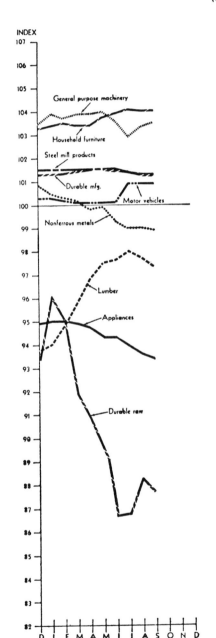

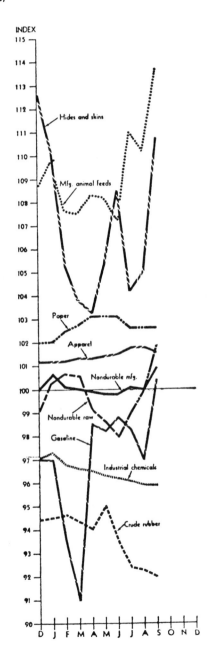

component products ranged from a low of 76.3 for inedible fats and oils to a high of 125.9 for silk products.[6] The breakdown of this index into fifteen groups by type of products showed three groups in which all items were selling below their 1957-59 average, five groups with all items selling above it, and the rest were mixed.

In Chart I, page 30, each item is compared with its average price during the three year period 1957-59, e.g., a reading of 91 for a commodity means that commodity is selling at 91 per cent of its average price during the base period 1957-59.[7]

Charts II through VI, pages 32-34, show the all commodity Wholesale Price Index and some of its components from 1953 to 1962.[8] Some of the components move in the opposite direction from the all commodity index, some move in the same direction. Some move in the same direction part of the time and the opposite direction at other times.

It is not the function of this report to debate the merits of original cost or replacement cost as possible principles of valuation. It is important to emphasize, however, that price-level adjustments of accounting data are not the same thing as the adoption of replacement costs, either in theory or in the nature of the results. Changes in the replacement cost of specific items take place even though there has been no change in the general price level. The possibility of shifting from an original cost to a replacement cost basis of accounting exists even though the value of the dollar remains constant.

31

Depreciation and Price-level Adjustments

This same confusion between replacement cost and price-level adjustments, or between price changes and price-level changes, is encountered in much of the discussion of depreciation and of the need for more liberal treatment of depreciation for income tax and other purposes.

> . . . The accepted purposes of charging depreciation are, firstly, to recover the cost of the machine against the profits arising from its use and, secondly, to ensure that sufficient funds are retained

---

[6] *Survey of Current Business*, April 1963, p. S-8.

[7] U. S. Department of Labor, Bureau of Labor Statistics, *Prices: A Chartbook 1953-62*, Bulletin No. 1351, 1963. p. 103.

[8] *Ibid.* pp. 77, 88, 95, 98.

Chart II

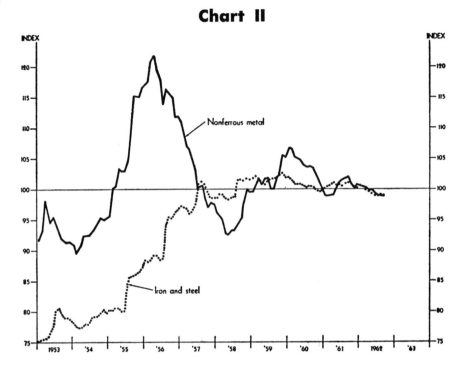

Nonferrous metal

Iron and steel

Chart III

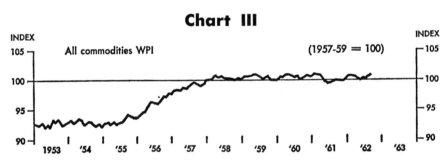

INDEX

All commodities WPI

(1957-59 = 100)

INDEX

Chart IV

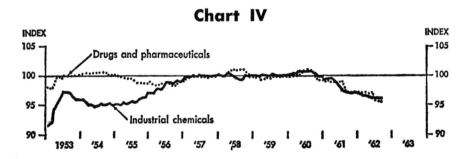

INDEX

Drugs and pharmaceuticals

Industrial chemicals

INDEX

Chart V

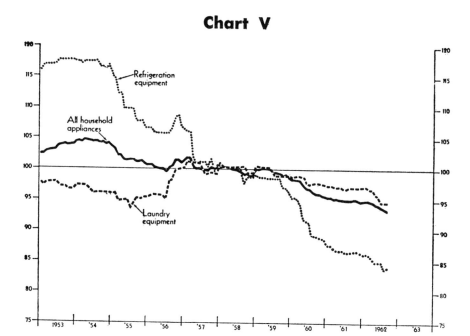

33

in the business for the replacement of the machine at the end of its useful life.[9]

Both of these "purposes" are misstated. It is generally agreed that the purpose of charging depreciation to operations is to distribute the cost over the estimated useful life of the property in a systematic and rational manner, to paraphrase the definition in paragraph 56 of *Accounting Terminology Bulletin No. 1.*[10] There is no certainty that the cost will be "recovered" and the depreciation charge will be the same whether it is or not.

The second "purpose," the financing of replacements, is seriously defective. The accounting for depreciation does not "ensure" that funds of any amount will be retained in the business. But even more serious is the implication that the total depreciation charges over the

---

[9] M. J. Greener, "Profit—Fact or Fiction?—II," *The Accountant,* Oct. 14, 1961, p. 489. Many similar examples appeared in the replies to an opinion survey on price-level adjustment of depreciation conducted by the Technical Services Department of the American Institute of Certified Public Accountants in 1958. See also Chapters 3 and 4 of *Inflation and Corporate Accounting* published by the National Industrial Conference Board in 1962.

[10] American Institute of Certified Public Accountants. 1953.

Chart VI

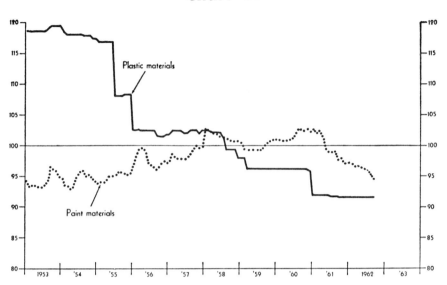

34   life of the property should equal the cost of replacement if it is higher than original cost, or that funds equal to the periodic depreciation charges should be expected to accumulate to the amount of the re-placement cost. To insist that replacement cost should be covered by the total depreciation charges during a period of rising prices means that more than the depreciation based upon current appraisal value would have to be charged each year to make up for the deficiencies of past periods, and this would result in costs clearly out of line with reality. If replacement costs were falling, more than enough would have been charged in past periods, and the current charge would have to be reduced in order to avoid an excessive accumulation.

The original cost was the investment made by the owner and, as long as the original cost basis of valuation is the basis generally accepted by the business community and by accountants, only that investment, expressed in dollars comparable to those used for other expense and revenue items, should enter into the determination of the profit or loss over the life of the asset. The excess of the replacement cost over such amounts charged to operations is an additional capital cost, to be financed by additional capital investment, by borrowing, or by the retention of earnings.

It is reasonable to maintain that the depreciation charge should be stated in terms of dollars which are comparable to those used in the measurement of other factors in the calculation of net profit, and this is where price-level adjustments enter into the picture. The proper result can be obtained by stating all other costs in terms of the dollar of the period in which the depreciating asset was acquired, or by restating the depreciation and all other items in terms of some other dollar, such as the base-period dollar, or the dollar of the current period.

For example, suppose that $100,000 is invested in a group of assets with an expected life of five years with no scrap value, that the straight-line method of depreciation is used, that the general price index is 120 at the time the assets are acquired and during the first year, and that the index increases ten points a year during the next four years. The plan is adopted of adjusting the depreciation each year for the change in the general price level. The results would be as follows:

Year	Price-level Index	Unadjusted Depreciation	Multiplier	Adjusted Depreciation as Recorded
1	120	$ 20,000	120/120	$20,000
2	130	20,000	130/120	21,667
3	140	20,000	140/120	23,333
4	150	20,000	150/120	25,000
5	160	20,000	160/120	26,667
		$100,000		

35

The figures in the last column can still be characterized as the results of applying the straight-line method of depreciation since each one represents the same amount of general purchasing power. Their sum, $116,667, is, however, a meaningless figure since it is a combination of five different types of the dollar or of dollars with five different values. If the depreciation amounts were converted to the dollar of the fifth year, they would be comparable, and the results would be:

Year	Adjusted Depreciation in Dollar of Each Year	Multiplier	Adjusted Depreciation in Dollar of Fifth Year
1	$20,000	160/120	$ 26,667
2	21,667	160/130	26,667
3	23,333	160/140	26,666
4	25,000	160/150	26,666
5	26,667	160/160	26,667
			$133,333

The figures in the last column are those which would appear in an adjusted comparative income statement for the five-year period. The $133,333 is equal to the converted original cost of the group of assets ($100,000 × 160/120), so there is no "deficiency" in the amount of depreciation which has been charged to operations because, for example, 23,333 "dollars-of-year-three" are identical with 26,666 "dollars-of-year-five" under the conditions of this case.

If depreciation had been charged at the conventional rate of $20,000 a year, there would have been a "deficiency" in the charge for depreciation. Expressed in fifth-year dollars, it amounts to $17,861, computed as follows:

Year	Deficiency for Each Year Expressed in Dollars of That Year*	Multiplier	Deficiency Expressed in Fifth-year Dollars
1	None	—	—
2	$1,667	160/130	$ 2,052
3	3,333	160/140	3,809
4	5,000	160/150	5,333
5	6,667	160/160	6,667
			$17,861

* See first table on page 35.

Another method of computing the depreciation deficiency is to make the logical assumption that each year's depreciation is expressed in the dollar of that year and convert each amount to the fifth-year dollar, as follows:

Year	Unadjusted Recorded Depreciation	Multiplier	Recorded Depreciation Expressed in Fifth-year Dollars
1	$20,000	160/120	$ 26,667
2	20,000	160/130	24,615
3	20,000	160/140	22,857
4	20,000	160/150	21,333
5	20,000	160/160	20,000
			$115,472

Total Adjusted Depreciation	133,333
Depreciation Deficiency	$ 17,861

This demonstration of depreciation adjustments is unrealistic in one respect. It would rarely be true that the depreciable assets would have been acquired at the same time. This only means, however, that the assets must be grouped according to age or date of acquisition, and rate and method of depreciation and a separate conversion be made of the cost and depreciation for each group or item. The basic principle is the same.

The Financial Problem

The financial aspects of the situation constitute a different type of problem. Referring to the previous illustration, there may or may not have been sufficient funds accumulated in the business to make good the purchasing power of $100,000 invested in the assets five years ago. Assuming that the revenue covers the expenses, it depends upon how funds equal to the annual depreciation charge were invested. If they were put aside in a noninterest-bearing cash account, there would be a financial deficiency of $33,333 ($133,333 − $100,000) if amounts equal to the unadjusted depreciation were deposited in the fund, or a financial deficiency of $16,666 ($133,333 − $116,667) if amounts equal to the adjusted depreciation for each year were used. If these latter amounts were invested in assets which increased in value at the same rate as the increase in the general price level, there would be no financial deficiency; a full $133,333 would be accumulated, and the purchasing power of the $100,000 "capital" would have been maintained.

The problem of financing replacements is not the same as the problem of depreciation accounting. Generally accepted accounting principles do not call for the replacement of existing facilities or the maintenance of an existing level of production to be financed out of revenue before a profit can be said to have been earned. Instead, in accordance with the requirements and standards of the business community, they call for accounting measurements to determine if the "capital" (money-cost) embodied in the resources of the business (including its depreciable assets) has been maintained, increased, or decreased. Furthermore, there is not even a requirement that the "capital" be held in any particular form, but merely that we know whether it has been maintained in total.

If the general price level has not changed, the entire excess of replacement cost over original cost represents an additional capital requirement which should be treated as such. If the general price level has risen, it is proper to insist that all operating costs should be stated in comparable dollars; any excess of replacement cost over the adjusted original cost then becomes the additional capital requirement.

3

Price-level Adjustments and Generally Accepted Accounting Principles

The first two chapters dealt with price-level adjustments in a positive way, setting forth a problem and a position and developing the consequences. Collateral issues, objections to price-level adjustments, and certain practical difficulties, although not completely neglected, were treated more or less incidentally. This chapter is the first of three that consider some of these "incidental" topics. Consideration of these topics also has the advantage of providing a different perspective from which to view the accounting problems created by changing price levels and the proposed method of dealing with them.

The procedures developed in this study assume no change in generally accepted accounting principles, other than the proposal to use an index of the general price level in supplementary reports on financial position and results of operations. This assumption serves to keep the scope of this study within bounds by preventing it from becoming enmeshed in issues that are not germane to changing price levels. It also serves to highlight the fact that price-level adjustments are feasible, desirable, and logically necessary, regardless of the set of accounting principles that are employed to measure income and financial position. The following five specific topics are discussed to indicate more concretely what the preceding assertions mean:

1. Adjusted cost or market for inventories
2. Lifo as a partial adjustment for price-level changes

3. Deferred income tax on price-level "increments"
4. Long-term debt and the depreciation adjustment
5. Monetary items and the realization concept

Adjusted Cost or Market for Inventories

What happens if the restated amount of inventories exceeds replacement cost? Suppose inventories were acquired when the index stood at 100; at the balance-sheet date, the index stands at 125, and replacement cost of the inventory is 120. Under presently accepted accounting principles, the inventory would be reflected at its historical cost of 100; it would not be written up to 120 (its current replacement cost) because to do so would recognize profit prior to sale. Under price-level adjustments, the historical cost of the inventory would be restated at 125, indicating that the investment of 100 at date of acquisition is equal to 125 at the date of the balance sheet. The "excess" of 25 is not an anticipation of profit; it is instead part of a restatement of capital (owners' equity) at the date on which the inventory was acquired.

Even so, the suggestion has been made that the inventory (in the case described above) should not be shown in excess of 120 in the adjusted financial statements, that a natural extension of the "cost or market" rule would be "cost (adjusted for price-level effects) or market, whichever is lower." No "gain" is anticipated by reflecting the inventory at 125 in financial statements adjusted for price-level effects. Therefore, if the "cost or market" rule is to be applied to the adjusted data and the inventory is in fact to be shown at 120 under the circumstances described, the difference of 5 (125—120) should be recorded as a "loss." Otherwise a writedown of an ordinary operating asset (inventory) below adjusted cost will bypass the (adjusted) income statement completely.

There is no corollary to the "lower of cost or market" rule for inventories in the conventional practice of accounting for property, plant, and equipment except in unusual circumstances, such as a quasi-reorganization. Similar questions do not arise therefore in restating the amounts of these assets.

Lifo as a Partial Adjustment

It is sometimes suggested that Lifo inventory pricing constitutes a type of partial price-level adjustment since it tends to put the cost of materials used or of goods sold on a current-cost basis. In principle, however, it does not come under the concept of price-level adjustments. If an index number is used, as in the "dollar-value" Lifo method, it is a *specific* commodity or group price index reflecting the market behavior of specific classes or types of goods. If the most recent purchase prices are used in calculating the Lifo cost of materials used or Lifo cost of goods sold, they will in most cases correspond closely to the replacement costs in the market at the end of the current period. Except by coincidence, these specific replacement costs, whether taken directly from market data or approximated by the use of indexes of specific goods, will not coincide with the movement of prices in general as measured by an index of the general price level. Thus, the general level of prices could be stable, while the Lifo index moved up or down; the Lifo index could be stable, while prices in general were falling or rising.

Furthermore, Lifo makes no adjustment at all for inventories on the balance sheet. The more the general price level moves, up or down, the further removed is a Lifo inventory from even approximating an inventory adjusted for changes in the general price level. Lifo is a method for excluding changes in the replacement costs of specific commodities from "realized profits"; it is not intended to and cannot cope with the measurement problem created by a change in the general purchasing power of money as measured by an "all-commodity" index.

Deferred Income Tax on Price-level "Increments"

Generally accepted accounting principles now require that provision be made for income taxes not yet paid (or declared) on net income reported in the financial statements. For example, suppose a company is on an accrual basis per books but on an installment (or cash collection) basis for tax purposes and earns $100,000 on installment sales made this year on which no tax is payable until the receivables are collected next year. If the applicable tax rate is 40 per cent, this company would show a tax provision of $40,000 in its net income calculation, and a corresponding liability for postponed tax. To do otherwise would overstate net income and retained earnings. Should not a similar practice be followed in financial statements adjusted for price-level effects with respect to the "increments," or excess of price-level adjusted net assets over the unadjusted amounts?

Under existing tax law, price-level adjustments are not recognized. This discussion assumes a continuation of that state of affairs. Since the tax law does not recognize price-level adjustments, the so-called "increments" will not find their way into the tax return of any year. The adjusted financial statements do not contain items reported earlier (later) for book purposes than they are for tax purposes. These adjusted statements merely *restate* what is contained in the unadjusted statements; they are *not* the results of the use of "replacements costs" or "current values" in place of acquisition costs. They do not "lead" or "lag" the tax return in reporting net income, before tax. In a period of rising prices, the typical case will not be one in which adjusted net income exceeds the unadjusted amount. Ordinarily it will show adjusted net income as *less* than unadjusted, on an adjusted investment that is *more* than the unadjusted amount. The conclusion is clear that no deferred tax provision is needed for price-level adjustments because (under existing law) they never enter into the calculation of the tax liability of any year. The only "deferred taxes" in a set of adjusted financial statements will be the amounts taken from the unadjusted data.

Long-term Debt and the Depreciation Adjustment

41

The purchasing-power gain on long-term debt is sometimes associated with the depreciable assets as an offset to the depreciation adjustment. One proposal has been to omit the adjustment of the nonmonetary assets (and related depreciation) to the extent that they were financed by borrowed capital. For example, if a building was acquired entirely from the proceeds of a bond issue, it would be left unadjusted at its acquisition cost.

In order to visualize the point at issue, assume the following case in which a doubling of the price level occurs.

	Unadjusted Index = 100	Restated Index = 200
Monetary assets	100	100
Depreciable assets (nonmonetary)	200	400
	300	500
Bonds payable	200	200
Common stock	100	200
Gain on bonds payable		200
Loss on monetary assets		(100)
Common stock equity	100	300
	300	500

Observe that if the financial statements are restated in the manner shown above, the income statement will show depreciation on the restated asset basis (400) in each year of the assets' remaining useful life, whereas the "gain" on bonds payable will be reflected *in toto* in the period in which the change in the price level occurs. This characteristic behavior of the amounts involved has led some to assert that it is not fair or equitable for the "benefit" on the bonds to be shown all at once, while the "burden" of higher depreciation is spread over a number of periods. One proposal for dealing with the "inequity" is to ignore the effects of price-level changes on both the asset and the financial instrument (the bonds) by which it was obtained. Another proposal would recognize the effect on the asset, but would spread the "benefit" or "gain" on the bonds over the depreciable life of the asset. For the reasons set forth below, neither proposal is acceptable in terms of the analysis developed in this study.

The apparent increase in depreciation, when restated in terms of the current dollar, is something of an optical illusion. If the depreciable assets are shown at higher amounts, they are not being written up in the sense of an appraisal but are merely being restated in terms of the dollar at the end of the current year, so as to put the items in the balance sheet and the income statement on a comparable basis. It is not necessary to use the dollar at the end of the current year for this purpose. Assume, for example, that the election was made to express all of the items in terms of the dollar at the beginning of the current year, and that there had been no change in the depreciable assets in use during the period. There would then be no change in the dollar amount shown for the assets or for the depreciation charged to operations during the period, but there still would be a gain on the long-term debt. The dollar expression of the gain would involve a smaller amount than if the end-of-year dollar had been used, but there would be the same proportionate gain. The depreciation and the gain on the long-term debt, then, are unrelated phenomena. The purchasing-power gain or loss on all monetary items should be computed and shown as one of the significant results of the change in the general price level. The restatement of depreciation should be made as another and unrelated part of the adjustment procedure.

Monetary Items and the Realization Concept

A distinction is sometimes made between "realized" and "unrealized" losses and gains on monetary accounts. Since the trend of prices may change before a monetary asset is collected or utilized, or before a monetary liability is discharged, it is often maintained that a purchasing-power loss or gain is unrealized until cash is spent or a liability is paid.

This concept of "realized" and "unrealized" purchasing-power gains and losses puts the emphasis upon cash receipts and disbursements rather than on the concept of accrual accounting. The gains and losses have occurred in much the same sense that interest has accrued, or that bond discount has accumulated or been amortized.[1] The cash balance could not be in more realizable form and the other current monetary items might be characterized as cash-receipts-in-process or cash-payments-in-process. If we are willing to recognize revenue on the basis of a receivable, we should be willing to recognize a loss or gain in purchasing-power on the same basis. As one writer has put it: "This interpretation accords well with common sense: for the gain or loss results from *holding* money claims during a period of changing prices, not from *disposing* of the money claims at some particular level of prices."[2]

43

[1] See *Balance Sheet Price Level Analysis*, by Othel D. Westfall (1950), pp. 18-22, for a development of what he calls the "interest realization convention" in the recognition of purchasing-power gains and losses on monetary items.

[2] John W. Coughlan, "Applicability of the Realization Principle to Money Claims in Common Dollar Accounting," *The Accounting Review*, Jan. 1955, p. 113.

4

Objections to Price-level Adjustments

This chapter deals with some of the objections that have been made to the recognition of price-level changes in financial statements, especially those that are not discussed in other parts of this study. The primary purpose of noting these objections is to give added perspective and depth to the meaning of price-level adjustments in financial statements as developed in chapters 1 and 2, and elaborated in the appendixes. No attempt has been made to cover the "social policy" questions, such as the question of equity as between business and individuals if price-level changes are recognized for tax purposes or the question in the public-utility field of the extent to which price-level changes should be recognized in setting rates. Questions of this type are not germane to a neutral inquiry into one phase of the accounting problem of the *measurement* of financial position and of operating results.

The examples which follow of specific objections to adjusted financial reports are grouped according to the classification given immediately below:

(A) Those objections which in effect deny that a problem exists or that it is serious enough to warrant attention.

(B) Those objections which admit that a problem exists but deny that accounting can handle it.

(C) Those objections which admit that a problem exists but fear that the proposed adjustments will have undesirable consequences.

(D) Those objections which stress the fact that the proposed adjustments are not yet perfected.

(E) Those objections which in effect require the adoption of the proposed adjustments for tax purposes before they are introduced into financial reports.

Deny That a Problem Exists or That It Is Serious Enough to Warrant Attention

Accounting Research Bulletin No. 43, Chapter 9(a) states in paragraph 11 that "The committee on accounting procedure has reached the conclusion that no basic change in the accounting treatment of depreciation of plant and equipment is practicable or desirable under present conditions to meet the problem created by the decline in the purchasing power of the dollar." And in paragraph 13: "Should inflation proceed so far that original dollar costs lose their practical significance, it might become necessary to restate all assets in terms of the depreciated currency, as has been done in some countries. But it does not seem to the committee that such action should be recommended now if financial statements are to have maximum usefulness to the greatest number of users."[1]

45

This statement by the committee on accounting procedure represented its view as to the proper policy to be followed at the time. The present study was initiated because the Accounting Principles Board felt that a new policy might be appropriate. In any case the technical (formal) analysis of the price-level problem can be made, whether the price level has changed little or much. The underlying principles are the same.

An objection of the same general class is based on the belief that the problem is essentially one of financial administration which can be handled in the financial statements by earmarking retained earnings. The increasing costs of specific assets, such as materials, other inventory components, equipment, and other fixed assets, are considered to be problems of financing higher replacement costs rather than of calculating net income. Implicit in this view is a denial that there has been a change of any consequence in the price level, i.e., it implies that there has been no inflation.

---

[1] *Accounting Research Bulletin No. 43* was published in 1953. Chapter 9(a) is a restatement of *Accounting Research Bulletin No. 33,* published originally in 1947.

A variant of this type of objection is the tenet that the inflation in prices has been offset (in part, at least) by the improved quality and diversity of goods. In other words, innovation of all types, including technical change, has brought about improvements, so that $100 in year B buys more than it would have if innovation had not occurred since year A. The facts implied by this objection are no doubt valid, but the inference is not. As a result of innovation, the total return to all factors of production taken together has increased; presumably, the return to each factor has increased also. In the absence of some sort of adjustment for price-level changes, however, the return to one factor (the investor in tangible goods) is calculated in a mixture of dollars of year A and year B because of inflation. The return to other factors, for example, the wages of labor or the salaries of top management, is calculated in a different way, namely, in terms of dollars of year B.[2]

Admit That a Problem Exists
But Deny That Accounting Can Handle It

46

One objection asserts that the risks of business include the risk of variation in monetary values. This assertion is undoubtedly correct, but it implies that because accounting cannot eliminate this risk it is incapable of reporting its effects. Of the same type is the assertion that accounting processes are poor and hopelessly inadequate tools to deal effectively with the economic evils of inflation. Although these assertions contain an element of truth, this does not preclude the reporting of "the results of activities measured in units of equal purchasing power" as well as "the results of changes in the value of the monetary unit." Accounting alone cannot eliminate the variation in monetary values, but it can measure the extent to which inflation and deflation have entered into the changes that have taken place and have been recorded in the accounts.

This type of objection probably refers, however, to a different but related problem in the field of social policy, namely, that inequities might be introduced into the tax structure if businesses were permitted to use "adjusted costs" for tax purposes while individuals whose income consisted mainly of salaries, wages, dividends, and interest might not

---

[2] See Appendix A, "The Index Number Problem" for a description of the way in which allowance for technical change is made in the construction of index numbers. Page 87.

get "relief." But tax rates could be adjusted to yield any given inflow of revenue to the U. S. Treasury, or some other method used to preserve equity among different groups in the country. In any event, the tax effects, while not independent of price-level adjustments, are separable and should be analyzed separately.

Admit That a Problem Exists but Fear That the Proposed Adjustments Will Have Undesirable Consequences

The development of methods to measure the changes in the purchasing power of money lagged behind the need for such measurement.[3] As a result, money has traditionally been used in the business community as the unit of account without measuring the fluctuations in its purchasing power. Even though measurement techniques have now been developed by which financial data can be adjusted to reflect the effect of changes in the price level, there is still reluctance to use these techniques.

This reluctance stems in part from concern among accountants that the presentation of adjusted data may reflect unfavorably on the financial statements currently presented as well as on the accountants who have expressed the opinion that these statements fairly present the financial conditions and results of operations of the companies involved.   47

This situation presents both a problem to be solved and an opportunity for the profession to add to its stature by taking the lead in improving financial reporting. The profession cannot properly be criticized for expressing the opinion that financial statements fairly present the financial position and results of operations in accordance with generally accepted accounting principles so long as those principles result in the best information that is objectively determinable with the means of measurement available at the time. The profession could be justly criticized for a rigid adherence to the status quo when there is substantial evidence that measurement techniques are available which will produce more meaningful statements. A willingness to experiment with new techniques and to test their usefulness will demon-

---

[3] Official work on the United States national income statistics was first initiated in 1932 by the 72nd Congress (Senate Resolution No. 220). The gross national product in current dollars was added to the income series shortly after Pearl Harbor to provide information necessary to the war effort. Gross national product in constant dollars and the implicit price deflators that are a by-product of its computation did not become available until 1951.

strate that the profession is making progress in the improvement of reporting practices. In the past, whenever the profession has faced up to problems and recommended solutions, it has enhanced its stature and authority.

There is also concern that public confusion would ensue from price-level adjustments in income-determination, particularly if some companies were to adopt the proposed adjustments while others did not. Americans seem to be more sophisticated than this objection indicates. They are not strangers to escalator clauses in labor contracts which affect their paychecks or payrolls or the prices of goods and services they buy or sell. Many contracts provide for automatic adjustment based on price indexes including long-term rentals, royalties, welfare payments, commodity purchase contracts, and alimony. In the meanwhile, "mixed" practices might not be as serious as some fear; in The Netherlands, some companies apparently make adjustments for price changes while others do not. Each company, however, tells what it has done. Although not an ideal situation, this practice in The Netherlands has not led to any noticeable confusion.

48 Detailed examination of specific objections yielded references to "amount to be set aside for replacement," "appraised values in the accounts," "estimated replacement or current cost." These reflect a misunderstanding of the objectives of the adjustments that have been proposed, as developed in chapters 1 and 2.

Discussions on price-level adjustments frequently include statements that indicate that an income statement is considered to be a species of funds statement. Under this conception, revenues are identified closely with receipts, and expenses with cash outlays, except for the so-called noncash items. Under these circumstances, price-level adjustments are looked upon as unnecessary intrusions into an otherwise fairly comprehensible report. At the same time, in the case of sophisticated readers and discussants of this particular problem, an undercurrent of distrust of income calculations can be noted. In other words, these people do not think much of an income statement in the first place, and accordingly are not much interested in one that has been adjusted through price-level indexes or by other means.

Unfortunately, the phraseology still used by many accountants reinforces the view that an income statement is no more than a kind of "funds-flow" statement. For example, "provision" for depreciation is still in vogue, as though it were a matter of discretion, a setting aside of something from a disposable pool. Instead, we should refer to depreciation "cost" or "expense" in order to describe more accurately the nature of the calculation and of the entry.

An extension of the theme that the "index method" would have objectionable results is the assertion that price-level adjustments would have an undesirable effect during a downswing of prices. Whether this is so or not depends on the meaning of "undesirable." In a downswing, profits would be higher and losses lower with "adjusted" costs than with unadjusted costs. Presumably, the profits or losses would be more accurately stated. These results are clearly desirable. But if taxes are tied to reported profits, then, in a downswing, taxes at any given schedule of rates would be higher with adjusted than with unadjusted costs. This apparently is the "undesirable" effect referred to in this type of objection.

Another example holds that departure from conventional reporting could result in increases in the cost of additional investment funds. This result could not take place in the economy as a whole, but it might happen to individual industries or firms. Adjusted costs, in other words, would reduce reported profits while prices are rising and, hence, might reduce the attractiveness of the company as an investment. But should investment continue to be placed when it is based on a misapprehension on the part of investors as to what has been going on? If the business unit is not as profitable as investors thought it was, there is nothing strange in their unwillingness to commit funds, except at an increased price.

49

Proposed Adjustments Are Not Yet Perfected

The point is made frequently that price-level adjustments are inaccurate. If the reference here is to the indexes now available, the problem is essentially statistical in nature.

Appendix A of this study, "The Index Number Problem," analyzes this question at some length. The analysis contained in the appendix concludes that there is only one index currently compiled that is a measure of the general level of the prices in the United States: the GNP (Gross National Product) Implicit Price Deflator.[4] This part of the study also points out that while there has been a high degree of

---

[4] Prepared by the U. S. Department of Commerce, Office of Business Economics, Washington, D. C. and available in the *Survey of Current Business.*

correlation between the results of applying this index and those obtained with the use of the somewhat more popular Consumer Price Index,[5] there is no assurance that this relationship will continue. The GNP Implicit Price Deflator series is available on an annual basis since 1929 and on a quarterly basis since the first quarter of 1947. Unless prices change very rapidly, a quarterly index series should be sufficiently precise for the adjustment of financial statements.

The question of whether any available index series is sufficiently accurate for the purpose of making price-level adjustments of accounting data is, of course, debatable and difficult to prove one way or the other. After considerable investigation and consideration of the problem, we have reached the conclusion that the GNP Implicit Price Deflator series is sufficiently reliable for accounting purposes if its use is not extended too far into the past, and that the degree of possible inaccuracy is no greater, and is probably much less, than that involved in many estimates which have to be made in the day-to-day accounting process.

Ideally, adjustments to accounting data for the effects of price-level changes should apply across the board. This ideal can be achieved wherever the assets and liabilities currently held originated during the period for which reliable index numbers are available. There is, however, one characteristic of our economy that is a limiting factor in the application of any price index series over a period of time. That characteristic is rapid technological change. The highest degree of reliability is attained when the prices which are used in compiling a price index relate to the same quantities and qualities of goods and services from one period to another. Technological changes and other such factors present difficulties in this connection which can only partially be overcome. (For a discussion of techniques currently used, see Appendix A, page 87.) This means that an index series should not be used for projections too far back into the past. As a rule of thumb at the present time (1963), perhaps the year 1945 is a good cutting off point. In the aging of depreciable assets, for example, it would be assumed that the price level of 1945 would apply to all assets acquired prior to that year; all units still on hand but acquired prior to the year 1945 would be presumed to have been acquired in that year. Two factors will reduce the materiality of any resulting inaccu-

50

---

[5] Prepared by the Bureau of Labor Statistics, U. S. Department of Labor, Washington, D. C. and available in the *Survey of Current Business,* the *Monthly Labor Review* and other publications.

racy: (1) retirement of depreciable assets since 1945, and (2) additions of depreciable assets. The combined effect of the two is to reduce materially, in many cases, the importance of pre-1946 acquisitions in the total plant and equipment in use in 1963.

The need for a cut-off date and an alternative recommendation are discussed in Appendix A.

Another type of objection holds that price adjustments are one-sided: increased costs would be recorded but not the gains which flow from holding fixed assets and inventories, or from holding long-term debt. This type of objection is pertinent to the recommendations of the Study Group as set forth in its publication, *Changing Concepts of Business Income*, but is not pertinent to the present study which assumes that the data will be completely adjusted for price-level effects. The Study Group, in essence, recommended adjustments limited to cost of goods sold and to depreciation in the income statement, leaving the asset side of the balance sheet untouched. By contrast, the Committee on Concepts and Standards of the American Accounting Association recommended (as does the present study) that a set of supplementary statements be presented in which all the data in the financial reports would be adjusted in a consistent manner. As a result, the increased basis of the inventories and fixed assets and the effect of holding long-term debt would be reflected in these supplementary statements.

51

Proposed Adjustments Are Desirable
Provided They Are Also Acceptable for Tax Purposes

Management is understandably reluctant to reduce net income by charges that are not recognized by tax purposes. But whether an item is, or is not, deductible for tax purposes is determined primarily by political rather than by accounting considerations, and political considerations should not determine accounting practice. Even so, the attitude of management reverses the proper sequence. If the business community wants recognition of price-level changes for tax purposes, it should take the lead by incorporating them in their financial reports. Management and accountants are in a weak position if they seem to favor a procedure for tax purposes which they are unwilling to incorporate into financial statements. Paul Grady makes this point in an article in *The Journal of Accountancy*, April 1959, page 60, when he states that

> . . . Treasury Department officials have made clear that they will not endorse any price-level depreciation allowance for tax pur-

poses unless it is coupled with appropriate recognition in the accounts. This suggests that the possibility of obtaining tax reform would be greatly improved if the accounting profession would remove the roadblock created by the Bulletin [chapter 9, *ARB No. 43*].

5

Methods of Disclosure

Completely Adjusted Financial Statements

If price-level effects are to be recognized in financial statements, the most practicable procedure in the foreseeable future is to present the adjusted data as supplementary to the unadjusted (conventional) statements. The presentation of completely adjusted financial statements, either as supplementary exhibits or in extra columns in the primary exhibits, should be particularly effective in a period of experimentation during which the reader of the reports would become familiar with the nature and significance of the adjusted figures. To guide the readers of the annual reports when presented with two versions of the results of operation or of financial position, an explanation of the meaning and significance of the adjusted amounts would be needed.

In the preparation of these supplementary but completely adjusted financial statements, the necessary adjustments would usually be recorded at the end of the accounting period, and these statements would ordinarily be expressed in terms of the dollar at the end of the period. (The index for the last month or quarter would be used unless the price level was changing very rapidly.) All nonmonetary items would be restated and brought up to date, the monetary items would appear unchanged, and the gain or loss in purchasing power of the monetary items would be recorded in the financial statements as a separate item.

In completely adjusted financial statements, all the amounts would be based on the same standard measuring unit and would therefore be comparable. As a result, the rate of return on the "adjusted" investment would be more accurate, the depreciation and related asset amounts would recognize price-level changes (but not necessarily current replacement costs), dividends could be interpreted in relation to more meaningful earnings, the proportion of earnings actually being taken by income taxes would be more apparent, the gains and losses from holding or maintaining monetary items would be disclosed, and so on.

Among the advantages of the use of supplementary financial statements is the fact that bond indentures and other such contracts often contain references and restrictions as to net income, dividends, working capital, etc., which in equity should probably be interpreted in the light of the accounting principles and procedures in use at the date of the agreement. The unadjusted primary statements will supply this information. Similarly, in the field of business law, there are many references to accounting terms and concepts such as net profit, earned surplus, dividends, etc., which will no doubt continue to be interpreted for an indefinite period in terms of unadjusted accounting data.

Credit grantors have through experience established more or less standard financial ratios. The supplementary data, recognizing price-level changes, will give them an opportunity to re-examine these ratios and develop new standards based on the adjusted figures.

Partially Adjusted Financial Statements

The most common partial adjustment of the financial statements is the restatement of depreciation, sometimes associated with a restatement of the related asset costs and the accumulated depreciation. The restriction of the partial adjustment to depreciation is an incomplete indication of the effect of inflation or deflation upon the net profit. In addition to depreciation, the cost of materials used or of goods sold is usually affected significantly. Also, the loss or gain on monetary items should be disclosed separately as a distinctive feature of price-level adjustments. In many cases it is true that depreciation would involve the largest adjustment, but at least these three adjusted items should appear when any attempt is made to revise the net earnings so as to reflect the change in the price level. Even then, the adjusted net profit figure will have its usefulness restricted unless the balance-sheet accounts are also restated. For example, a meaningful rate of return cannot be computed by comparing the adjusted net profit with the unadjusted or partially adjusted stockholders' equity.

Minimum Requirements of Adequate Disclosure

Adequate disclosure of the effects of inflation or deflation upon the accounting data should begin with the preparation of fully adjusted financial statements, using an index of the general price level. In lieu of the presentation of these statements in the annual report, the key figures can be presented in schedules, charts, or verbal comments. The particular items selected for this purpose may vary from one business or industry to another, or from one year to another, but the minimum requirements for adequate disclosure of the effects of price-level changes would ordinarily include the following:

1. Sales or other major source of revenue. Unadjusted and adjusted amounts should be compared for a period of years, either in current dollars or as percentages of a base year.

2. Net profit. The unadjusted (conventional) amount, and the amount of net profit that results from the adjustment of the component items (revenues and expenses) for price-level changes, should be compared for a period of years.

3. Common stockholders' equity. Sufficient information should be presented to permit the calculation of the adjusted rate of return over the period of years for which net profit figures are shown.

4. Purchasing-power gains and losses on monetary items. The amount of these gains and losses should be shown, together with an indication as to how they have been treated in the calculation of net profit and the common stockholders' equity.

Other information might include a comparison of unadjusted and adjusted depreciation, the percentage of income taxes to adjusted net profit, the relation of dividends to adjusted net profit, a comparison of unadjusted and adjusted cost of goods sold, and sufficient additional data to permit the calculation of the adjusted rate of return on total investment.

Comparative data. If the financial data are presented in terms of the price level at the balance-sheet date, any prior years' figures in-

55

cluded for comparative purposes will also have to be restated in terms of the same price level. This "alteration" of figures already reported in previous financial statements is an unavoidable consequence of inflation and deflation—the price level is moving, whether or not it is measured and recognized in the financial statements. But the possible unsettling effect on the reader of the statement can be minimized by casting comparative data (e.g., sales, net profit, for each of the past five years) in the form of ratios or percentages. The *percentage* of adjusted net profit to adjusted sales, for example, for a past year is not altered by restating the financial statements of that year in terms of the price level at any other point of time. The same is true of the *ratio* of adjusted current assets to adjusted current liabilities, or the *ratio* of income taxes to (adjusted) net profit before tax. In brief, the introduction of price-level adjusted data into financial reporting can be the occasion for a change in emphasis in presenting comparative data, a change away from "absolute" dollar figures to true comparatives, such as ratios, percentages, and trends.

Examples of financial statements adjusted for price-level effects will be found in Appendix D. The Philips Lamp statements (pages 184 to 193) represent a set of financial statements adjusted in part for price-level effects and in part for changed replacement cost. Indiana Telephone Corporation (pages 194 to 199) uses parallel columns to present their financial statements with and without adjustments to fixed assets and depreciation. The Reece Corporation (pages 173 to 183) represents an effective use of narrative, and of charts and graphs to convey the story, without touching the conventional statements at all. Reece solves the dilemma of presenting comparative data by making all its comparisons as percentages or ratios of a base year.

56

APPENDIX A

The Index Number Problem

By Cecilia Tierney

Table of Contents

58

60

Section 1: Introduction

The Purpose of the Study

The purpose of this study is to give accountants an outline of some of the problems involved in index number construction and their implications for accounting records and statements. This involves (1) a review of the criteria of a satisfactory price index, with special reference to one that will measure the general level of prices, (2) an examination of some of the well-known price indexes that are currently compiled to see how well they meet these criteria, and (3) the selection of the index (of those studied) that best measures changes in the general level of prices, including an indication of its limitations and suggestions for improvement.

Some Applications of Index Numbers

Some familiar indexes. The use of index numbers to express the relationship between existing conditions and some norm (base condition) is familiar to all. The changes in the "cost-of-living" are commonly expressed in terms of the U. S. Bureau of Labor Statistics' (BLS) Consumer Price Index popularly known as the cost-of-living index. The public has been introduced to the U. S. Department of Agriculture's Parity Index in discussions of agricultural price supports, while increases or decreases in industrial activity are expressed in terms of the Index of Industrial Production published by the Federal Reserve Board.

Early adjustments for fluctuations in the value of money. Adjustment for fluctuations in the value of money is not new. Irving Fisher in *The Money Illusion* gives many examples of cases both here and abroad of contracts that provided for payment of money equal in value to a specified amount of a commodity or group of commodities.[1] One of his examples refers to a law passed in Massachusetts in 1780 providing for the payment of certain notes issued by the State in money equal to the value of a group of commodities. The note specified:

> Both Principal and Interest to be paid in the then current Money of said State, in a greater or less Sum, according as Five Bushels of Corn, Sixty-eight Pounds and four-seventh Parts of a Pound of Beef, Ten Pounds of Sheeps Wool, and Sixteen Pounds of Sole Leather shall then cost, more or less than One Hundred and Thirty Pounds current Money, at the then current prices of the said Articles.[2]

Labor has used an index of the "cost-of-living" as a lever for raising wages during inflation since before the entry of the United States into World War I. Beginning in 1922, subsistence and rent allowances for commissioned officers below certain ranks in the armed services were determined by changes in the cost-of-living figures of the United States Bureau of Labor Statistics.[3]

62

An Index and a Price Index Defined

What an index is. Ratios are measures of the size of one quantity relative to the size of another. A ratio may be expressed either as a fraction, e.g., 5/4, or as the quotient derived by dividing the numerator of the fraction by the denominator, e.g., $5/4 = 1.25$. A ratio multiplied by 100 becomes a *percentage*, i.e., $1.25 \times 100 = 125\%$. In other words, 5 is 125 per cent of 4. When each term in a series of quantities is compared to a given term and the ratios are converted to percentages, the percentages are called *relatives* or *index numbers* and the series of percentages is called an index. Therefore, an *index* can be defined as a succession of measurements, expressed as percentages, of the size of each term in a series of quantities relative to a given term. The individual measurements that make up the series are *index numbers*.

What a price index is. There are many currently compiled indexes that measure changes in prices of particular commodities or groups of

---

[1] (Adelphi Company, 1928), pp. 114-19.
[2] *Ibid.* p. 118.
[3] *Ibid.* pp. 119-21.

commodities, for particular industries or groups of industries, for various segments of the economy and for the economy as a whole. The classes of indexes that measure changes in prices are called *price indexes*. This group of indexes is of particular interest for accounting applications.

Price indexes may be divided for convenience into two types: (1) those that measure relative changes in the prices of specific commodities or related groups of commodities, and (2) those that measure relative changes in the *price level* prevailing in the economy as a whole or in a segment of that economy. These two types differ in the scope of the prices measured. A third group, those that measure the change in the *purchasing power of the dollar* either in the economy as a whole or in a segment of it, are the reciprocals of the price-level indexes and are not, strictly speaking, "price indexes." They measure the changes in the exchange value of money rather than in prices, whereas the price-level indexes measure changes in the quantity of goods and services that money will buy. For example, if the general level of prices in 1962 is 150 (1952 = 100), then prices are 150/100 or 3/2 as high in 1962 as in 1952.[4] The purchasing power of the dollar in 1962, however, is the "reciprocal" of 3/2, or 2/3, or 66⅔ per cent of its power in 1952.

63

A *price index* can be defined for purposes of this study as a series of measurements, expressed as percentages, of the relationship between the average price of a group of goods and services at a succession of dates[5] and the average price of a similar group of goods and services at a common date. The components of the series are price index numbers. A price index does not, however, measure the movement of the individual component prices, some of which move in one direction and some in the opposite direction.

Weighting an index. An index of the price level compares the relative changes in the prices of all goods and services exchanged in the economy. Since more than one commodity is involved, it is necessary to give consideration to the relative importance of each one. This is termed "weighting." To illustrate the importance of "weighting," the following familiar example from the area of financial statement analysis is presented. It is the case of the relationship among

---

[4] The percent sign (%) is understood but not expressed with index numbers.

[5] Price indexes may compare prices in different places as well as at different times but comparisons between places are not within the scope of this study.

gross profit per unit, number of units sold, and the rate of gross profit for the business as a whole:

	Period			
	I		II	
Commodity A				
Sales price	$100	100%	$110	100%
Cost	60	60	62	56
Gross profit	$ 40	40%	$ 48	44%
Sales in units		9,000		4,000
Commodity B				
Sales price	$ 50	100%	$ 60	100%
Cost	40	80	45	75
Gross profit	$ 10	20%	$ 15	25%
Sales in units		1,000		10,000
		10,000		14,000

Between Period I and Period II, the sales price per unit increased by $10 for both Commodity A and Commodity B. The gross profit on a unit of Commodity A increased from 40 to 44 per cent of the selling price, or $8 a unit. The gross profit on a unit of Commodity B also increased; in this case from 20 to 25 per cent of the selling price, or $5 a unit. In addition, the total units of product sold increased from 10,000 units in Period I to 14,000 units in Period II. But note the effect on the rate of gross profit of the business when there is a shift in quantities between high profit and low profit commodities:

I

Sales

A:	9,000	@	100	$900,000		
B:	1,000	@	50	50,000	$ 950,000	100%

Cost

A:	9,000	@	60	$540,000		
B:	1,000	@	40	40,000	580,000	61
	Gross profit				$ 370,000	39%

II

Sales

A:	4,000	@	110	$440,000		
B:	10,000	@	60	600,000	$1,040,000	100%

Cost

A:	4,000	@	62	$248,000		
B:	10,000	@	45	450,000	698,000	67
	Gross profit				$ 342,000	33%

64

The effect of the shift in importance of the number of units sold from a high profit commodity (A) to a low profit commodity (B) is shown in the reduced rate of gross profit for the two commodities combined. The favorable effects of an increase in gross profit per unit for both A and B are more than offset when the unit profits are "weighted" by the quantities sold.

The base date. The common date that serves as the basis of comparison in an index is referred to as the *base, base date,* or *base period.* The base date may be either a point in time (e.g., June 12, 1960) or it may be a period of some duration (e.g., 1954 or 1947-49). The indexes currently compiled by the Federal Government use a period of either a year or three years as a base.

In a price-level index, a base date that covers one or more years is desirable because of the seasonal character of so many important commodities. If the duration of the base is only a day, or even a month or a quarter, it may not be possible to get representative prices for commodities that are out of season. When the base date is one or more years, the prices for the base are the average prices over that time. It is not necessary for the base date to be considered "normal," although this may be desirable for some types of analysis. Any date may serve as the base date as long as the commodities being compared at the respective dates have enough in common for the comparison to be valid.

65

Example of the Construction of a Simple Price Index for Lifo Inventory Valuation

The dollar-value method of pricing Lifo inventories under the Internal Revenue Code presents an interesting example of the construction by the accountant of a relatively simple price index, and the application of that index to the solution of an accounting valuation problem. The following example, taken from T.D. 6539, § 1.472-8 (Jan. 20, 1961),[6] illustrates the computation of the Lifo value of inventories under the "double-extension" rule.

(a) A taxpayer elects, beginning with the calendar year 1961, to compute his inventories by use of the LIFO inventory method under section 472 and further elects to use the dollar-value

---

[6] Also Reg. § 1.472-8(e)(2)(v), *Income Tax Regulations as of February 1, 1961.* CCH 1961, 31051-6, 7.

method in pricing such inventories as provided in paragraph (a) of this section. He creates Pool No. 1 for items A, B, and C. The composition of the inventory for Pool No. 1 at the base date, January 1, 1961, is as follows:

Items	Units	Unit cost	Total cost
A	1,000	$5.00	$5,000
B	2,000	4.00	8,000
C	500	2.00	1,000
Total base-year cost at Jan. 1, 1961			$14,000

(b) The closing inventory of Pool No. 1 at December 31, 1961, contains 3,000 units of A, 1,000 units of B, and 500 units of C. The taxpayer computes the current-year cost of the items making up the pool by reference to the actual cost of goods most recently purchased. The most recent purchases of items A, B, and C are as follows:

Items	Purchase date	Quantity purchased	Unit cost
A	Dec. 15, 1961	3,500	$6.00
B	Dec. 10, 1961	2,000	5.00
C	Nov. 1, 1961	500	2.50

(c) The inventory of Pool No. 1 at December 31, 1961, shown at base-year and current-year cost is as follows:

Items	Quantity	Dec. 31, 1961, inventory at Jan. 1, 1961 base-year cost		Dec. 31, 1961, inventory at current-year cost	
		Unit cost	Amount	Unit cost	Amount
A	3,000	$5.00	$15,000	$6.00	$18,000
B	1,000	4.00	4,000	5.00	5,000
C	500	2.00	1,000	2.50	1,250
Total			$20,000		$24,250

(d) If the amount of the December 31, 1961 inventory at base-year cost were equal to, or less than, the base-year cost of $14,000 at January 1, 1961, such amount would be the closing LIFO inventory at December 31, 1961. However, since the base-year cost of the closing LIFO inventory at December 31, 1961, amounts to $20,000, and is in excess of the $14,000 base-year cost of the opening inventory for that year, there is a $6,000 increment in Pool No. 1 during the year. This increment must be valued at current-year cost, i.e., the ratio of 24,250/20,000, or 121.25 percent. The LIFO value of the inventory at December 31, 1961, is $21,275, computed as follows:

Pool No. 1

	Dec. 31, 1961, inventory at Jan. 1, 1961 base-year cost	Ratio of total current-year cost to total base-year cost*	Dec. 31, 1961, inventory at LIFO value
Jan. 1, 1961, base cost	14,000	100.00	$14,000
Dec. 31, 1961, increment	6,000	121.25	7,275
Total	20,000	....	$21,275

* The index numbers.

In this case, an index number is used to value the increase in the inventory pool at current-year cost. The entire ending inventory is priced at both base-year and current-year cost and the relationship between the two is expressed as an index number. The increment in the inventory pool, expressed in base-year costs, is multiplied by this index number to convert it to current cost.

The weighted average used for the computation of this index is known as "Paasche's formula" which may be expressed as $\dfrac{\Sigma\, p_1 q_1}{\Sigma\, p_0 q_1}$ where the subscript "1" (one) refers to the current year and the subscript "o" to the base year.[7] Applied to the example above, this expression reads:

67

> To find the index number for the current year
>
> divide (i) the sum (Σ) of the actual units included in the ending inventory (q_1) expressed in the current-year prices (p_1)
>
> by (ii) the sum (Σ) of the same items (q_1) expressed in base-year prices (p_0).
>
> To complete the process, multiply the resulting ratio by one hundred.

Federal *Income Tax Regulations* also permit the accountant to use any index that is acceptable to the Commissioner.[8]

Conversion Technique

Index numbers provide a convenient method of stating the relationship between two magnitudes. For this reason they provide practical

---

[7] This and other formulas are discussed at greater length in Section 3, below.

[8] United States Bureau of Labor Statistics (BLS) indexes which are applicable to the goods in question are acceptable to the Commissioner. Reg. § 1.472-1(k), *Income Tax Regulations as of February 1, 1961.* CCH. 1961, p. 31049.

tools for the translation of dollar amounts from one point of time to another. The procedure used is to multiply the amount involved by the index number of the point in time to which the conversion is to be made, I_1, and to divide by the index number of the point of time from which the conversion is made, I_0. Expressed as a fraction, this procedure becomes $\frac{I_1}{I_0}$. For example, to convert a cost of \$36,000 from a point of time when the relevant index stood at 90 (I_0) to a point of time when it stood at 120 (I_1), multiply \$36,000 by $\frac{120}{90}$.

$$\$36,000 \times \frac{120}{90} = \$48,000$$

The same process could be used to convert the \$48,000 from the later date to the earlier date, specifically $\$48,000 \times \frac{90}{120} = \$36,000$, which is the original amount.

Relationship of an Index to Its Intended Use

If an index (or indexes) is to be used in the preparation of financial reports, the type of information that accounting statements are to convey must be clearly defined because the desired result determines the data from which the index is constructed. If, for example, the statements are to reflect the situation as to physical capital maintenance, a set of indexes that measure the specific price changes that affect the individual accounts would be appropriate. If, however, "capital maintenance" refers to the general purchasing power of enterprise capital, an index of the general level of prices is called for.

When relative weights are held constant, changes in an index are caused by changes in the relative prices of the specific commodities priced. Therefore, an index cannot measure directly price changes for either a smaller or larger group than the group it represents: an index of prices paid by farmers does not measure changes in prices paid by city dwellers, nor does it measure the average price change in the economy as a whole, since prices do not react in the same way in all segments of the economy. In this sense, there is a cause and effect relationship between the data from which an index is constructed, and the movement of terms in that index.

For example, suppose an index of the general level of prices is desired but the only one available is an index that applies to only a limited segment of the economy. Even though the desired index and the substitute both refer to "price levels," the results would not necessarily be comparable because the indexes are measures of different things.

There may, however, be a high degree of correlation between two indexes so that the price movements measured by an index for one segment of the economy may approximate price movements in another sector or in the economy as a whole. When this correlation exists, the index for one segment of the economy may be used to estimate relative price changes in the other sector, or in the economy as a whole, when the desired index is not available. It must be remembered, however, that there is no guarantee that this relationship will continue. Unless there is something inherent in the data from which the indexes are constructed that will insure the permanence of parallel tendencies, the possibility of dissociation, with its accompanying effect on financial reporting, should be recognized whenever a substitute index is used.

In recent decades the Consumer Price Index, the GNP (Gross National Product) Implicit Price Deflator, and the Composite Construction Cost Index have usually "moved together" (the direction of change and the turning points, but not the amplitude). The kind of reason that may explain these parallel tendencies might be found in the importance of wages and salaries in the economy. One possible explanation, for example, is that labor costs account for a high proportion of Gross National Product while the Consumer Price Index and the Composite Construction Cost Index cover commodities with a high content of labor cost; therefore all three indexes are greatly influenced, directly or indirectly, by movements in wages and salaries. Some correlation is therefore to be expected—a high correlation is not surprising.

The purpose for which an index is intended determines the data to be compared. An index of price changes in one specific market of one specific commodity will be constructed from prices of that commodity in that market. An index of the average price change of a group of commodities in one market will be constructed from suitably weighted prices of those commodities in that market. An index of the relative change in the over-all level of prices can only be constructed from data that are representative of all goods and services exchanged in all segments of the economy.

69

Section 2: Currently Available Price Indexes a Brief Description

Types of General Price Information That Are Available

The wealth of data that has been published in this country from an early date gives evidence that "a strong passion for statistics early developed itself in the life of our people. . . ."[1] Estimates of the total value of all the real and personal property in the United States (exclusive of Louisiana Territory) were published as early as 1806 and a historical table of price fluctuations over the fifty-six year period from 1825 through 1880 was included in the "Annual Report of the Director of the Mint, 1881," (Horatio C. Burchard).[2] A growing interest in price and value information has resulted in the collection of data and the compilation and publication of time-series by numerous governmental agencies and private organizations. A wealth of time-price information is therefore available. Time-price series, some of which have been translated into indexes, have been published by various agencies for many individual products of numerous industries. These series are available for many of the products of agriculture, forestry, mining and metal products industries, manufacturing, construction and housing, and numerous other areas.

The Board of Governors of the Federal Reserve System compiles and publishes extensive information relative to the price of money including

---

[1] Francis A. Walker, quoted in "Historical Statistics of the United States 1789-1945," a *Supplement to the Statistical Abstract of the United States,* U. S. Department of Commerce, Bureau of the Census. 1949. p. v.

[2] *Loc. cit.* p. 1.

Federal Reserve Bank Discount rates, maximum interest rates payable on time deposits, money market rates, bank rates on short-term business loans, member bank reserve requirements, security prices, margin requirements, bond and stock yields, etc. These data are derived from regular reports made to the Board by banks of the Federal Reserve System, Treasury Statements, and other sources and are published monthly in the *Federal Reserve Bulletin*.

Farm prices, income, expenditures, debts, etc., are collected and published monthly in *Agricultural Marketing* by the U. S. Department of Agriculture; statistics about metals and minerals are available from the Bureau of Mines (U. S. Department of the Interior) upon request; financial data on education are published in the *Biennial Survey of Education* by the Department of Health, Education and Welfare, and so on.

Price, quantity, and value data are collected by numerous agencies of the Federal Government, by industrial groups, by various special interest groups and by independent research groups. Some of the data have been converted into index numbers; many more have not. Of the indexes that have been compiled, several have gained prominence and warrant individual description.

71

Examples of Price Indexes

The Index of Change in Prices of Goods and Services Purchased by City Wage-Earner and Clerical-Worker Families to Maintain Their Level of Living (better known as the "Consumer Price Index" or the "CPI") measures the average change in the retail prices of a "market basket" of approximately 300 goods and services purchased by wage-earner and clerical-worker families in 46 cities in the U.S.A. The goods and services in the market basket are identical in quantity and quality in consecutive pricing periods, except for substitutes that are introduced to replace items no longer available. The goods and services priced include foods, clothing, fuel, housefurnishings and other goods; the fees paid to doctors and dentists; rents; rates charged for utilities, and so on.

In addition to an "all-city average of all items," several subindexes are also published. These subindexes include indexes by city for twenty cities of all items and for food prices; the all-city average by type of commodity, i.e., food, housing, apparel, etc., and a regrouping by durable goods, nondurable goods, and all services.

There have been three major revisions (1934-36, World War II, 1950-

52) of this index since it was first issued in 1919 (with data from 1913). The revisions involved (1) bringing the market basket up-to-date through studies of actual expenditures, (2) improving the sample, and (3) improving the methodology (calculation and pricing methods, specifications, etc.). The index numbers presently in effect (i.e., the latest revision) for this series use 1957-59 prices = 100 with 1952 weights (i.e., the relative importance given to the approximately 300 goods and services included in the market basket) since January 1953, 1949-50 weights for the period 1950 to 1952, 1934-36 weights for the period 1930 to 1949, 1917-19 weights from 1913 to 1925, and an average of the 1917-19 weights and the 1934-36 weights for the period 1926 to 1929. A new comprehensive revision of the index is in process which is scheduled to go into effect in the January 1964 index.

According to the *Labor Law Reporter*,[3] the current index is representative of the buying patterns in 1952 of 64% of the urban population and 40% of the total U. S. population.

The *Consumer Price Index* is prepared by the Bureau of Labor Statistics of the U. S. Department of Labor, and is available in publications of the Bureau which include:

72

Monthly Labor Review
Consumer Price Index (a separate monthly publication)
Statistical Supplement—Monthly Labor Review (annual beginning with 1959)

Secondary sources include publications of:

U. S. Department of Commerce, Office of Business Economics:
  Survey of Current Business (monthly)
  Supplement to the Survey of Current Business (biannually)
Board of Governors of the Federal Reserve System:
  Federal Reserve Bulletin (monthly)
Commerce Clearing House:
  Union Contracts Arbitration section of the *Labor Law Reporter*

The *Wholesale Price Index* (WPI) measures average changes in prices of about 2,200 commodities sold in primary markets in the United States. Wholesale, as used here, means sales in large lots. The

---

[3] *Labor Law Reporter*, Union Contracts Arbitration 1, CCH 1960. ¶ 56,100.02.

prices apply as nearly as possible to the first large volume commercial transaction for each commodity, e.g., the selling prices of grains on the organized exchanges, of fresh produce at central auction markets, of machinery f.o.b. manufacturer's factory, and so forth. The weights used are based on the total value of shipments data (from the Industrial Censuses for 1958) f.o.b. production point, less interplant transfers, for the producing and processing sector of the economy. The prices used are those in effect on a particular day of the month, in most cases Tuesday of the week in which the 15th of the month falls.

This index has been published as a continuous series since 1890. At the time it was first constructed it was believed that it reflected the behavior of the price level more correctly than retail prices but with the passage of time its use as a "general price-level index" has declined. Preference has developed for the use of the Consumer Price Index (CPI) and the index number derived from the calculation of Gross National Product in current and constant dollars and known as the "GNP deflators" (for a discussion of GNP deflators, see pages 76 to 78). One major cause of the shift was the realization that the Wholesale Price Index was not a true sample of the prices in the economy and that it was not particularly pertinent to any one group of consumers or businesses.[4] It is not a measure of "wholesale prices," as its name implies, but a measure of *some* wholesale prices in specific markets.

Since "GNP deflators" are available only on a yearly and quarterly basis, no index is available to measure price-level movements on a current month-to-month basis. The Wholesale Price Index together with the Consumer Price Index, however, serve as an approximate indicator of the movement of the price level. Although use of the Wholesale Price Index has declined, the highly detailed and specific subindexes of individual industries, commodities, and product classes are widely used by manufacturers, by trade associations and by various government agencies in the production of other basic economic data.[5] For example, the U. S. Department of Commerce makes extensive use of the product class and commodity price data in the deflation of Gross National Product.

The detailed indexes are published in four different groupings of which the most detailed groups the individual products by industry. The other groupings are by stage of processing, durability of product,

73

---

[4] Hearings before the Subcommittee on Economic Statistics . . . Part I, January 24, 1961. *Government Price Statistics*, pp. 61-64.

[5] *Ibid.* pp.63-64.

and special commodity groupings. The grouping by industry would be the most valuable for accounting purposes if adjustments in financial statements were to be made for changes in the prices of specific commodities rather than for changes in the price level.

The Wholesale Price Index is prepared by the U. S. Department of Labor, Bureau of Labor Statistics and is available in publications of the Bureau including separate monthly and annual publication of the Wholesale Price Index. Secondary sources include those for the Consumer Price Index, except for the *Labor Law Reporter* which does not publish the Wholesale Price Index.

The U. S. Department of Commerce—Composite Construction Cost Index is a combination of various construction cost indexes weighted by the relative importance of the major classes of construction. The index is computed by dividing the total seasonally adjusted estimates of new construction activity in current prices by the same estimates expressed in 1957-59 prices.[6] The total in 1957-59 prices is obtained by adding the estimates for the various classes of construction that have been deflated separately.[7] Therefore, the composite index is the equivalent of a variably weighted index reflecting changes in both the component indexes and in the relative importance of the major classes of construction.[8] An index of this type, i.e., one that is inherent in the relationship between an aggregate before deflation and the same aggregate after deflation, is frequently referred to as an *implicit* index.

This index is published in total only, with a 1957-59 base. Some of the component indexes that are used to deflate the various classes of construction, however, are published along with it. The component indexes do not all have the same base. Some of them use 1947-49 as a base while others use 1946 and still others use 1926-29 or 1913. Some of the component indexes are by type of construction, e.g., commercial and factory buildings of brick and concrete, brick and steel, frame, etc., others by city or in total.

74

---

[6] Data are adjusted for seasonal effects by dividing the unadjusted datum for a given month by a constant percentage factor whose deviation from 100 registers the extent to which that period of the year is typically above or below some measure of "normal" because of seasonal influences.

[7] The term *deflate* is used in this paper in a technical sense meaning "to remove the effects of price changes." It refers to both increases and decreases in prices and therefore applies to both "deflation" and "inflation."

[8] *Business Statistics*, 1959 Supplement to the *Survey of Current Business*, U. S. Department of Commerce, Office of Business Economics. p. 219.

Unlike the two indexes of commodity prices previously described which are indexes of output (goods or services produced), the Composite Construction Cost Index is a measure of the relative change in cost of the *units* of *input,* i.e., the cost per unit of the factors of production, of which wage rates and materials cost are the most important. If wage rates increase or the cost of a thousand board feet of lumber increases, this index number increases. This is the only index reviewed in this report that measures change in the cost of units of input. Any difference between the changes measured by an index number derived from input costs and those measured by one derived from commodity prices or output (for the same items) is due to changes in productivity. For example, if construction wage rates and contractor's profits both increased, a construction cost index would also increase. It would, however, still be possible to have a decrease in the selling prices of completed construction work, provided that productivity increased more than wage rates and profits. In that case the effect on the general price level would be downward.

The individual indexes (many of which are privately compiled) used in deflating the current dollar figures for the different classes of construction include: 75

Residential building, except farm:
   E. H. Boeckh and Associates

Farm buildings:
   U. S. Department of Agriculture

Nonresidential building, selected types and military facilities:
   American Appraisal Company
   Fuller
   Turner Construction Co.

Public utilities, selected types:
   Interstate Commerce Commission
   Handy-Whitman

Military facilities and highway:
   U. S. Department of Commerce, Bureau of Public Roads

Sewer and water, conservation and development, and miscellaneous:
   Associated General Contractors of America, Inc.
   Engineering News-Record

The Composite Construction Cost Index is prepared by the Construction Industry Division, Business and Defense Services Administration of the U. S. Department of Commerce and is available in the following publications of the Department:

The Survey of Current Business

Supplements to the Survey of Current Business

Statistical Supplement to the Construction Review
(published jointly by the U. S. Departments of Commerce and Labor on a monthly basis).

Monthly indexes are available from 1951 and annual indexes beginning with 1915.

GNP (Gross National Product) Implicit Price Deflator. The elimination of the effects of price changes from the total dollar value of the Nation's production (so that the physical volume of all goods and services produced by the economy in different time periods can be compared) is accomplished through the use of numerous price indexes and price series, including the three foregoing indexes. The GNP Implicit Price Deflator is the resultant composite index implicit in the relationship of the figures before and after deflation, and is the most comprehensive price index available. It measures the relationship between (a) the total value of all goods and services produced in a given year expressed in current dollars, and (b) the total value of the same goods and services expressed in prices of a base year (constant dollars).

Gross National Product, in both current and constant prices, is subdivided into four classes of expenditures: personal consumption expenditures, gross private domestic investment, net exports of goods and services, and governmental purchases of goods and services. Each of these four classes is further subdivided into its component parts. In tables of GNP Implicit Price Deflators, however, deflators are not shown for gross private domestic investment and net exports of goods and services because significant components of these items include elements of opposite algebraic sign. Deflators for exports and for imports, taken separately as independent series, are meaningful indicators of price movements. A deflator of the *difference* between exports and imports is not reliable, however, because a relatively small *increase* in the prices of exports, accompanied by a relatively small *decrease* in the prices of imports will cause a disproportionately large change in the movement of price of *net* exports. For example, suppose that in the base year exports totaled $1,000,000 and imports totaled $900,000 leaving net exports of $100,000. If exports increase by two per cent (2%) while imports decrease by two per cent (2%), net exports will increase by thirty-eight per cent (38%):

	Base Year	Percentage Increase (Decrease)	Current Year
Exports	$1,000,000	2%	$1,020,000
Imports	900,000	(2%)	882,000
Net exports	$ 100,000	38%	$ 138,000

For similar reasons, a deflator of "change in business inventories" is likely to be unreliable. Since "change in business inventories" is frequently a significant component of "gross private domestic investment," deflators are not calculated for the total of this subdivision of GNP, although they are presented for all of the other components of this segment. In the total picture of GNP, however, changes in business inventories and net exports of goods and services are not likely to be substantial and do not, therefore, disqualify the deflators for total GNP as indicators of price movements.

77

The GNP deflators are prepared by the U. S. Department of Commerce, Office of Business Economics and are available in the *Survey of Current Business* and supplements.

The *U. S. Income and Output* supplement to the *Survey of Current Business* includes annual deflators from 1929 through 1957 and seasonally adjusted quarterly deflators from 1947 through 1957.

The National Income Number of the *Survey of Current Business*, published annually in July, brings up-to-date the information in the *U. S. Income and Output* supplement. Interim seasonally adjusted quarterly deflators are available in the "Annual Review Number," issued in February, for the preceding year.

Although final revised deflators are not available for any quarter until July of the following year, interim deflators can be computed by dividing the current dollar estimates (seasonally adjusted at annual rates) of the GNP by the constant dollar estimates that are published in the *Survey of Current Business* in the second month following the end of each quarter.

Data for accounting reports adjusted by deflators computed from the preliminary estimates of current and constant dollar GNP would not be materially different from amounts derived by using the revised estimates published in July of the following year. A test of 1959, 1960 and 1961 quarterly and annual deflators showed that the largest difference in the adjusted data would have been roughly one-half of one per cent.

The largest difference in the test period was for the quarter ended December 31, 1961. The preliminary estimates for this quarter first appeared in the February 1962 issue of the *Survey of Current Business* (pages S-1 and S-2):

	Billions of Dollars
GNP in current dollars	542.2
GNP in constant (1954) dollars	464.6

The deflator implicit in the preliminary estimates is: $542.2 \div 464.6 = 116.7$

The revised estimates in the July 1962 issue (page S-1, and table 1, pages 6-7; table 5, pages 8-9) are:

	Billions of Dollars
GNP in current dollars (revised)	538.6
GNP in constant (1954) dollars (revised)	463.4

78

The revised deflator, 116.2 is published in table 6 (page 9) of the July issue.

Measurement of Price Changes by U. S. Price Indexes

The four price indexes described in the previous section are charted in Figure 1, page 79, for the years 1929-1961 inclusive. Each of these indexes is designed to measure price changes in different groups of commodities: (1) the Consumer Price Index measures changes in prices of goods and services purchased by city wage-earner and clerical-worker families to maintain their level of living, (2) the Wholesale Price Index measures changes in the prices of nearly 2,200 commodities that are sold in primary markets, (3) the Composite Construction Cost Index is designed to show the changes in the cost of the units of input in the construction industry and (4) the GNP Implicit Price Deflator measures the price changes in all of the goods and services produced by the economy in a given year. Since these indexes do not attempt to measure changes in the same groups of prices, they cannot be expected to arrive at the same measurement.

Even though these indexes do not measure the changes in the same

Figure 1

U. S. PRICE INDEXES

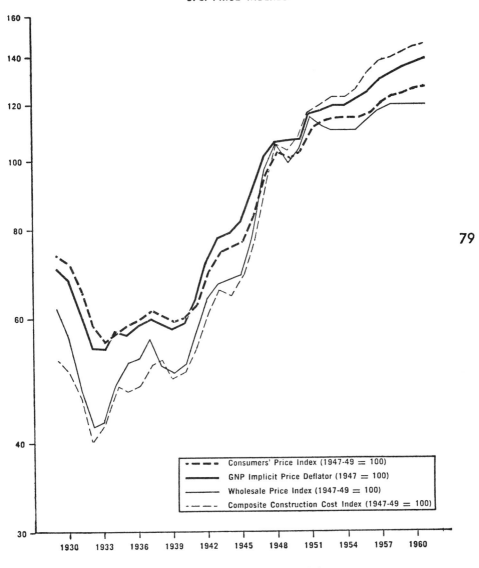

79

Source: U. S. Department of Commerce and U. S. Department of Labor Publications.

groups of prices, the curves (in Figure 1) show parallel tendencies. The similarity in trends suggests that the increases in price levels indicated by these indexes are real.

That this inference is plausible can be demonstrated by a few admittedly rough but nevertheless valid comparisons. An increasing quantity of goods and services are available per person in the United States because the rate of growth shown in both the Index of Industrial Production and the Gross National Product (in constant dollars) has been greater than the rate of increase in the population. The rate of growth in the supply of money, however, has been much greater than in the output of goods and services so that proportionately more money has been available for the purchase of each unit of output. In addition, the rate of turnover of demand deposits has also increased, thereby enabling a given quantity of money to serve as a means of payment for an increasing volume of transactions.

As a consequence of these circumstances, a general rise in prices with an accompanying decline in the exchange value of money is almost inevitable. The statistics used in making the above comparisons can be found in the following publications:

Business Statistics, 1959 Supplement to the *Survey of Current Business,* U. S. Department of Commerce, Office of Business Economics.

Data for 1929-1958 inclusive:
Gross National Product in constant dollars, p. 3.
Index of Industrial Production, p. 8.
Population, p. 59.
Money supply, p. 96.

Annual rate of turnover of demand deposits 1943-1958 inclusive, p. 96.

Earlier annual deposit turnover rates are available in "Historical Statistics of the United States 1789-1945" *op. cit.,* p. 269. These rates are not comparable with the later rates previously cited because of differences in the extent of coverage.

Federal Reserve Bulletin, February 1962.

Data subsequent to 1958:
Gross National Product in constant dollars, p. 230.
Index of Industrial Production, p. 216.
Money supply, p. 185.
Annual rate of turnover of demand deposits, p. 185.

80

Section 3: The Criteria of Adequate Price Indexes

Definition of Terms

The problem of an adequate index divides itself naturally into three parts: the universe, the sample, and the formula.

The universe. The first step in the selection of an index is a precise definition of the concept to be measured so that the class of items that enter into the measurement can be clearly defined. The collection of all possible items that have the stated characteristics of the class of items defined is called a *universe.* The universe, then, is the totality [whole, aggregate, mass] that is under observation and about which information is desired. The concept to be measured, precisely formulated, would determine the exact limits of the universe.

81

The sample. In most cases it would be neither practical nor desirable to obtain data for the entire universe. The cost would be prohibitive and the time necessary to collect and process the data would result in an index that was out of date when prepared and, therefore, useful only as historical data. Valid conclusions can be drawn at more reasonable cost and in considerably less time by the careful selection of comparatively few items that are representative of all items in the universe. The items selected to represent the universe are called a *sample.* A properly selected sample would have the same characteristics as the universe and the index number constructed from the sample would be representative of the index number obtainable from the entire universe.

The formula. Once the universe has been defined and a representative sample selected, the data obtained from the sample are averaged in order to combine them into an index number. To avoid either over-stating or understating the price change measured by the index number, the average must be weighted by the related quantities exchanged at these prices. The weighting scheme used is called the *formula*.

Much of the discussion that follows will be applicable whether adjustment is to be made in the financial reports for changes in prices of the specific items included in the accounts or for changes in the price level. The major emphasis, however, is on an index of the general level of prices.

The Universe

In order to adjust financial reports for changes in the specific prices that are applicable to the individual accounts, a number of indexes or other time-price series would be necessary, each one suitable to the item to be adjusted. The universes for these indexes would be the mass of measurable evidence of the prices of the particular goods and services or related groups of goods and services in the markets in which the company or industry buys those commodities. The universe for an index for one commodity in one market might require only price data. If two or more markets are involved, then the relative importance of prices in the different markets must be given proper weight and both price and quantity data become important. If two or more commodities are combined in one index, whether more than one market is involved or not, both price and quantity data are needed to reflect the relative importance of the prices of the individual commodities. The universe for each of the individual indexes would be defined in terms of the specific account to be adjusted and the specific market in which the company or industry buys, borrows and attracts capital. The universe for each individual index would be comparatively simple to define; there would, however, be a number of them.

The universe for an index of the general level of prices encompasses the over-all group of goods and services exchanged in all segments of the economy in the periods being compared; the "universe" of an index limited to one segment of the economy uses only those exchanges applicable to that segment. The universe includes all transactions that place goods and services in the hands of the final consumers. The effect on the universe that results from interim transactions between the companies that perform the successive processing stages within an industry (e.g., extracting, refining, fabricating, assembling, and marketing) is reflected in the increases and decreases in inventories. If accounting reports are adjusted for changes in the price level, the same index will be used for all adjustments. If the reports are to reflect changes in the general level of prices, the universe will include the aggregate underlying data that represents measurable evidence of the quantity of goods and services that money will buy at the times of measurement. Because the dollar serves as a standard of exchange value, the price of any commodity can be expressed in dollars; the price of dollars, however, can only be expressed in terms of the over-all group of goods and services for which it can be exchanged. The composition of the measurable evidence of the "price of dollars," therefore, will reflect an average of the prices of *all* goods and services exchanged in *all* segments of the economy, both public and private, in the ratio in which they affect the general level of prices.

Preferably, all measurements should rest on evidence that is reliable and subject to verification.[1] Objective evidence of the general level of prices is found in quantities and prices involved in exchange transactions that take place in the economy.

83

The economy encompasses all of the affairs of the nation that are concerned with its source of income, its expenditures, the development of its natural resources and so on. Production, distribution, and consumption of wealth are all included. Because of the scope and complexity of the economy, care must be exercised to insure that all pertinent transactions are included in the universe while at the same time avoiding duplication which would give undue weight to some items. This involves a restricted use of the term *exchange transaction.*

Exchange transactions that affect the general level of prices (those reflected in national income and product accounting) might be compared to the transactions reflected in the consolidated earnings statement of a parent company and its subsidiaries after the elimination of intercompany items. If all of the successive stages of production and distribution were performed by companies within consolidated groups, then consolidated income would be reported only when the product was sold to the final user, and "intermediate products" would have

---

[1] Maurice Moonitz, "The Basic Postulates of Accounting," *Accounting Research Study No. 1.* American Institute of Certified Public Accountants. 1961, p. 50, Postulate C-2.

their effect on net changes in business inventories. Consolidated earnings statements in this case would directly parallel national income and product accounts.

In addition to pinpointing the exchanges in each period that affect the general level of prices, the actual items exchanged must have enough in common to warrant comparison. The rate at which the goods and services available to the consumer are improved, changed, or replaced makes it necessary to select a new base period at frequent intervals because the prices being compared must apply to comparable goods and services if the index is to measure changes in prices.

No definite life span over which a base period is valid can be established; that is determined by the degree and scope of change in the universe in subsequent time periods.

> ...In a stable society, revisions could be extremely infrequent; in the rapidly changing American economy, a revision once in a decade or more (as has more than once been the case with the Farm Indexes and the Consumer Price Index) is too infrequent. The rapid pace of introduction of new products in the United States, the large demographic changes in recent decades, the revolution in production methods—these are instances of the changes that dictate frequent revision of weight bases.[2]

With comparable universes in the two periods, the quantities of most goods and services will be in terms of the units in which those goods and services are marketed. When the exchange transactions that affect the price level have been identified, and comparable quantity units determined, then the prices that prevail for the quantities exchanged can be realistically assigned on a consistent basis.

The collection of all of the prices and quantities necessary for a complete enumeration of the items in the universes described here is a practical impossibility. Therefore, a complete enumeration is replaced by a sample of measures which describe the group as a whole.

The Sample

Inherent in the use of a sample is the assumption that the part of the universe measured is valid evidence of a measure of the whole. The sample therefore should have the same characteristics as the universe if the index number constructed from the sample is to be representative

---

[2] Hearings before the Subcommittee on Economic Statistics ... Part I, Jan. 24, 1961. *Government Price Statistics*, p. 31.

of one obtainable from the entire universe. There are two firmly established methods of selecting a sample: (1) judgmental sampling, and (2) probability sampling.[3]

Judgmental samples. The choice of items in a judgmental sample is made by competent individuals experienced in the area after careful consideration of all the factors related to the problem. Consultation with manufacturers and trade associations, review of census data, and surveys of the purchasing habits of individuals are some of the devices used as preparation for the selection of representative samples. Some of the best known indexes currently compiled are based on this type of sample; at least one of these indexes makes use of a survey of the type mentioned above.

Accountants use judgmental samples in testing all types of accounting data and they base sound decisions on the limited data selected. The interlocking characteristics of accounting data increase the likelihood that the auditors' tests will produce reliable results. Since the data from which index numbers are constructed do not have these interlocking characteristics, census data, income tax returns and other "benchmarks" are used to determine whether the index number is reasonable. Under judgmental sampling, however, there is no way in which a numerical value can be assigned to the degree of confidence that can be placed in the sample. The user of an index based on samples of this type relies on knowledgeable specialists to evaluate the index and determine whether it is accurate enough for his purpose.

85

Probability samples. Inherent in the use of probability samples is the assumption that the validity of using the part as a measure of the whole can be determined within limits that can be estimated in advance if the choice of items is based on the mathematics of probability. When this type of sampling is used, the number of possible selections from the universe, and the importance of the item (as indicated by the weight assigned to it) determine the "chance of selection." For example, in tossing a coin there are two possibilities for each toss, a head or a tail, and each has an equal chance or a probability of one-half, whereas, in throwing a die there are six possibilities for each toss so the probability of any particular number from one to six is one-sixth. In more complex situations all possibilities are not equally likely.

---

[3] The methods used to select the samples for the currently compiled indexes reviewed in this study are discussed in Section 4, page 102.

Because of the method of selection, bias in the person making the selection does not affect the sample. This type of sample is representative of its universe because it is designed to give the same weight to each item (or group of items) in the sample as it has in the universe.

Collecting the Sample

An accurate index number requires accurate data for its computation. The quantitative data used in compiling index numbers do not always originate in measurements taken by those using the data; they are usually reported by others. The collection of data for a price index depends on the co-operation obtained from thousands of individuals and organizations who furnish the information. In order for the collecting agency to receive the data it wants, the commodities, their prices and the related quantities must be clearly defined in a manner that will convey the same meaning to those who furnish the data and those who use it.

Identification of commodities. In order for an index to reflect only price changes, the price quotations that are being compared should apply to comparable goods and services. If prices for dissimilar goods are compared, the resultant index will reflect, in part, the effects of variables other than prices. For this reason the specifications should be in enough detail to identify the goods and services for which data are requested so that the user will get the information he wants.

One of the chief problems of index number construction is insuring that the commodities being priced in successive periods have the same qualities. To achieve this end, specifications should be and are drawn up in elaborate detail (e.g., the specifications for a single producers' durable good may run to several pages). To provide for the diversity of the market, the specifications for some items make allowance for choices by expressing some features of the product as ranges, with the limits of the ranges set to minimize differences in quality among the products within the range.[4] When a commodity is displaced in the market by another having different qualities, the newcomer is substituted in the index for the old by "linking."

Linking (or "bumping" as it is known in Canada) requires prices on the same date for products having the old quality and those having

86

---

[4] Ethel D. Hoover, "The CPI and Problems of Quality Change." *Monthly Labor Review.* Nov. 1961, p. 1177.

the new. In those cases where the full difference in price is due to the quality difference, the price measure based on the new quality is tied to the preceding one by "factoring out" the difference in price.[5] An example of the method used to factor out price differences due entirely to quality change follows:

	Base Period	Period 1	Period 2
Reported price:			
Original item before quality change (old)	$3.00	$3.60	—
Substitute commodity that has different qualities (newcomer)	—	5.00	$4.00
Price relative	—	$\dfrac{3.60}{3.00} \times 100 = 120$	$\dfrac{4.00}{5.00} \times 100 = 80$
Price index	100	120	$\dfrac{120 \times 80}{100} = 96$

In other cases there may be a change in price that is not due entirely to a change in quality. This frequently occurs in the case of commodities that have a model change every year. Similar changes take place in other commodities at irregular time intervals. Calculating price changes for these items requires a more elaborate procedure. First an adjustment is made for any change in price that is due to change in quality. To do this, industry committees are often consulted in the U.S. concerning the effect on prices of changes in technology and quality. Next the adjusted price is compared directly with the price of the former item in the preceding period. In the following period the new variety is "linked" into the index, displacing the old one completely.

As an example of this type of adjustment, suppose that a new safety device is installed as standard equipment on cars marketed in the current period and this device is identifiable with an increase in the price of cars of $50. The current period price would be reduced by $50 before comparing the current period with the preceding period so that the prices compared would represent comparable commodities. In the following period, the price of the car *including* the safety device would be used for comparison in both periods. This method of adjust-

---

[5] *Ibid.* p. 1178.

ing the sample can be used with any of the current methods of index number construction.

In many cases a given commodity is considered to be representative of a group of similar commodities so that the importance of the sample for this item is magnified by the weight assigned to the entire group which it represents.

Tangible products can be readily identified and counted; services (intangible products), which are becoming increasingly important in the U.S., present more difficult problems of measurement. Because services are intangible, the units cannot always be readily identified and no definitive method has been devised to insure that similar units are being compared. Services may be divided into two major groups: (1) those for which there are no market transactions to provide measures of prices and quantities, and (2) those for which there are, i.e., those performed on a fee basis.

A substantial volume of services is purchased by the community through the payment of taxes. For these services there are no market transactions in which a known "quantity" of service is exchanged for a known quantity of money. The quantity units of many of these services are abstract ideas. Agreement on the definition of the unit has not been reached. One method used to estimate the quantity exchanged in these cases is to analyze the component parts or input units.

Public school education is a prime example of a service that is purchased by the community through the payment of taxes. No fee is paid by the parents. There are no market transactions to provide measures of the price and quantity of education exchanged. A unit of education is an abstract idea; there is no agreement on how to measure the output of the public school system. Since no way has been devised to measure the output units, measurement of the input units is substituted. The output, education, is assumed to be worth its cost. The costs of similar input units in the two periods are compared. For example, the cost of salaries for teachers with similar education and teaching experience are weighted by the number of teachers in that classification. The use of the cost of input units does not, however, give weight to changes (if any) in factors such as the productivity of teachers or the quality of instruction given. Accordingly the related effect on the quality of a "unit of education" is not reported or assessed. This method (the use of the costs of inputs) is, however, a good practical approach to a complicated problem for which no better solution has been devised.

Services that are performed on a fee basis include both those for which the unit of output can be readily measured (e.g., number of sheets laundered) and those for which it cannot (e.g., advice of a physician). In both cases the billing unit is used as the quantity unit even when billing is based on units of input (e.g., hours spent on an audit). The prices used are actual "exchange prices" (or fees) and present no problem. When billing is based on *input* units, however, the quantity data used will have the shortcomings mentioned in the example of public school education.

The level of prices and the standard of living. A price index does not and cannot be expected to measure changes in customer satisfaction, economic welfare, utility, or other subjective concepts that are related to changes in the "standard of living." A price index measures directly the variations in the exchange-prices of goods and services, and indirectly the variations in the exchange-value of money. The "standard of living" is a different concept, related to people's wants and their ability to satisfy them. Since production has increased more rapidly than population in the United States, the standard of living would no doubt have risen whether the price level had increased, decreased, or remained constant. Changes in technology or quality may make a product more acceptable for some purposes and less acceptable for others. This will no doubt affect the standard of living directly but can have only an indirect effect on price-level measurements through its effect on the supply of and demand for the good or service, and hence on its exchange-price. The only factor that makes technical and quality changes directly pertinent to price-index construction is the problem they create in determining whether the prices quoted are in fact applicable to comparable units.

89

Technological change and price comparisons. To measure changes in price, and not in some other variable, the units priced should be the basic units actually exchanged in the market and not a hypothetical unit of satisfaction received. Take the case of a doctor and his patients. Assume that the doctor charges a standard fee of five dollars for an office call. His patients have different ailments and therefore receive different treatments, but all pay the same fee for an office call. More rapid advance of medical technology in some fields may result in the rapid recovery of some patients while others recover slowly or not at all. There is, however, no reason for this to affect the statistical measure of the price of medical services. The point at which the transaction takes place between the doctor and the patient is the point of measurement for the exchange transaction entering into the pattern of prices. If, at a later date, the fee should be raised to six dollars, the increase should and would be reflected in a properly constructed index.

Publication of the report of the Price Statistics Review Committee early in 1961 promoted considerable interest among economists and statisticians in the problems of price-level measurement created by technological and quality changes in goods and services.[6] *The Monthly Labor Review* has since published technical articles on this subject that were stimulated by the report. One of these, "The problem of quality changes and index numbers" by Milton Gilbert of the Bank for International Settlement, has had considerable influence on this discussion.[7]

Prices. The concept of price is not uniform. Prices may be quoted before or after deducting discounts. Sales and excise taxes, freight, and handling charges are among the items that may or may not be included in price quotations. Since two sets of prices are needed for the construction of a price-index number—those in effect in the base period and in the period with which the base is being compared—"price" must mean the same thing in both cases. These prices should be actual exchange prices for comparable quantities of goods and services (e.g., prices for units sold in carload lots should not be compared with the prices for units sold by the dozen).

Information concerning unit prices is available in more detail than the related quantities sold at those prices, especially for consumer goods that are advertised in the daily newspapers. In sampling prices, consideration should be given to the effect of bargain sales and discounts on the actual prices paid.

When actual exchange prices cannot be determined it is sometimes necessary to use catalog, quoted, or other list-type prices as the best available evidence of exchange prices. This may result in an error in the index number, but the error is ordinarily of little consequence as long as the numerator and denominator are both biased (or "in error") in the same direction. The bias tends to cancel out in the result. If the bias is proportionately the same in both numerator and denominator, the resultant "index number" is precisely accurate:

90

---

[6] This committee was appointed in 1959 by the National Bureau of Economic Research, at the request of the Bureau of the Budget, to review critically the price indexes of the Federal Government.

[7] Sept. 1961, pp. 992-97. Also available as reprint *No. 2375.*

Period	Actual		Catalog	
	Prices	Index	Prices	Index
Current	300		330	
Base	200	$= 150$	220	$= 150$

In this case, both numerator and denominator are in error by 10 per cent. The only cases in which biases in the data underlying index number construction are significant for accounting uses are those in which the biases are both (a) erratic and (b) unpredictable (indeterminate).

The Formula

The data obtained from the samples are combined into index numbers by means of weighted averages which are referred to as formulas. Many formulas have been proposed and used in the construction of index numbers; they differ in the method of assigning weights to the prices. The "best" formula is one that results in an index that is mathematically unbiased so that the change measured by the index will be neither overstated nor understated.

The following symbols are conventionally used by statisticians in expressing these formulas:

$p =$ the price of a commodity or service.
$q =$ the quantity of that commodity or service.
$p_0, q_0 =$ the price, quantity of the commodity in the base period.
$p_1, q_1 =$ the price, quantity of the commodity in a period other than the base period.
$p_a, q_a =$ the price, quantity of a commodity in some "average" period; or the averages over some selected period.
$\Sigma =$ (Sigma) the sum of all the terms similar to that following the Σ.

Thus, $\Sigma p_0 q_0 =$ the summation of the base year values (base year prices multiplied by base year quantities) for all commodities sampled.

In the case of a single commodity, a simple unweighted arithmetic average is sometimes used, which may be expressed by $\frac{p_1}{p_0} \times 100$.

The commonly used indexes described in Section 2 are classified by type of formula in the discussion in Section 4 where they are analyzed and evaluated. The four most frequently used formulas are the Laspeyres, Paasche, Fisher, and a fixed-weight formula that is a varia-

91

tion of the Laspeyres formula. Notice that in each formula the same "q" factors appear in both the numerator and denominator; hence, they cancel out to leave a ratio of "p" factors weighted by the "q" factors.

Laspeyres formula. This formula averages the change in the prices of fixed quantities of specified commodities; the quantities are fixed because they are *base period quantities,* i.e., the weights are from the base period.

$$\text{Laspeyres:} \quad \frac{\Sigma \, p_1 q_0}{\Sigma \, p_0 q_0}$$

Paasche formula. This formula averages the change in the prices of changing quantities of specified commodities; the quantities change each period because the current period quantities are used, i.e., the weights are from the current period.

$$\text{Paasche:} \quad \frac{\Sigma \, p_1 q_1}{\Sigma \, p_0 q_1}$$

Fisher formula. This formula is a geometric average of the Laspeyres and Paasche formulas; therefore both base period and current quantities are used as weights.

$$\text{Fisher:} \quad \sqrt{\frac{\Sigma \, p_1 q_0}{\Sigma \, p_0 q_0} \times \frac{\Sigma \, p_1 q_1}{\Sigma \, p_0 q_1}}$$

Fixed-Weight formula. This formula, like the Laspeyres formula, averages the change in the prices of fixed quantities of specified commodities. It differs from the Laspeyres formula in that the quantities are from a fixed period that is not the base period. (It is often referred to as a "Laspeyres type" formula.)

$$\text{Fixed-Weight:} \quad \frac{\Sigma \, p_1 q_a}{\Sigma \, p_0 q_a}$$

The four formulas are presented above in what may be called their "definitional form," as various combinations of *value sums* (i.e., quantities of particular goods and services multiplied by their prices). This form is used here in order to simplify the discussion. In the actual construction of price indexes, a more complicated "computational form" of the formula is used which may be described as a *value weighted price relative.* For example, for the Laspeyres formula, $\frac{\Sigma \, p_1 q_0}{\Sigma \, p_0 q_0}$,

the computational form is $\dfrac{\Sigma\, p_0 q_0\, \frac{p_1}{p_0}}{\Sigma\, p_0 q_0}$ and requires a knowledge of
the base year value, "$p_0 q_0$," and a relative $\dfrac{p_1}{p_0}$ which measures the
change in prices. When the computation of the index is complete, the
results are identical with the concept in the "definitional form" of the
formulas used in this discussion.

Characteristics of the Formulas

Tests of index numbers. The ratios of quantity-weighted prices for a
single commodity have certain properties which cannot all be exhibited
by an index number for a *group* of commodities. These properties,
which were originally used by W. M. Persons[8] and Irving Fisher as
tests to be used in the choice among different formulas for an index
number, are now used merely to describe the numerical characteristics
of the various formulas. Fisher advocated what he called the "time
reversal test" and the "factor reversal test" as the most important,
whereas Persons placed more emphasis on the "circular test."

93

The first test is the time reversal test. If prices in 1960 are double
those in 1930, then prices in 1930 are half of those in 1960. This requires
that the backward index number (e.g., from 1960 to 1930) be the
reciprocal of the forward index number from 1930 to 1960. The test
used to determine if the two index numbers are in fact reciprocals is
the *time reversal test.* This reciprocal quality will permit price data to
be carried backward or forward in time, while various relationships
are exactly maintained.

The "backward" index numbers derived when the Fisher and the
Fixed-Weight formulas are used are the reciprocals of the "forward"
index numbers. This is not true when either the Laspeyres or the
Paasche formula is used.

The second test is the factor reversal test. Not only may prices
change, but so may the quantities of goods and services. Suppose a
given formula applied to prices in two periods of time yields an index
of 200, and the same formula applied to the related quantities yields

---

[8] *Indices of General Business Conditions.* Harvard University Press. 1919.

an index of 300 (i.e., prices, on the average have doubled, while quantities exchanged have tripled), then it follows that the total market value in the second period is six times the market value in the first period.

This truism in the case of a single commodity must be modified for the Laspeyres and Paasche formulas. The ratio of the market value at two dates can be expressed as the product of a price index and a quantity index[9] in two ways:

$$(1) \quad \frac{\Sigma\, p_1 q_1}{\Sigma\, p_0 q_0} = \frac{\Sigma\, p_1 q_0}{\Sigma\, p_0 q_0} \times \frac{\Sigma\, q_1 p_1}{\Sigma\, q_0 p_1} = L(p) \times P(q)$$

i.e., a Laspeyres price index—$L(p)$—multiplied by a Paasche quantity index — $P(q)$.

$$(2) \quad \frac{\Sigma\, p_1 q_1}{\Sigma\, p_0 q_0} = \frac{\Sigma\, p_1 q_1}{\Sigma\, p_0 q_1} \times \frac{\Sigma\, q_1 p_0}{\Sigma\, q_0 p_0} = P(p) \times L(q)$$

i.e., a Paasche price index—$P(p)$—multiplied by a Laspeyres quantity index—$L(q)$.

The value ratios cannot be equated to the product of the price and quantity indexes of the same formula, but they are the product of a Laspeyres index and a Paasche index. The Fisher formula which is the geometric mean of the Laspeyres and Paasche index satisfied the factor reversal test because of the truisms (1) and (2). When the differences between the Laspeyres and Paasche indexes are not large, the value ratios may be approximately equal either to the product of the two Laspeyres indexes or to the product of the two Paasche indexes. For example, assume the following prices and quantities for three commodities in two different years:

Commodity	Given Data				Multiplications			
	p_0	q_0	p_1	q_1	$p_0 q_0$	$p_0 q_1$	$p_1 q_0$	$p_1 q_1$
A	10	100	12	100	1,000	1,000	1,200	1,200
B	12	5,000	17	10,000	60,000	120,000	85,000	170,000
C	20	400	18	500	8,000	10,000	7,200	9,000
Σ					69,000	131,000	93,400	180,200

The Laspeyres formula yields the following index numbers when applied to these data:

---

[9] The quantity index formula associated with a price-index formula can be obtained from the latter by interchanging the letters p and q (price and quality), while the subscripts remain fixed in place.

Price index number:

$$\frac{\Sigma\, p_1 q_0}{\Sigma\, p_0 q_0} = \frac{93,400}{69,000} = 135$$

Quantity index number:

$$\frac{\Sigma\, q_1 p_0}{\Sigma\, q_0 p_0} = \frac{131,000}{69,000} = 190$$

The product of these two index numbers (135×190) is 257. However, a direct comparison of the total market value in the two periods, $\frac{\Sigma\, p_1 q_1}{\Sigma\, p_0 q_0}$, yields an index of 261 indicating that the Laspeyres and Paasche price indexes were not widely different.

The third test is the circular test. This test presumes that the base of a series of three or more index numbers should be shiftable at will and without error. Only formulas using constant weights can satisfy this test, and no index series can satisfy it over long periods of time because the weights are changed at varying intervals. The circular test is currently regarded as important, however, in the construction of a monthly index number that will be consistent with an annual index.

The circular test requires that a series of three or more index numbers form a closed series and is actually an extention of the time reversal test. For example, the index number from period 0 to 1, multiplied by the index number from period 1 to 2, multiplied by the index number from 2 back to 0, should equal unity.

In general, then, if there are n distinct periods, numbered 0, 1, 2, . . ., n-1, n, then the index numbers will be for the period 0 to 1, 1 to 2, 2 to 3, and so on to n-1 and n, and finally for the period n back to 0. The product of all these index numbers should be equal to 1 to satisfy this test. This test is the *circular test*.

The only formulas that satisfy the circular test are fixed-weight formulas.

Additivity of component indexes. The use of index numbers in the analysis of national income data has resulted in the favor of index formulas in which the grand total is the simple weighted sum of the component indexes. The Laspeyres, Paasche, and Fixed-Weight formulas have this property but the Fisher formula does not. In the example on page 94, the price index number is the weighted sum of the price index numbers for each of the three commodities—A, B, and

95

C,—where the weights are the values at the base date:[10]

$$\frac{\Sigma\ p_1 q_0}{\Sigma\ p_0 q_0} = \frac{93{,}400}{69{,}000} = \frac{1{,}000 \times \dfrac{12}{10} + 60{,}000 \times \dfrac{17}{12} + 8{,}000 \times \dfrac{18}{20}}{1{,}000 \ + \ 60{,}000 \ + \ 8{,}000}$$

with the heading *Index for Commodity* over columns A, B, C.

For each commodity, we have in the numerator the exchange value in the base year ($p_0 q_0$) multiplied by the ratio of the price in period 1 (p_1) to the price in period 0 (p_0).

An economic viewpoint. Some mathematical economists in studying the changes in price levels have concluded that, under certain conditions with respect to tastes and real income, the Laspeyres formula results in an index number that is greater than the "true" one, i.e., it is biased upward, while the Paasche formula is biased in the opposite direction and the unbiased index lies somewhere between the two.[11] Under these same conditions, Fisher's formula approximates the "true" index because it lies between the Laspeyres and Paasche formulas.

96

In a practical sense, these conditions serve to limit the time over which one base period may be used, because tastes and real income are affected in the long run by factors that in the short run are either absent or not material. If the given period is "too far away" from the base period, then the index number computed on the base period may not be very accurate. For short periods of time, however, the Fisher index number can be an accurate indicator of the change in the level of prices compared to the base period.

Small changes. If the actual change in prices was quite small, use of the Laspeyres formula might result in a slight move in one direction while the Paasche formula resulted in a slight move in the other direction. This possibility of different "readings" as to direction of change by two index numbers may lead to confusion or uncertainty, of

---

[10] See Richard Stone, *Quantity and Price Indexes in National Accounts,* Organization for European Economic Co-operation, Paris. 1956, pp. 37-39.
[11] See Robin Marris, *Economic Arithmetic* (Macmillan & Co., Ltd., 1958), pp. 257-62; also Michael J. Brennan, *Preface to Econometrics* (South-Western Publishing Company, 1960) p. 369.

course, but it is not significant because it can only occur when the changes themselves are small and therefore not of much consequence one way or the other.

Representative weights. Theoretically, the quantity data used to weight a price index for an economy characterized by changing expenditure patterns should give effect to the conditions existing in both of the periods being compared.[12]

The Fisher formula is the only one of the four that takes into consideration the actual conditions existing in both of the periods being compared.

The Laspeyres formula uses quantity data from the base period but ignores the given period quantities, a procedure which gives too much weight to commodities which were significant in the base period but are of minor importance in the given period.

The contrary "bias" is found in the Paasche formula which uses quantity data from the given period but ignores the base period quantities.

The Fixed-Weight formula does not give effect to the conditions existing in either the base or given periods. The time period from which the quantity data is selected may be determined in any one of several ways, including (among others) the availability of census data and other benchmarks, or Congressional appropriation of funds for a survey of purchasing habits.

97

The time and cost needed to gather the necessary data often play an important role in the selection of the particular formula used in compiling an index because the formulas do not all require the same amount of data. All price index formulas require both base year and given year prices; they differ, however, in the quantity data needed. For the Laspeyres formula, only base year quantities are needed; once these have been collected, additional quantity data are unnecessary. For the Fixed-Weight formula, the selected quantity data are needed; once these have been collected, no additional quantity data are required. For the Paasche and Fisher formulas, given year quantities are needed

[12] United States Department of Labor, *Wholesale Price Index*, Reprint of Chapter 10 BLS Bulletin No. 1168, pp. 9-10. "In theory, most authorities agree that the ideal formula . . . would be one in which the weights represent the conditions existing in both of the periods which are compared. . . ." Also Bruce D. Mudgett, *Index Numbers* (John Wiley & Sons, Inc., 1951), pp. 37-40.

which must be collected each year. The Fisher formula also requires base year quantities. The gathering of data for the Paasche and Fisher formulas costs more in both time and money than for the other formulas. As a result they are less frequently used.

Shifting Base Index—The Chain Index Method

There are two methods of constructing indexes: (1) by use of a fixed base, and (2) by use of a shifting base or "chain." In the United States all of the well-known indexes are of the fixed base variety, i.e., they measure changes in prices in a succession of years as compared with a base period. If, for example, 1950 is the base, then the indexes for 1955, for 1960, and for 1965 relate prices in the later years to prices in 1950. The less familiar "chain" method, by contrast, uses a new base for each successive link in the chain.[13] It relates prices in 1955 to those prevailing in 1954, those in 1960 to those prevailing in 1959, and those in 1965 to those prevailing in 1964. The chain index method provides for the shortest possible time interval by comparing each period with the next preceding period.

98

Several groups of goods and services that affect the price level in the two periods being compared can be identified:

1. Those existing in both the base period and the period with which the base period is being compared.

2. Those existing in the given period that are essentially modifications of goods and services that existed in the base period.

3. Those existing in the given period that were introduced subsequent to the base period (new goods and services).

4. Those existing in the base period that are not available in the given period (discontinued items).

Changes in technology, tastes, styles, and quality are reflected in these groups. The prices of all of the goods and services in the above groups that are in existence at the times under consideration affect the general level of prices.

---

[13] The term "chain index" is also used to refer to the "chaining" together of a series of fixed base indexes to make one index, but this is not the sense in which the term is used here. The Consumer Price Index and the Wholesale Price Index are examples of the joining together of a series of fixed base indexes.

An index of the general level of prices is constructed from a sample that is representative of all of the goods and services exchanged in the economy. In a reliable index, the bulk of the commodities will be those in the first group, i.e., those existing in both the base period and the given period. The larger the total market value of this group relative to the total market values of all goods and services in the two periods, the more accurate the index number will be as a measure of the change in prices. The relative value of this group will ordinarily increase as the time interval between the two periods is shortened because there will be less opportunity for the introduction of new products (group 3), the modification of existing commodities (group 2), or the disappearance of goods from the market (group 4). The chain index method achieves the maximum uniformity between the goods and services that affect the price level in the two periods by comparing adjacent time periods.

The chain method also provides a means by which commodities which are being replaced in the economy (i.e., group 4) can be easily replaced in the index; and new commodities introduced in the economy (i.e., group 3) can be introduced into the index within a comparatively short time.

More specifically, new commodities would be introduced into the chain index in the period following the period in which they were first marketed. In this way the time lag between their effect on the price level and their effect on the index would be reduced to one time period. At the time they are introduced into the index, there would be exchange transactions to supply price quotations for these commodities for both the base period (i.e., the period in which they were first marketed) and for the given period. Unless new commodities represented a significant portion of the total value of the exchange transactions in the period in which they were first marketed, which would be most unusual, the effect on the index would be immaterial.

In addition, the removal of commodities that are discontinued is simplified by revising the base each year. If this were done, the index number for the period following the last period in which the commodities were marketed would be the only one affected. Furthermore the importance of commodities discontinued from one year to the next cannot be very great because commodities that sell in substantial quantities will not be discontinued by the producers except under extraordinary circumstances. As a consequence the commodities that are discontinued normally constitute a negligible part of the whole, minimizing further the effect on the reliability of the related indexes.

If monthly or quarterly indexes are needed, the chain index method could be modified to provide for the seasonal character of the avail-

99

ability of many commodities. Instead of using the adjacent previous month (or quarter) as the base period, the same month (or quarter) in the preceding year could be used as the base.

A chain index retains contact continuously with the prices and quantities of the goods and services actually exchanged in the economy over the years. Over a period of years, a fixed base index, on the other hand, loses contact with the relative importance of the new commodities introduced and the older commodities that disappear from the market in the interlude between the periods being compared. In this sense the chain index is clearly superior.

A chain index cannot completely eliminate bias resulting from the introduction of new commodities and the discontinuance of old ones, but it can reduce it to insignificance. Since insignificant errors cannot have a material effect on statement presentation, a price index prepared in this manner may prove more satisfactory for the accountants' need for indexes that reflect changes in the price level, and in nothing else.

There is disagreement among economists and statisticians concerning the theoretical accuracy of the chain index method as compared with 100 the fixed base method. There are distinguished authorities on both sides of the issue. The fixed base method has prevailed in this country due to practical considerations. For one thing it requires fewer data, and therefore it costs less to compile. Also, prior to the advent of rapid communications and electronic data processing equipment, there was no practical method to obtain and use quantity weights sufficiently current for application of the chain method to a broad based index. Because of the disagreement as to which approach is theoretically superior, there has been no pressure from any influential group to spend the extra money for the adoption of the chain method.

At the present time there is more of a consensus in favor of chain indexes for particular small classes of commodities, especially in those cases where the specifications change frequently. In actual practice the indexes for many classes of commodities, e.g., men's shoes and agricultural machinery, are almost chains in the sense of this section of the report, because of the necessity for frequent linking of the index due to new specifications.

Rapid data gathering and data processing methods are now available which make a revival of interest in the "chain index" feasible. The expanding needs of business, government, accountants, and others indicate a need for more accurate indexes of price movements. Because of its many advantages, the chain index method should be experimented with and its strengths and weaknesses more satisfactorily determined.

Limited Time Span for Reliable Measurement

Neither the chain method nor the fixed base method of index number construction provides a method of measuring the percentage change in prices between two periods in which the bulk of the goods and services exchanged in each period are unique. A reliable price index cannot compare the prices of commodities in one period with prices in other periods in which comparable products do not exist. The rate of technological change, therefore, is one important factor that serves to limit the time span over which price changes can be reliably measured by a given series of index numbers. It may be possible, for example, to determine whether the price level was higher or lower in the 1920's than in 1963, but the precision of the measure of change is open to serious question because of the dissimilarity in the goods and services available in the two periods.

The rate at which new commodities are introduced into the economy and old ones are discontinued is neither uniform nor systematic. For this reason, a definite limit cannot be established for the number of years over which price-level changes can be reliably measured. There is reason to believe, however, that comparisons of current price levels with time periods preceding World War II would not be sufficiently reliable for accounting purposes. This assertion is based on the *prima facie* evidence of the numerous goods and services currently available that originated in discoveries and innovations attributable to the war effort and to postwar developments. To the extent that these goods and services represent a large portion of the dollar value of current exchange transactions, the precision of comparisons of current price levels with those prevailing in periods prior to World War II are unreliable.

For industries in which a material amount of the assets and liabilities currently held were acquired prior to World War II, the need for adjustment is not diminished by the lack of adequate devices for measuring price changes over long periods of time. To the contrary, the longer the time span involved, the greater the chances for significant shifts in prices and the more serious is the need for adjustment. Current progress in the development of improved methods of measuring price changes may culminate in a breakthrough in techniques that will make a cut-off date unnecessary.

Section 4: Critique of Currently Compiled Indexes and Recommendations

Critique of Currently Compiled Indexes

The Consumer Price Index. The index known as the Consumer Price Index measures change in prices of goods and services purchased by city wage-earner and clerical-worker families to maintain their level of living. Their "level of living" is represented by a market basket of approximately 300 goods and services selected as a result of a study of their buying habits. This index does not attempt to measure price changes for any group of consumers other than city wage-earner and clerical-worker families. To the extent that others have similar purchasing habits, this index may indicate the price changes that affect them. However, caution should be used when applying this index as a measure of price changes that it does not attempt to cover.

The *universe* of this index is described in its official title "The Index of Change in Prices of Goods and Services Purchased by City Wage-Earner and Clerical-Worker Families to Maintain Their Level of Living." The shorter title by which it is known, "The Consumer Price Index," is inaccurate in that it indicates a wider universe than is actually used.

The market basket of goods and services priced in this index has been revised less often than once every ten years. The goods and services available to consumers are improved, changed, or replaced in our economy at a rate which outdates a base period more frequently than this index is revised. The Bureau of Labor Statistics makes adjustments to the market basket to compensate for these changes where possible. There is, however, no adequate measure of the effect on the index numbers caused by the use of an obsolete base.

The *sample* used in the "Consumer Price Index" is a complex which incorporates probability, semiprobability and judgmental sampling for different parts of the index.[1] The Commissioner of Labor Statistics believes that "It is intrinsically impossible to obtain sampling errors, in the usual sense, for the Consumer Price Index."[2] As a result, it is not possible to tell how closely this index approximates an index of the complete universe.

The Bureau of Labor Statistics has compiled the Consumer Price Index for nearly half a century. In that time the index has been thoroughly reviewed, scrutinized in detail, re-examined and evaluated many times. Based on the experience and reputation of the Bureau, it is usually judged to be "good" without attaching a numerical value to its precision.

The *specifications* for the goods and services priced are carefully defined and in detail. As a result, there is the possibility that prices of commodities that are "out of style" may be used to reflect the changes of prices of a group of similar items that are in general use.[3]   103

The *prices* are usually actual exchange prices. Whether the prices are representative is open to question since the time and place of price sampling is affected by practical considerations. For example, the Food-at-Home Index, a subindex of the Consumer Price Index, does not include prices from transactions on weekends, or during sales lasting less than a week, because the respondents that supply price data will not take the time to work on a price list with the Bureau agent when their stores are crowded with customers.[4]

There is also the question of whether a fixed market basket index is a realistic measure of the effect of price changes on consumers since purchases can be rearranged to avoid buying products whose prices have risen and equally desirable new low priced products can be substituted.[5]

---

[1] Ewan Clague, "Comment" on "Food Prices and the Bureau of Labor Statistics" by William H. Kruskal and Lester G. Telser, *Journal of Business*. July 1960, p. 283. Mr. Clague is Commissioner of Labor Statistics, United States Department of Labor.

[2] *Ibid.*

[3] *Government Price Statistics*. pp. 32-34.

[4] Ewan Clague, *op. cit.* p. 281.

[5] *Government Price Statistics*. p. 51.

The *quantity* data used to weight the prices are those established through a survey conducted in 1950-51. The comprehensive revision of this index that is scheduled to go into effect in the January 1964 index will use weights based on a survey conducted in 1960-61.

The *formula* used in the construction of the Consumer Price Index is a *fixed-weight* formula that is weighted by quantities established by a survey and revised less often than once in ten years.

Any decision involving the use of the Consumer Price Index for making adjustments for price-level changes should give careful consideration to the effects of (a) the limited universe, (b) the complex sampling plan coupled with the inability to determine sampling errors, and (c) the qualifications imposed by a market basket that is weighted by quantities established by a survey.

The Wholesale Price Index. The Wholesale Price Index is *not,* as implied by its title, an index of prices either paid to or received by wholesalers, distributors, or jobbers. It does *not* refer to "any definable set of producers or purchasers in the economy."[6] Wholesale, as used in the title of this index, refers to sales in large lots at primary market levels, i.e., the first important commercial transaction for each commodity.[7] The *universe,* as defined by the Bureau of Labor Statistics, is the total of primary-market transactions in the United States.

As currently compiled, the Wholesale Price Index covers agriculture, mining, and manufacturing. Construction materials are covered as a part of manufacturing, but construction itself is not included, nor is transportation.[8] Exports (up to the point at which they leave the domestic market) and imports are included in the index but they are not segregated.

Judgmental sampling is used to select the most important commodities in each field for inclusion in the Wholesale Price Index. Knowledge of each industry and its important products is derived through consultation with leading trade associations and manufacturers in each field and from Census data.[9]

Commodity *specifications* were selected on advice from industry and other sources and are precisely defined as to both commodity char-

104

---

[6] *Ibid.* p. 64.
[7] *Wholesale Price Index.* Reprint of Chapter 10, from BLS Bulletin 1168. United States Department of Labor. p. 2.
[8] *Government Price Statistics.* p. 65.
[9] *Wholesale Price Index, op. cit.* p. 4.

acteristics and the terms of sale from specified types of sellers to specified types of purchasers.[10]

In general, *prices* used represent seller's net realization per unit which is defined as actual sales less normal discounts, in approximately similar quantities to similar classes of buyers. Prices quoted on organized exchanges or markets are also used. List or nominal prices quoted in trade journals or by manufacturers are used when they satisfy the above criteria and reflect the industry's customary pricing practices.[11] The consistent use of these prices normally will not distort the index (as previously explained on pages 90-91) since the index attempts to measure relative price movements and relationships among prices, not the absolute level of prices.

The *quantity* weights used are based on value of shipments data from industrial censuses, with interplant transfers excluded where possible. Each commodity priced is considered to be representative of a class of commodities and is assigned the weight of the whole class.

The prices, then, although not necessarily transaction prices, do reflect the industry's customary pricing practices and the quantity weights used are based on data from industrial censuses rather than the quantities actually exchanged in the periods being compared. 105

The *formula* used in the construction of this index is a *fixed-weight* formula that uses given year prices weighted by quantities from an industrial census taken a few years previous to the given year, and 1957-59 base year prices weighted by the same census data. For example, the wholesale price index numbers for 1960 used weights from the 1954 Census of Manufactures. In January 1961 new weights from the 1958 Census were introduced into the index for the first time.

For accounting purposes, the group indexes and individual price series that are components of the all-commodity index would be of most value in making adjustments to financial reports for changes in the specific prices. The absence of probability sampling to determine the commodities to be priced does not affect the reliability of the individual series.

When using wholesale price index numbers, consideration should be given to some limitations of this index that have been pointed out by the Bureau of Labor Statistics.

Some limitations on the use of the wholesale price index have al-

---

[10] *Ibid.* p. 3.
[11] *Ibid.*

ready been mentioned. The index is designed to measure change, not absolute levels of prices, and the quotations used in the index for individual commodities do not necessarily measure the average dollars-and-cents levels of prices. The index is not a true measure of the general purchasing power of the dollar — it does not include prices at retail, prices for securities, real estate, services, construction, or transportation. Even at wholesale or primary market levels, the index, while a good approximation, is not a perfect measure — since it is based on a relatively small sample of the many commodities which flow through these markets. In addition, there are some real price changes which the Bureau cannot measure — for example, some improvements in quality, hidden discounts, differences in delivery schedules, etc.

The index has not been designed for use in measuring margins between primary markets and other distributive levels. Thus, direct comparisons of the wholesale and consumer price indexes cannot be used to estimate or evaluate margins. The index does not measure prices paid by industrial consumers since it normally excludes transportation costs and similar factors affecting final prices. Finally, the index should not be used to forecast movements of the Consumer Price Index, particularly over the short

106   run. Many components of the wholesale price index never enter retail markets (for example, machinery); similarly, many components of the Consumer Price Index (such as services and rents) are not covered by the wholesale price index.[12]

The Composite Construction Cost Index. The U. S. Department of Commerce—Composite Construction Cost Index is the most comprehensive index available in the construction field. The *universe* of this index is the total cost of work put in place on all structures and facilities under construction during a given period. Estimates of this total cost are based on contract awards, building permits, progress reports on Federal construction projects, and financial reports. The estimates are then adjusted for seasonal variation and deflated to 1957-59 dollars by many indexes, most of which are privately compiled.

The *sample* is not a probability sample, nor can it properly be called a judgmental sample because the Construction Statistics Office (of the Department of Commerce, Bureau of the Census) that compiles this index has very little detailed information concerning the sources of data or the methods used in the construction of the component indexes. In addition none of the component indexes, with the exception of the Bureau of Public Roads Composite Mile Index, is completely

---

[12] *Ibid.*

representative of any one specific primary classification of construction.[13]

Since this is primarily an input index, few of the component indexes make allowance for productivity changes. Therefore, attempts to use this index to measure price movements of the output of the construction industry are hampered by an upward bias to the extent that productivity has increased over time.

Until very recently the Construction Statistics Office did not collect any original data for this index. Some of the indexes used to deflate the current dollar estimates of construction costs are indexes of fixed quantities of material and labor which were typical of facilities constructed twenty-five to thirty years ago but are no longer representative, and at least one index excludes building fixtures (e.g., plumbing, heating, elevators) which are important items of construction cost.[14] To the extent that the relative importance of the component construction costs have shifted since the base year, the composite index is biased in an unknown direction which either aggravates or counteracts the upward bias resulting from productivity change.

Because of the unknown effect of the weighting schemes included in the indexes used as deflators, the formula used in this index cannot be classified according to the schemes given in the previous section (pp. 92-93). It resembles the Paasche formula most closely because its construction begins with current dollar estimates of construction costs which includes current quantity data at current prices.

Of the four indexes reviewed in this report, the Composite Construction Cost Index currently displays the least cause for confidence based on procedures of its construction. In spite of its method of construction, however, there is reason to believe that the resulting index may be fairly accurate. In an article in the December 1961 *American Economic Review*, R. A. Gordon[15] marshals considerable support for the validity of the constant dollar figures for that segment of Gross National Product that is deflated by the Composite Construction Cost Index. Evidence supporting this contention includes:

1. One study . . . found that a specially constructed index of

107

---

[13] *Government Price Statistics. op. cit.* p. 91.
[14] *Ibid.*
[15] "Differential Changes in the Prices of Consumers' and Capital Goods." pp. 937-57.

actual house prices rose by about the same amount as a residential construction-cost index over the period 1890-1934.

2. A completely independent study by Colean and Newcomb ...found that the *Engineering News-Record* fixed-weight index of building costs rose no more during the period 1913-51 than an average of the indices of *actual* building costs compiled by four construction firms.

3. Prices of building materials, particularly lumber, have risen significantly more than the index of all wholesale prices, and it is unlikely that all of this differential increase in prices has been offset by savings in the use of materials.

4. There is a good reason to believe that, over the last half century or more, the recorded rise in union wage rates in the building trades — the wage component in most fixed-weight construction-cost indices — does not seriously exaggerate the rise in unit labor costs, except in heavy engineering projects. Labor productivity in building construction has apparently risen relatively slowly over most of the period covered by our figures, and the trend in union wage rates understates the rise in actual hourly earnings.

5. Improvements in productivity have been retarded by union restrictions and building regulations. Also, some "external diseconomies" have been at work. Thus one factor in the rise in building costs has been "the rapidly increasing complexity of the urban environment resulting from greater concentration of population on the one hand and higher standards of health and safety on the other. . . ."

6. Where extensive mechanization has been introduced, some of the resulting labor saving has been offset by an increase in cost per unit of output for such items as interest, depreciation, fuel and power, etc. . . .

7. Raymond Powell . . . after a careful survey of the evidence for the United States (largely from the same sources that we have cited), reaches the following conclusion:

". . . there has been little divergence in the *trends* of input and output prices in residential and nonresidential building construction in the U.S. over the periods covered. . . .

". . . building construction, in which the trends of input and output prices appear to have been similar, account for the greater part of total construction. . . ."[16]

A comprehensive program for the improvement of construction statistics is in process by the Bureau of the Census. The program is based on the recommendations of the Price Statistics Review Committee[17] and is seeking to eliminate the shortcomings of present construc-

[16] *Ibid.* pp. 943-44.
[17] *Government Price Statistics,* Appendix B.

tion statistics. The general objectives of the Bureau include (1) the measurement of prices rather than costs (i.e., the prices of the output of the construction industry instead of the costs of its inputs), (2) the use of actual transaction prices rather than estimates, and (3) methods of measurement that apply to the entire field of construction (e.g., pricing separate operations for types of construction that do not lend themselves to handling as complete projects).[18] Since the Bureau is pioneering in construction *price* indexes, it faces problems not previously explored. The improvement in construction statistics that ensues from this program will also result in the improvement of our national income accounts and the GNP deflator.

GNP (Gross National Product) Implicit Price Deflator. The most comprehensive price index available is an outgrowth of national income and product accounting which is one of the chief tools for formulation of Government economic policy. This index, the GNP (Gross National Product) Implicit Price Deflator, is implicit in the relationship between the current and constant dollar estimates of Gross National Product. The report of the National Accounts Review Committee, National Bureau of Economic Research to the Subcommittee on Economic Statistics in 1957 termed the estimates "as good as the primary data and funds available for their processing and analysis permit."[19] Improvements have since been made based on some of the recommendations in that report.

109

The *universe* for this index encompasses all exchange transactions in the economy that affect the general level of prices. It is the only index presently compiled that reflects an average of *all* goods and services exchanged in *all* segments of the economy. It is an index of the prices of final products, consumer purchases, and business investment. The national economic accounts from which this index is constructed "constitute a systematic record of basic information about economic activity. . . ."[20]

The data used in estimating and deflating Gross National Product are collected by various governmental and private agencies for

---

[18] Samuel J. Dennis, *Recent Progress in Measuring Construction*, U. S. Department of Commerce, Bureau of the Census. 1962. Mr. Dennis is Chief of the Construction Statistics Division of the Bureau of the Census, pp. 15-19.

[19] Hearings before the Subcommittee on Economic Statistics. . . . October 29 and 30, 1957, *The National Economic Accounts of the United States.* p. 110.

[20] *Ibid.* p. 133.

other purposes as a by-product of administrative routine. As a result these data must be further processed to adjust them to use for this purpose. Reliance must be placed on judgment and the development of benchmarks derived from alternative measurements. As a result, quantitative indicators of the degree of statistical precision are not available.[21]

The U. S. Department of Commerce, Office of Business Economics prepares the GNP Deflators but it neither collects the data itself nor controls their collection. Therefore the *sample* cannot be accurately described as a judgmental sample, even though judgment must be exercised by the Office of Business Economics in the selection and processing of data supplied by other agencies.

The subindexes of the Consumer Price Index, the Wholesale Price Index, the Composite Construction Cost Index, and other indexes compiled by various governmental agencies as well as other price lists and catalogs are used to deflate the portions of Gross National Product to which they apply. Improvements in the individual indexes used as deflators result in improved GNP Implicit Price Deflators.

110   One of the areas most in need of improvement is in the construction statistics. Accurate measurement is difficult in this area because of the number of small-business units, many of which do not maintain adequate records, and the diversity of the products. Each construction project usually has unique characteristics which complicate the collection of comparable data. A considerable start has been made in the last few years toward accurate construction data; there are, however, still many problems to be solved.

The *formula* used for the GNP deflator is a Paasche type formula; however, various formulas are used in the computation of the subindexes. It is the only one of the output price indexes reviewed in this study that is based on current weights that change every year.

The importance of the Gross National Product estimates (in both current and constant dollars) in the formulation of economic policy gives continuing impetus to their improvement. As the estimates become more accurate, the index inherent in the relationship of the estimates before and after deflation improves accordingly. The overall estimates are probably more reliable than the various segments because the best check now available for the estimation of Gross National Product is the reconciliation of the aggregate with the total derived in estimating National Income, which has attained a high

---

[21] *Ibid.* pp. 217-18.

degree of reliability for the period since 1939. The major portion (by far) of National Income is compensation of employees. Estimates of total wages and salaries are reliable because they are based on data from the Railroad Retirement Board and the Social Security Administration. The reporting systems under the Railroad Retirement and Social Security Acts approach the ideal as a source for income estimates.[22] Federal Income Tax information also supplies benchmarks for checking the accuracy of components of National Income and Gross National Product.

The GNP Implicit Price Deflator is the only index currently compiled which measures the over-all or general level of prices. It is a "good" index but the method of sampling and the absence of control over data collection by the Office of Business Economics preclude giving a numerical value to its statistical precision.

The Best Currently Available Index or Indexes for Recasting Financial Reports

Index of the general level of prices. Money is the common denominator in which financial data presented in accounting reports are measured.[23] The purchasing power of the dollar, however, varies from time to time, and as a result, assets, liabilities, revenues, and expenses are expressed in "dollars" which represent different purchasing powers.[24] If financial statements in dollars that have the same purchasing power as "dollars in general" are desired, an index of the general level of prices is needed, because the dollar is a commodity whose value (purchasing power) varies in inverse proportion with the general level of prices of the commodities for which it can be exchanged. When the general level of prices rises, the value of the dollar falls because more dollars are needed to buy the same quantity of commodities. Conversely, when the general level of prices falls, the value of the dollar rises because fewer dollars are needed to purchase that quantity of commodities.

The only index currently compiled that is a measure of the general level of prices in the United States is the GNP Implicit Price Deflator.

[22] *National Income*, 1954 Supplement to the *Survey of Current Business*, United States Department of Commerce, Office of Business Economics. p. 68.

[23] Maurice Moonitz, "The Basic Postulates of Accounting," *Accounting Research Study No. 1.* (American Institute of Certified Public Accountants, 1961) p. 22, Postulate A-5.

[24] *Ibid.* pp. 44-46.

111

It is the only price index compiled in this country whose "universe" encompasses the entire economy.

There has been a high degree of correlation between price movements measured by the GNP Implicit Price Deflator and the Consumer Price Index. There is, however, no guarantee that this relationship will continue because the Consumer Price Index does not attempt to measure price movements for the economy as a whole.

Deflators by calendar quarters are available only since the first quarter of 1947; annual deflators are available for every year back to 1929. The data from which the deflators are computed are provisional when first published and revised as additional information becomes available. The final revised data together with the deflators are published annually in July for the previous year. In recent years, the differences between deflators computed from the provisional data and the final published deflators have been minor. When considered in relation to their use for adjustment of financial data, the effect would be immaterial.

As a result of our investigation we are convinced that the GNP Implicit Price Deflators are reliable enough for accounting purposes. However, since the precision of the measure of change is open to serious question when the goods and services available in the two periods being compared are dissimilar, and because so many of the goods and services currently available resulted from wartime (World War II) and postwar technology, it would probably be desirable to select a cutoff date instead of using prewar or even wartime index numbers for the adjustment of the applicable data in financial statements.

The earliest point in time that seems to offer reasonable comparability of goods and services is no earlier than 1945. If 1945 were selected as a cutoff date, all assets acquired and liabilities incurred prior to 1945 would be treated as if they had originated during that year. For most industries, the resulting inaccuracies would probably not be material.

For those industries in which the inaccuracies would be material, one possible procedure is to use 1945 as a cutoff date and accept the resulting inaccuracy. Again, in most cases, the adjusted data are probably more realistic than the unadjusted data. In this case, however, fixed asset values and the inflation gain (loss) on long-term monetary items would be misstated by an unknown amount.

Another possible procedure is to use the best index available and make "across-the-board" adjustments, regardless of the limitations to the reliability of the index. If we use an index beyond its range of reliability, we will be in the position of not knowing whether the index tended to overstate or to understate the change. As a result we would not know whether the adjusted data were more accurate than the unadjusted data or whether the adjustment introduced a fictitious element of unknown size that was not there before.

Both approaches result in inaccuracies of unknown size and direction. The advantage of using a cut-off date is that the limitations inherent in the use of index numbers for long-range comparisons are clearly recognized.

The literature in the field of index number construction evidences both (1) enthusiasm for the progress being made in the measurement of price changes and (2) caution against reliance on the accuracy of long-range comparisons except as indicators of trends. Recognized authorities in the field are not willing to vouch for the accuracy of the measurement when the bulk of the goods and services available in the two periods being compared are dissimilar.

On balance, therefore, the members of the research staff are loath to recommend the use of index numbers prior to 1945 in measuring price-level changes. Nevertheless, we are aware of our limitations and submit the following recommendations:

113

1. We recommend that the American Institute of Certified Public Accountants commission one of the recognized economic research organizations, such as the National Industrial Conference Board, the National Bureau of Economic Research, or the Brookings Institution to study this phase of the problem and to recommend an appropriate index and cutoff date.

2. We recommend that the American Institute of Certified Public Accountants adopt and publish the findings of the outside research organization as to the relevant index numbers and cutoff date. The business community should then be urged to use these published index numbers (and cutoff date, if any) in preparing price-level adjusted financial statements.

Changes in the prices of specific commodities. Changes in the prices of specific commodities can be reflected in financial reports by the use of appropriate price series for the individual accounts that appear in those reports. Fortunately, as indicated in Section 2, a wealth of price data is collected and published by various agencies of the Federal Government. Some of these prices have been converted into indexes, others have not. The nonindexed price series are easily converted into indexes by the formula $\dfrac{p_1}{p_0}$ x 100 (i.e., divide (i) the price for each successive date, p_1, by (ii) the price for the date selected as the base, p_0, then multiply by 100). The subindexes of the Wholesale Price Index would supply many of the needed indexes. The most troublesome area would be finding good indexes to adjust building values, due to the inadequacies in construction cost indexes currently compiled; however, the solution is in process.

Price-level changes for limited segments of the economy. Indexes to adjust for price-level changes affecting limited segments of the economy that would also be appropriate for recasting of financial statements are not available. The over-all Wholesale Price Index does not refer to any definable set of producers or purchasers in the economy. An "Index of Change in Prices of Goods and Services Purchased by *City Wage-Earner* and *Clerical-Worker Families* to Maintain Their Level of Living" (emphasis supplied) does not seem to have any qualifications that would make it theoretically appropriate. An index of "Gross Private Domestic Investment," a subdivision of Gross National Product, would seem to be appropriate but it is not reliable. The Office of Business Economics does not compute a separate deflator for this subdivision because a significant component, change in business inventories, includes elements of opposite algebraic sign (see pages 76 and 77). An index constructed from two subdivisions of Gross Private Domestic Investment, i.e., other new construction and producers durable equipment, would have two major deficiencies: (1) it would not include all types of purchases in any segment of the economy and (2) data on new construction, the largest segment, has serious limitations at the present time.

Recommendations for Improvement

One of the major limitations on the construction of adequate indexes in the United States is the shortage of funds made available for this purpose. Committees organized by the National Bureau of Economic Research have made studies of government price statistics and national economic accounts. Reports of these studies together with recommendations for improvements have been made to the Subcommittee on Economic Statistics of the Joint Economic Committee of the Congress of the United States. Some of the recommendations have been put into effect but insufficient funds preclude the adoption of many of them at the present time. If the business community wants better data than are currently available, it will have to encourage the allocation of sufficient funds for their compilation. In order to obtain improved indexes for restating financial statements, funds should be allocated to the study of and research into the problems of sampling methods, of gathering basic data, and of the timing of revisions of weights, as well as to a program of publication of changes and improvements. Research into methods of measuring price changes should encompass underlying statistical theory and techniques.

Government price statistics and national economic accounts are the basis of policy decisions by business, labor, individuals and government. A wealth of statistics are collected and published by numerous governmental agencies on a wide variety of topics. Their importance for economic and business analysis continues to grow. The improvement of economic statistics would benefit both their users and all who are affected by the policies dependent in part on their use.

115

Selected Bibliography on Index Numbers

BRENNAN, MICHAEL J., *Preface to Econometrics*, South-Western Publishing Company, 1960.

CLAGUE, EWAN, "Comment" on "Food prices and the Bureau of Labor Statistics" by William H. Kruskal and Lester G. Telser, *Journal of Business*, July 1960, pp. 280-84.

CROWDER, EDWARD T., "Centralized internal control of data collection by Federal agencies," *Journal of the American Statistical Association*, June 1944, pp. 155-64.

DeJANOSI, PETER E., "A note on provisional estimates of the gross national product and its major components," *Journal of Business*, Oct. 1961, pp. 495-99.

DEMING, W. EDWARDS, "On a classification of the problems of statistical inference," *Journal of the American Statistical Association*, June 1942, pp. 173-85.

DENNIS, SAMUEL J., *Recent Progress in Measuring Construction*, U.S. Department of Commerce, Bureau of the Census, 1962.

FISHER, IRVING, *The Making of Index Numbers*, Third Edition, revised, Houghton Mifflin Company, 1927.

FISHER, IRVING, *The Money Illusion*, Adelphi Company, 1928.

FOSS, MURRAY, "How rigid are construction costs during recessions?" *Journal of Business*, July 1961, pp. 374-83.

GILBERT, MILTON, "The problem of quality changes and index numbers," *Monthly Labor Review*, Sept. 1961, pp. 992-97.

GORDON, R. A., "Differential changes in the prices of consumers' and capital goods," *American Economic Review*, Dec. 1961, pp. 937-57.

Government Price Statistics, Hearings before the Subcommittee on Economic Statistics of the Joint Economic Committee, 87th Congress, 1st session, Jan. 24, 1961, Part I.

HOFSTEN, ERLAND v., *Price Indexes and Quality Changes*, George Allen & Unwin Ltd., 1952.

HOOVER, ETHEL D., "The CPI and problems of quality change," *Monthly Labor Review*, Nov. 1961, pp. 1175-85.

Income Tax Regulations as of February 1, 1961, CCH, 1961.

Labor Law Reporter, Union Contracts Arbitration 1, CCH, 1960, ¶ 56,100.

MARRIS, ROBIN, *Economic Arithmetic*, Macmillan & Co., Ltd., 1958.

MITCHELL, WESLEY CLAIR, *The Making and Using of Index Numbers*, Bulletin 284, U.S. Bureau of Labor Statistics, 1921.

MUDGETT, BRUCE D., *Index Numbers*, John Wiley & Sons, Inc., 1951.

National Economic Accounts of the United States, Hearings Before the Subcommittee on Economic Statistics of the Joint Economic Committee, 85th Congress, 1st session, Oct. 29 and 30, 1957.

PERSONS, W. M., *Indices of General Business Conditions*, Harvard University Press, 1919.

RICE, STUART A., HINRICHS, A. FORD, TOLLEY, HOWARD R., and HAUSER, PHILIP M., "Problems of integrating Federal statistics," *Journal of the American Statistical Association*, June 1945, pp. 237-44.

SEARLE, ALLAN D., "Weight revisions in the Wholesale Price Index, 1890-1960," *Monthly Labor Review*, Feb. 1962, pp. 175-82.

SIEGEL, IRVING H., "Index-number differences: geometric means," *Journal of the American Statistical Association*, June 1942, pp. 271-74.

STONE, RICHARD, *Quantity and Price Indexes in National Accounts*, Organization for European Economic Co-operation, Paris, 1956.

U. S. DEPARTMENT OF COMMERCE, BUREAU OF THE CENSUS, *Historical Statistics of the United States 1789-1945*, (a supplement to the *Statistical Abstract of the United States*), 1949.

U: S. DEPARTMENT OF COMMERCE, BUREAU OF THE CENSUS, *Historical Statistics of the United States, Colonial Times to 1957*, (a supplement to the *Statistical Abstract of the United States*), 1960.

U. S. DEPARTMENT OF COMMERCE, OFFICE OF BUSINESS ECONOMICS, *Business Statistics*, (a supplement to the *Survey of Current Business*), 1959.

U. S. DEPARTMENT OF COMMERCE, OFFICE OF BUSINESS ECONOMICS, *National Income*, (a supplement to the *Survey of Current Business*), 1954.

U. S. DEPARTMENT OF COMMERCE, OFFICE OF BUSINESS ECONOMICS, *U. S. Income and Output*, (a supplement to the *Survey of Current Business*), 1959.

U. S. DEPARTMENT OF LABOR, BUREAU OF LABOR STATISTICS, *Wholesale Price Index*, Reprint of Chapter 10, from BLS Bulletin 1168.

Demonstration of the
Adjustment Technique

Table of Contents

Demonstration

The purpose of the following demonstration is to provide a simplified illustration of the essential features of price-level adjustments of financial statements, and to contribute to an understanding of the effect of price-level changes. It is not intended to provide a detailed technical guide for the use of an accountant in preparing a set of adjusted financial statements for an actual case.[1] It will be followed by comments on certain variations and special problems not covered in the basic demonstration.

The illustration will include a two-year period, beginning with the opening of business. Adjusted income statements will be prepared for each of the two years, and adjusted balance sheets for the opening of business, the close of the first year, and the close of the second year.

The following price-level index numbers are assumed for use in the demonstration:

Opening of business	150	Second year—average	190
First year—average	160	Second year—end	200
First year—end	175		

---

[1] Technical aspects of price-level adjustments are discussed in the following publications, among others:

Ralph C. Jones, *Price Level Changes and Financial Statements—Case Studies of Four Companies.* American Accounting Association, 1955.

Ralph C. Jones, *Effects of Price Level Changes on Business Income, Capital, and Taxes.* American Accounting Association, 1956.

Ralph D. Kennedy and Stewart Y. McMullen, *Financial Statements— Form, Analysis, and Interpretation.* Third Edition. Chapters 17-21. Richard D. Irwin, Inc., 1957.

Perry Mason, *Price-Level Changes and Financial Statements—Basic Concepts and Methods.* American Accounting Association, 1956.

The financial statements will be restated in terms of the *dollar at the end of the second year,* that is, in terms of the *"current dollar"* when the index is at 200.

Other assumptions are:

1. The inventory is priced on a first-in, first-out (Fifo) basis.

2. All revenue and expenses, except for depreciation and that portion of the cost of goods sold represented by the beginning inventory, are earned or incurred evenly throughout each year, i.e., in effect, the transactions occur at the average price level of the year.

3. Dividends are declared and paid at the end of each year.

4. At the beginning of the second year, $50,000 of the long-term liabilities are paid in cash, and $300,000 are converted to capital stock.

5. Acquisitions of plant and equipment take place at the opening of business and at the close of the first year. The land on which the plant is located is held under a lease, so all items of plant and equipment are subject to depreciation. The average depreciation rate is 10 per cent a year on the straight-line basis.

Comparative Income Statement (Historical Basis)

	First Year	Second Year
Sales	$800,000	$1,000,000
Operating Expenses:		
Cost of goods sold	$470,000	$ 600,000
Depreciation	30,000	40,000
Other expenses (including income tax)	280,000	300,000
Total Operating Expenses	$780,000	$ 940,000
Net Profit from Operations	$ 20,000	$ 60,000

Comparative Statement of Retained Earnings (Historical Basis)

	First Year	Second Year
Retained Earnings, Beginning of Year	$ —	$15,000
Net Profit from Operations	20,000	60,000
Total	$20,000	$75,000
Dividends to Stockholders	5,000	10,000
Retained Earnings, End of Year	$15,000	$65,000

122

Comparative Balance Sheet (Historical Basis)

Assets	Opening of Business	End of First Year	End of Second Year
Cash, Receivables, and Other			
Monetary Items	$200,000	$195,000	$235,000
Inventories	250,000	300,000	200,000
Plant and Equipment	300,000	400,000	400,000
Less: Accumulated			
depreciation	—	(30,000)	(70,000)
Total Assets	$750,000	$865,000	$765,000
Liabilities			
Current Liabilities	$100,000	$200,000	$100,000
Long-term Liabilities	350,000	350,000	—
Total Liabilities	$450,000	$550,000	$100,000
Stockholders' Equity			
Capital Stock	$300,000	$300,000	$600,000
Retained Earnings	—	15,000	65,000
Total Stockholders' Equity	$300,000	$315,000	$665,000
Total Liabilities and			
Stockholders' Equity	$750,000	$865,000	$765,000

123

Adjustment of Income and Retained Earnings Statements

Sales

Sales took place evenly throughout the year, so, in effect, they took place at the average dollar of the year, i.e., when the price index was at the average for the year. The adjustment of the sales amounts to the end-of-second-year dollar, or the current dollar, would be:

First year: $ 800,000 × 200/160 = $1,000,000
Second year: $1,000,000 × 200/190 = $1,052,632

Cost of Goods Sold

Under the first-in, first-out (Fifo) method of inventory pricing, the cost of goods sold is measured by the beginning inventory plus a portion of the merchandise purchased during the period.

First year. The beginning inventory was acquired at the opening of business when the index number was 150. The merchandise purchases were made at the average price level of the year, or when the index number was 160. The adjustments to express the cost of goods sold in terms of the current dollar would be:

Beginning inventory	$250,000 × 200/150 = $333,333
Portion of merchandise purchases	220,000 × 200/160 = 275,000
Cost of goods sold	$470,000 $608,333

The traditional calculation of cost of goods sold could have been used. (The merchandise purchases of $520,000 is derived from the other related figures.)

Beginning inventory	$250,000 × 200/150 = $333,333
Merchandise purchases	520,000 × 200/160 = 650,000
	$770,000 $983,333
Ending inventory	300,000 × 200/160 = 375,000
Cost of goods sold	$470,000 $608,333

124 *Second year.* The beginning inventory of $300,000 at historical cost, or $375,000 as adjusted to the current dollar, is carried forward from the close of the first year. An additional $300,000 (historical cost) is a part of the merchandise purchased during the second year when the price index was at 190. The adjustments are:

Beginning inventory	$300,000 × 200/160 = $375,000
Portion of merchandise purchases	300,000 × 200/190 = 315,789
Cost of goods sold	$600,000 $690,789

Depreciation

The most time-consuming step in the adjustment process is the "aging" of the depreciable property and the corresponding adjustment of the periodic depreciation. Strictly speaking, the date of acquisition of each item of property must be determined as well as its cost, and the corresponding depreciation must be adjusted to the current-dollar basis. Once the "aging" process has been carried out, however, it can be kept up to date with a relatively small amount of time and effort. Various simplifications can be introduced. All items acquired at approximately the same time, such as a month or a quarter, can be grouped together and treated as a single item, unless the depreciation charge to operations must be broken down for more detailed accounting purposes. An arbitrary cut-off point can sometimes be used for the older items of property, which are often a small proportion of the total, and all items acquired prior to a certain point of time can be treated as though they were all acquired at the cut-off point. Where a very large number of similar units of equipment are in use, statistical methods are available for the aging calculation. Survivorship tables, similar to the mortality tables used by insurance companies, may be employed to determine under rules of statistical probability how many items are in use, classified by date of acquisition.

Ordinarily the simplest way to revise the depreciation charges is to apply the normal depreciation rates to the adjusted cost amounts. In the demonstration, the $300,000 of plant and equipment used during the first year was acquired at the beginning of that year, and the addition of $100,000 was acquired at the close of the first year. The calculations are:

Plant and equipment, acquired at beginning of first year, $300,000 × 200/150	$400,000
Plant and equipment, acquired at end of first year, $100,000 × 200/175	114,286
Total adjusted cost of plant and equipment, beginning and end of second year	$514,286
Depreciation, first year — 10% of $400,000	$ 40,000
Depreciation, second year — 10% of $514,286	51,429

125

Other Expenses

The other expenses, which include income tax expense, were incurred evenly throughout each year or at the average dollar of the year. The adjustments are:

First year, $280,000 × 200/160 = $350,000
Second year, $300,000 × 200/190 = $315,789

Dividends

Dividends to stockholders were declared and paid at the end of each year. The adjustments are:

First year, $ 5,000 × 200/175 = $5,714
Second year, $10,000 × 200/200 = $10,000

Gain or Loss on Monetary Items

A loss in purchasing power of monetary items arises from holding monetary assets during a period of rising prices or from maintaining liabilities during a period of falling prices. A gain is the reverse; it arises from holding monetary assets during a period of falling prices or from maintaining liabilities during a period of rising prices.

The purchasing-power gain or loss on monetary assets and liabilities appears only on adjusted financial statements. Differences of opinion exist as to the method of reporting these gains and losses,[2] but for purposes of this demonstration, they will be treated in a statement of income and inflation gain or loss as separately disclosed elements immediately following the determination of net profit.

The amount of the accumulated net gain or loss on monetary items can be calculated by determining the amount needed to balance the financial statements after making all adjustments of the nonmonetary accounts. A more detailed analysis, however, is desirable as a verification of the net gain or loss and to analyze it as to types of monetary items. The calculation in the demonstration will be made in two parts: (1) the gain or loss on the net current monetary items, and (2) the gain or loss on the long-term liabilities.

There are several ways of computing the gain or loss from holding monetary items. The computations which follow are in more detail than would ordinarily be needed because in an actual case calculation could be facilitated by grouping together items to be adjusted by the same multiplier. Regardless of the method chosen, however, care must be used to insure consistency. That is, both sides of a transaction must be adjusted by the same index number. In our illustration, for example, the choice of the index number at the end of the first year to adjust the acquisition of plant and equipment dictates that the outlay of monetary assets for plant and equipment in that year be adjusted by the index at the same date.

Net Current Monetary Items

	Opening of Business	End of First Year	End of Second Year
Cash, receivables, and other monetary items	$200,000	$195,000	$235,000
Current liabilities	100,000	200,000	100,000
Net monetary assets (liabilities)	$100,000	($ 5,000)	$135,000

---

[2] Various methods of presentation in financial statements are illustrated and discussed in Appendix C, page 137.

126

First Year	Unadjusted Amount	Multiplier	Adjusted Amount
Net monetary assets – beginning	$100,000	175/150	$116,667
add –			
Sales	800,000	175/160	875,000
	$900,000		$991,667
deduct –			
Purchases of merchandise	$520,000	175/160	$568,750
Other expenses	280,000	175/160	306,250
Dividends paid at end of year	5,000	175/175	5,000
Plant and equipment purchased at end of year	100,000	175/175	100,000
	$905,000		$980,000
Net monetary assets – end	($ 5,000)		$ 11,667
			(5,000)
Purchasing-power loss			$ 16,667

Since this loss is stated in terms of the dollar at the end of the first year, it must be converted into terms of the dollar at the end of the second year for inclusion in the adjusted statements:

$$\$16,667 \times 200/175 = \$19,047 \text{ (Loss)}$$

127

Second Year:	Unadjusted Amount	Multiplier	Adjusted Amount
Net monetary assets – beginning	$ (5,000)	200/175	$ (5,714)
add –			
Sales	1,000,000	200/190	1,052,632
	$ 995,000		$1,046,918
deduct –			
Retirement of debt at beginning of year	$ 50,000	200/175	$ 57,144
Purchases of merchandise	500,000	200/190	526,316
Other expenses	300,000	200/190	315,789
Dividends paid at end of year	10,000	200/200	10,000
	$ 860,000		$ 909,249
Net monetary assets – end	$ 135,000		$ 137,669
			135,000
Purchasing-power loss			$ 2,669

Long-term Liabilities

	First Year	Second Year
Balance at beginning of year	$350,000	$350,000
Balance at end of year	350,000	—
Decrease during year	None	$350,000

First year. The $350,000 of long-term liabilities remained constant throughout the year. The calculation of the purchasing-power gain for the year, converted into terms of the dollar at the end of the second year is:

$$\$350,000 \times 175/150 = \$408,333;$$
$$\$408,333 - \$350,000 = \$ 58,333;$$
$$\$ 58,333 \times 200/175 = \$ 66,667 \text{ (gain)}.$$

Second year. There is no gain or loss of purchasing power because the decrease took place at the beginning of the year.

Summary

	First Year	Second Year
Loss on net current monetary assets	$19,047	$2,669
Gain on long-term liabilities	66,667	—
Net gain or loss	$47,620 (Gain)	$2,669 (Loss)

128

The adjusted comparative income statement can now be prepared in terms of "end-of-second-year" dollars and appears as follows:

Adjusted Comparative Statement of Income and Inflation Gain (Loss)

	First Year	Second Year
Sales	$1,000,000	$1,052,632
Operating Expenses:		
Cost of goods sold	$ 608,333	$ 690,789
Depreciation	40,000	51,429
Other expenses (including income tax)	350,000	315,789
Total Operating Expenses	$ 998,333	$1,058,007
Net Profit (Loss) From Operations	$ 1,667	$ (5,375)
Inflation Gains or Losses		
Gain (loss) on short-term monetary items	$ (19,047)	$ (2,669)
Gain (loss) on long-term debt	66,667	—
Net Inflation Gain (Loss)	$ 47,620	$ (2,669)
Net Profit and Net Inflation Gain (Loss)	$ 49,287	$ (8,044)

Adjusted Comparative Statement of Retained Earnings

Retained Earnings, Beginning of Year	$ —	$43,573
Net Profit and Net Inflation Gain (Loss)	49,287	(8,044)
Total	$49,287	$35,529
Dividends to Stockholders	5,714	10,000
Retained Earnings, End of Year	$43,573	$25,529

Adjustment of the Balance Sheet

Monetary Items

The amounts of the monetary items at the end of the second year require no adjustment since they are, as legal tender, or by agreement with the debtors and creditors, receivable or payable in current dollars. The amounts at the opening of business and at the end of the first year, however, must be restated in order to express them in terms of the purchasing power of the dollar at the end of the second year.

129

Cash, Receivables, and Other Monetary Items:

Opening of business, $200,000 × 200/150 = $266,667
End of first year, $195,000 × 200/175 = $222,857
End of second year, $235,000 × 200/200 = $235,000

Current Liabilities:

Opening of business, $100,000 × 200/150 = $133,333
End of first year, $200,000 × 200/175 = $228,570
End of second year, $100,000 × 200/200 = $100,000

Long-term Liabilities:

Opening of business, $350,000 × 200/150 = $466,667
End of first year, $350,000 × 200/175 = $400,000
End of second year, None

Inventories

The merchandise inventory at the opening of business was acquired at the price level of that date. The inventories at the end of the first and second years were, under the Fifo pricing method, assumed to have been acquired at the average price level of each of the respective years. The adjustments to the current-dollar basis, therefore, are:

Opening of business, $250,000 × 200/150 = $333,333
End of first year, $300,000 × 200/160 = $375,000
End of second year, $200,000 × 200/190 = $210,526

Plant and Equipment

The adjustment of the plant and equipment was demonstrated in the previous section, "Adjustment of the Income Statement." The adjusted amounts for the plant and equipment were:

Opening of business, $400,000
End of first year, $514,286
End of second year, $514,286

The adjusted amount of accumulated depreciation can be derived from the adjusted annual depreciation, as follows:

130

End of first year, 10% of $400,000	$40,000
Depreciation during second year, 10% of $514,286	51,429
Accumulated depreciation, end of second year	$91,429

Capital Stock

The first $300,000 was issued at the opening of business. The next $300,000 was issued by conversion of long-term liabilities at the beginning of the second year. Expressed in terms of the current dollar, the adjusted capital stock appears as follows:

Issued at opening of business, $300,000 × 200/150 = $400,000
Issued at beginning of second year, $300,000 × 200/175 = 342,854
Total, end of second year $742,854

Retained Earnings

The adjusted retained earnings are derived from the series of adjusted income statements. As a matter of informative disclosure for purposes of this demonstration, the retained earnings from ordinary operations will be shown separately from the accumulated gain or loss on monetary items:

Retained earnings from operations:

	First Year	Second Year
Carried over from previous year	$ —	($4,047)
Net profit or (loss) from operations	1,667	(5,375)
	$1,667	($9,422)
Adjusted dividends	5,714	10,000
Retained earnings from operations	($4,047)	($19,422)

Accumulated gain or loss on net monetary items:

Gain on net monetary items, first year	$47,620
Loss on net monetary items, second year	2,669
Accumulated gain on net monetary items	$44,951

Adjusted Comparative Balance Sheet

	Opening of Business	End of First year	End of Second year
Assets			
Cash, Receivables, and Other Monetary Items	$ 266,667	$ 222,857	$235,000
Inventories	333,333	375,000	210,526
Plant and Equipment	400,000	514,286	514,286
Less Accumulated Depreciation	—	(40,000)	(91,429)
Total Assets	$1,000,000	$1,072,143	$868,383
Liabilities			
Current Liabilities	$ 133,333	$ 228,570	$100,000
Long-term Liabilities	466,667	400,000	—
	$ 600,000	$ 628,570	$100,000
Stockholders' Equity			
Capital Stock	$ 400,000	$ 400,000	$742,854
Retained Earnings:			
From Operations (after dividends)	—	(4,047)	(19,422)
Accumulated Gain or (Loss) on Net Monetary Items	—	47,620	44,951
Total Stockholders' Equity	$ 400,000	$ 443,573	$768,383
Total Liabilities and Stockholders' Equity	$1,000,000	$1,072,143	$868,383

Additional Comments

The demonstration assumed that no adjustment of the financial statements had been made prior to the end of the second year. This required the restatement of the historical income statement for the first year and of the historical balance sheets at the beginning and end of the first year in terms of the current dollar in order to make them comparable with the adjusted financial statements for the second year. If adjustments had been made at the end of the first year, the results at the end of the second year would have been the same, but the procedure would have been somewhat different. Each amount in the adjusted statements prepared at the close of the first year would have been multiplied by the fraction 200/175 in order to restate them for use in the comparative financial statements prepared at the close of the second year. Other calculations involving items carried over from the first to the second year would correspondingly be modified.

It was assumed in the demonstration that the inventory was priced on a first-in, first-out (Fifo) basis. Other pricing methods would require variations in the computations. For example, if the last-in, first-out (Lifo) method had been used, the inventory at the end of the first year would have consisted of $250,000 acquired at the opening of business when the price-level index was 150, and $50,000 acquired during the first year when the average price-level index was 160. The calculation for the adjustment to the current dollar would have been:

$$\$250,000 \times 200/150 = \$333,333$$
$$50,000 \times 200/160 = 62,500$$
$$\overline{\$300,000} \qquad \overline{\$395,833}$$

The corresponding amount of goods sold would have been acquired entirely from the first year's purchases of merchandise and the adjustment calculation of the cost of goods sold for the first year would have been

$$\$470,000 \times 200/160 = \$587,500$$

For the purposes of the demonstration, price-level index numbers were available only for the beginning, the end, and the average of each year. Index number series are usually available at monthly or quarterly intervals and should be used if greater refinement of the restated amounts is considered desirable. On the other hand, a still greater simplification than the one used in the demonstration could be employed when the movement of the price level is relatively slow by assuming that the index number at the beginning of each year applied to all transactions during the year. The results might be sufficiently accurate for most purposes.

In the demonstration, the accumulated gain or loss on monetary items and the accumulated undistributed earnings from ordinary operations were shown as separate portions of the retained earnings. This was possible because the illustration started with the opening of business and the accumulations could readily be computed over the two-year period. Where the price-level adjustment technique is put into effect for a company which has been in existence for a great many years, the accumulated adjusted retained earnings is obtained as a balancing figure in the first set of financial statements. To isolate the accumulated gain or loss on monetary items would not be feasible since it would require calculating the purchasing-power gain or loss on monetary items back to the date of origin of the company. Either the accumulated amount must be left as an undivided and unidentified portion of the retained earnings, or a practical compromise must be adopted such as starting the accumulation at a practicable date and disclosing this limitation of the accumulated amount by means of a footnote.

133

Gains and Losses Attributable to the Holding of Monetary Items When the Price Level Changes

Table of Contents

136

Gains and Losses on Monetary Items

An articulated set of financial statements (income statement, retained earnings statement, and balance sheet), which has been completely adjusted to dollars of equal purchasing power, balances only if an item is included which does not appear in unadjusted statements: the net purchasing power gain or loss resulting from the holding of monetary items while the price level changes.

137

This gain or loss, which is unique to statements completely adjusted for changes in the purchasing power of the dollar, arises because "Every firm is forced to speculate somewhat in the value of the dollar."[1] In a period of rising prices, the value of the dollar falls and the holder of a monetary asset suffers a loss in the sense that his command over goods and services diminishes. On the other hand, a debtor gains when prices rise in the sense that the contractual amount of a liability remains constant and therefore represents a diminishing burden in terms of the effort or sacrifice required to meet the obligation; the contractual amount of a liability does not rise even though the general price level does. This gain or loss is real and stems from the fact that although the dollar value at which a monetary item is stated in the statements does not change, the value of the dollar in which it is measured does change. The gain or loss results from the holding of an asset or liability while its equivalent purchasing power increases or declines.

The presence of the gain or loss on monetary items in statements which have been adjusted for price-level changes creates a number

---

[1] Donald A. Corbin, "Impact of Changing Prices on a Department Store," *The Journal of Accountancy*, Apr. 1954, pp. 430-40.

of problems which do not exist in connection with unadjusted statements. This appendix is concerned with four such problem areas: (1) the nature of the items which give rise to purchasing-power gains and losses, (2) the relative importance of purchasing-power gains and losses on monetary items, (3) the computation of purchasing-power gains and losses on monetary items, and (4) the reporting of purchasing-power gains and losses in financial statements.

The Nature of Monetary Items

The distinction between nonmonetary and monetary items is important in adjusting statements for changes in the price level. In general terms the book value (basis) of a nonmonetary item is restated to give effect to inflation or deflation. A monetary item, on the other hand, is not restated, if the intent of the adjustments for price-level changes is to state all items in the financial reports in current terms.

138 The concept of monetary items which has been adopted in this price-level study is as follows:

> A "monetary" item is one the *amount* of which is fixed by statute or contract, and is therefore not affected by a change in the price level.

In other words, regardless of what happens to the general price level, the monetary items remain fixed in terms of the current dollar. They are subject to change only if the financial data are to be expressed in terms of the dollar at some other point of time, or when comparative statements are prepared in terms of a common dollar. In the latter case, past figures have to be revised to make them comparable with current amounts.

This concept of monetary items enables us to draw some conclusions regarding the nature of individual assets and liabilities.

Types of Monetary Assets

The most obvious examples of monetary assets are cash or claims to cash—undeposited cash, cash in banks, accounts and notes receivable, mortgages and bonds receivable, and the like.

Marketable securities or investments in securities of other companies may conceivably be carried at cost, market value, or, in the case of notes and bonds, at face value plus or minus unamortized premium or discount. If carried at cost, they should be treated as nonmonetary assets and be adjusted for changes in the price level. If carried at market, they are already stated in current dollars and require no further adjustment, but, as was pointed out in Chapter 2, the change in carrying value should be analyzed so as to separate the effect of the price-level change from the real appreciation (or the reverse). If notes and bonds are carried at face value plus or minus the unamortized premium or discount, they qualify for the category of monetary assets.

Convertible bonds held as an investment may be difficult to classify since the intent to convert to stock is dependent upon a number of factors, both immediate and long range. A useful rule of thumb is to treat such investments as monetary assets as long as the market price of the stock is below the conversion price, and as nonmonetary assets if the market price of the stock is at or above the conversion price. Convertible preferred stock presents a parallel problem.

Inventories are generally nonmonetary in character, but there are occasional exceptions such as goods produced under a fixed-price contract, or refined gold where the price is fixed by government fiat. 139

Prepaid expenses or "deferred charges" may present some difficulties of classification. Parts and supplies, if included in this group, are clearly nonmonetary. Such items as prepaid rent, advances of salaries and commissions, and the like, are essentially fixed-dollar amounts of receivables collectible in goods or services rather than cash. They may also be viewed as advance payments on liabilities which will accrue as time passes or as services are rendered. They may therefore be considered the equivalent of cash and be classed as monetary items.

Other examples include the proceeds of security issues which are sometimes held in the form of cash for some time before invested or used for expansion of facilities. Sinking funds and pension funds are often at least in part in the form of uninvested cash or bonds. Advances to officers or to affiliates, cash surrender value of life insurance, and other long-term receivables are monetary items.

Types of Monetary Liabilities

A monetary liability is one which can be settled by the payment of a fixed amount of dollars. This does not rule out estimated liabilities. Practically all liabilities are monetary in character, but occasionally one is found the amount of which by agreement is determined by the change in the price level.[2]

Such items as accounts payable, notes payable, debentures and mortgage bonds, obligations under lease agreements (if shown in the balance sheet), withheld taxes, and accrued expenses will, with rare exceptions, clearly qualify as monetary items. "Deferred credits" such as unexpired magazine subscriptions, prepaid rents and royalties, pre-paid maintenance service, unearned insurance premiums, deposits on contracts, meter deposits, and other such items as advances by customers or loans should be treated as monetary liabilities even though some of them are obligations which will be settled by the delivery of goods or the performance of services instead of cash. The price has been agreed upon and the amount is fixed in terms of current dollars.

Unearned interest, discount and finance charges are offsets to or deductions from the face value of related receivables and are, there-fore, monetary in character. Unrealized profit on installment sales can be treated as a monetary item since it is primarily an offset to the related receivables.

Other examples include purchase contracts, deferred or postponed income taxes, and the liability for pension costs. The amounts involved may be estimates and may vary due to such factors as amortization of premium or discount, but these variations are in no way related to changes in the price level; the items can still be characterized as fixed-dollar or monetary.

Convertible bonds which can be exchanged for shares of common stock at the discretion of the holder present a troublesome problem. Until conversion irrevocably occurs, these obligations can properly be classified as liabilities. If, however, it becomes advantageous for the bondholder to do so, he may step into the role of a stockholder, some-times with a resulting dilution of the other stockholders' equity. There are a number of factors which may lead the holder to carry out the conversion but he is unlikely to do so until the market price of the stock reaches the conversion price. A rule of thumb, which was

140

---

[2] Exceptions have occasionally occurred in the United States and more frequently in other countries where the obligation is linked to the price of gold, to a price-level index, to the currency of another country, or other-wise is not a fixed amount in terms of the local currency. See, for example, A. Rubner, "The Abdication of the Israeli Pound as a Standard of Measure-ment for Medium and Long Term Contracts," *The Review of Economic Studies*, vol. 28, p. 69 (1960); and Lionel A. Wilk, *Accounting for Inflation*, Chapter 7, p. 81, Sweet & Maxwell Limited (London). 1960.

suggested for convertible securities held as an asset, is to treat convertible bonds as monetary liabilities when the market price of the stock is below the conversion price, and as nonmonetary when the market price is at or above the conversion price.

What has just been said about convertible bonds would be applicable to convertible preferred stock or other convertible securities.

Monetary Items in the Stockholders' Equity

In general, the stockholders' equity, as the residual claim to net assets, is nonmonetary in character. The one important exception is the equity of the preferred stockholders. This is usually a fixed-dollar amount; it may involve a retirement premium in case of redemption, or other such modifications of the par value, but these are unrelated to changes in the price level.[3] The preferred stock account, therefore, should ordinarily be treated as a monetary item and the purchasing-power gain or loss should be computed in the same manner as that of a monetary liability. The result during a period of rising prices is that the loss in purchasing power of the preferred stockholders' claim becomes an increase in the common stockholders' equity; during a period of falling price the preferred stockholders' interest gains at the expense of the common stockholder.

141

For example, assume that the opening balance sheet of a corporation is as follows:

Nonmonetary assets	$200,000	Preferred stock	$ 50,000
		Common stock	150,000
	$200,000		$200,000

Now suppose that the price level doubles before any other transactions occur. The balance sheet would be adjusted as follows:

Nonmonetary assets	$400,000	Preferred stock	$ 50,000
		Common stock	$300,000
		Plus purchasing-power loss of preferred stock	50,000
			$350,000
	$400,000		$400,000

[3] There may be occasional instances in which the preferred stock contract permits participation in assets in case of liquidation to such an extent that it loses its character as a fixed claim and should be treated the same as the common stock.

If, on the other hand, prices had dropped 50 per cent, the balance sheet would have shown the following situation:

Nonmonetary assets	$100,000	Preferred stock	$ 50,000
		Common stock	$ 75,000
		Less purchasing-power gain of preferred stock	25,000
			50,000
	$100,000		$100,000

In the first case, where prices rose, the preferred stock interest was reduced from 25 per cent to 12½ per cent. In the second case, where prices fell, the preferred stock interest increased from 25 per cent to 50 per cent.

These adjustments back and forth between the common and preferred stock equities are, like other purchasing-power gains and losses on monetary items, subject to change as the trend of the price-level changes, and are fully effective only through liquidation of the business, retirement of the stock, or other disposition of the stock interest, events which ordinarily are indefinite as to date of occurrence. The presence of preferred stock does, however, act as a hedge by absorbing purchasing-power gains or losses which otherwise would adhere to the common-stock equity. For example, see Table 10 on page 143, taken from the report on The Reece Corporation on page 127 of *Price Level Changes and Financial Statements—Case Studies of Four Companies,* by Ralph C. Jones.[4]

Significance of Gains and Losses on Monetary Items

The importance of the gains and losses on monetary items will vary a good deal from one company to another. Companies in the financial area have relatively small amounts of nonmonetary assets and are largely in a hedged position as to monetary assets and liabilities. Companies in other areas employing relatively large proportions of borrowed capital, or operating with extensive advances from customers, will typically have a balance of purchasing-power gains during a period of rising prices, while the others will ordinarily show a balance of purchasing-power losses. Companies which are in a position to assume

142

[4] American Accounting Association. 1955.

Table 10

Distribution of Purchasing Power Loss Between Preferred and Common Stockholders
1948-1951

(In Thousands of Dollars)

Dec. 31	Preferred Stock Outstanding	Total Purchasing Power Loss (Gain)*	Loss (Gain) Absorbed by Preferred Stockholders*	Loss (Gain) to Common Stockholders*
1948	$635	$26	$(12)#	$38
1949	635	(24)	(14)	(10)
1950	617	43	38	5
1951	600	33	36	(3)
		$78	$ 48	$30

* December 1951 dollars.
# Preferred stock was issued on August 31, 1948, when the purchasing power factor was 1.079.

143

the risks of operating with a higher proportion of borrowed working capital will to that extent be able to hedge the gains and losses on current monetary items.

The following examples are taken from the few actual cases which have come to our attention in which the gains and losses on monetary accounts were computed.

The most extensive published study of gains and losses on monetary accounts is that made by William A. Paton, Jr.[5] He calculated the effect of inflation upon the short-term monetary items of fifty-two nonfinancial companies for the period 1940-1952. Only two companies showed a net gain. Thirty-six showed an average annual loss rate (the relationship between the average loss and the average net current monetary assets) of 5 per cent or more over the twelve-year period. He estimated that the average loss for all United States corporations (excluding banks and insurance companies) was over $1 billion a year.

The study made by Professor Ralph C. Jones[6] of four companies, covering, in general, the 1940's and early 1950's, showed varying results. The New York Telephone Company had an excess of current

---

[5] *A Study in Liquidity.* University of Michigan. 1958.

[6] *Price Level Changes and Financial Statements—Case Studies of Four Companies.* American Accounting Association. 1955.

monetary liabilities (exclusive of bank loans) over current monetary assets, but the net purchasing-power gain amounted to about .1 per cent a year on the adjusted equity of the invested capital—stock, bonds, and notes. The Reece Corporation suffered a purchasing-power loss of about 1.5 per cent a year of the total equity of the stockholders. (There were no bondholders or noteholders.) Both Armstrong Cork Company and Sargent & Company, the remaining two companies included in the study, had average annual losses on monetary items considerably less than one per cent of the adjusted invested capital. The New York Telephone Company showed sizeable gains on its long-term debt.

A study of two public utility companies, covering the years 1938 to 1956, made by Professor Eldon S. Hendriksen[7] also demonstrated the relatively greater significance of long-term debt in this type of industry. The Washington Water Power Company showed an average loss on net current monetary items of a little over 2 per cent of the adjusted net income before including this item; there was an average purchasing-power gain on the combined long-term debt and preferred stock of almost 50 per cent. The corresponding data for the Portland General Electric Company were a loss on the current items of over 5 per cent and a gain on long-term debt of 85 per cent.

144

A manufacturer in the aircraft industry prepared a series of adjusted financial statements for the period 1951 to 1957 which have not been published. Due primarily to sizeable advances on Government contracts, the results showed purchasing-power gains in all but one year on the net current monetary assets. In two of the years, the gain was well in excess of the adjusted net income before including this item.

The materiality of the purchasing-power gains and losses on monetary items, then, will vary substantially from one company to another, but there is convincing evidence that the amounts can often be very significant.

Computation of Purchasing-power Gains and Losses on Monetary Items

If all nonmonetary-account adjustments have been made, the amount required to balance a set of adjusted financial statements will be the

---

[7] *Price-Level Adjustments of Financial Statements*. Washington State University. 1961.

net purchasing-power gain or loss on the monetary items. If only the amount of the net gain or loss is desired, therefore, no further calculations are required. There are at least three reasons, however, making the direct calculation of the purchasing-power gain or loss on monetary items necesary or desirable: (1) the direct calculation serves to verify the amount of the net gain or loss, thereby insuring that the statements do, in fact, balance; (2) the reporting of gains and losses on current monetary items separately from those on long-term monetary items is often desirable; and (3) information regarding the effect of the individual monetary items on purchasing-power gains and losses may be useful in certain circumstances.

Conceptually, the calculation of the purchasing-power gain or loss on a monetary item is quite simple. The loss or gain can be measured in terms of the dollar at any given point of time. Three possible monetary units are: (1) the dollar at the end of the year, (2) the dollar at the beginning of the year, or (3) the base-period dollar. The following schedule demonstrates these three variations in measuring or expressing the amount of loss on a monetary asset, or gain on a monetary liability, where a balance of $10,000 remained unchanged during a year when the general price-level index rose from 150 to 200.

145

	End-of-year Dollar	First-of-year Dollar	Base-period Dollar
Balance—first of year	$13,333(a)	$10,000	$6,667(c)
Balance—end of year	10,000	7,500(b)	5,000(d)
Loss (if an asset) or gain (if a liability)	$ 3,333	$ 2,500	$1,667

(a) 200/150 × 10,000.　　(b) 150/200 × 10,000.　　(c) 100/150 × 10,000.
(d) 100/200 × 10,000.

Each of these calculations shows the same result—there was a 25 per cent loss in the value of the dollar which amounted to $3,333 in terms of the current end-of-year dollar, $2,500 in terms of the dollar at the beginning of the year, or $1,667 in terms of the base-period dollar. The amount which would appear in a set of adjusted financial statements would depend upon the method used in adjusting other items; the current end-of-year dollar has been used in most experiments and studies of price-level adjustments, so we would ordinarily say that there has been a loss (if an asset) or gain (if a liability) of $3,333. The amount can also be calculated as: 50/150 × $10,000 = $3,333.

If the price level had fallen during the year, there would be a rise in the value of the dollar which can be measured and expressed in the same manner. Assume that the price-level index declined from 150 to 125. The calculation of the loss or gain on a monetary item of $10,000, in terms of the end-of-year dollar, would be as follows:

Balance—first of year (125/150 × 10,000)	$ 8,333
Balance—end of year	10,000
Gain (if an asset) or loss (if a liability)	$ 1,667

There has been a 20 per cent increase in the value of the dollar and the gain or loss can be expressed as $1,667 in end-of-year dollars. It can also be calculated as: $25/150 \times \$10,000 = \$1,667$.

Where the price-level adjustments are made in terms of the end-of-period dollar, it can be said that the monetary assets and liabilities are automatically adjusted since the amounts shown in the end-of-period balance sheet are always receivable or payable in current dollars—$10,000 in the previous illustration. In a comparative balance sheet, however, the amounts for the previous years must be adjusted so that they will be expressed in terms of the current dollar and therefore be comparable to the amounts in the end-of-period statement—in the previous illustrations, $13,333 would appear in the adjusted balance sheet at the close of the previous year if the price index rose from 150 to 200, or $8,333 if the index fell from 150 to 125.

Computation of the purchasing-power gain or loss is somewhat more complicated in actual practice, however, because the monetary items rarely remain unchanged throughout the year. Additions and deductions in the account must therefore be taken into consideration as well as beginning and ending balances.

For purposes of illustration, it will be assumed that all adjustments are made in terms of the current end-of-year dollar. (Unless the price changes have occurred with great rapidity, the index for the last month or quarter of the year can be used as the equivalent of the end-of-year index.) The following demonstration shows the calculation of the gain or loss for a period during which prices are rising. The price index stands at 150 at the beginning of the period. An addition to the account takes place when the index has reached 160 and a deduction when it has reached 180. At the end of the period, the index has risen to 200. The technique is to convert the opening balance and each change into end of period dollars and subtract the closing balance to obtain the amount of the loss or gain.

	Index No.	Unadjusted Amount	Multiplier	Adjusted Amount
Balance—beginning	150	$25,000	200/150	$33,333
Addition	160	5,000	200/160	6,250
		$30,000		$39,583
Deduction	180	10,000	200/180	11,111
Balance—end		$20,000		$28,472
				20,000
Loss (if an asset) or gain (if a liability)				$ 8,472

Another way of making the computation is to compute the loss or gain for each successive balance, and convert the result to end-of-year dollars.

	Unadjusted Amount	Multiplier	Adjusted Amount	Loss or Gain Amount	Conversion Factor	End-of-year Dollar
Balance—beginning	$25,000	160/150	$26,667	$1,667	200/160	$2,083
Addition	5,000					
	$30,000	180/160	33,750	3,750	200/180	4,167
Deduction	10,000					
Balance—end	$20,000	200/180	22,222	22,222	200/200	2,222
Loss (if an asset) or gain (if a liability)						$8,472

147

In this simple illustration, one addition to the monetary item and one deduction from it, both at known index levels, are assumed. In the usual case, in which numerous transactions take place during the period, grouping is required in order to facilitate the use of average indexes. Additions to monetary items and deductions from monetary items may be grouped, depending on the degree and rapidity of price change, on a monthly, quarterly, or annual basis. Monetary and non-monetary items should be grouped in the same manner in order to make the results of any adjustments comparable.

If it can reasonably be assumed that all transactions during the period took place at the average price level of the period, the calculations can be considerably simplified and condensed. If this assumption is made in the previous illustration and if the average price-level index of the period is 170,[8] the calculation of the loss or gain for the period would be:

---

[8] Note that this would be the average of the monthly or quarterly index figures for the period and would not necessarily correspond to the index at the midpoint of the period.

	Index No.	Unadjusted Amount	Multiplier	Adjusted Amount
Balance—beginning	150	$25,000	200/150	$33,333
Addition	170	5,000	200/170	5,882
		$30,000		$39,215
Deduction	170	10,000	200/170	11,764
Balance—end	200	$20,000		$27,451
				20,000
Loss (if an asset) or gain (if a liability)				$ 7,451

The computation can be simplified, as follows:

	Index No.	Unadjusted Amount	Multiplier	Adjusted Amount
Balance—beginning	150	$25,000	200/150	$33,333
Net deduction	170	5,000	200/170	5,882
	200	$20,000		$27,451
				20,000
Loss (if an asset) or gain (if a liability)				$ 7,451

148 This assumption that all transactions took place at the average dollar of the period is most commonly applied to the current monetary items, and the calculation is further simplified by applying the index numbers to the *net* current monetary assets and liabilities. The assumption is of course proper only when the price-level changes are not erratic, when the transactions occur with considerable frequency and regularity, or, in general, where the conditions permit a presumption that the results will be reasonably accurate, as compared with a more detailed calculation. Such conditions are more apt to exist in the case of the current than the noncurrent monetary items.

Foreign monetary items. If monetary assets represent foreign currencies or if monetary liabilities are payable in foreign currencies, such as the monetary assets and liabilities of a foreign subsidiary included in a consolidated balance sheet, the purchasing-power gain or loss is determined by the fluctuations in the price level in the foreign country. Ideally, under complete freedom of trade and of the determination of exchange rates, the exchange rate would reflect the relative purchasing power of the two currencies. The rate, if expressed in U. S. dollars, would fall if the general price-level index rose faster in the foreign country than it did in the United States, or would rise if the reverse situation existed. The difference between the U. S. dollar equivalent of any given amount of a foreign monetary item at the beginning and end of a period would be the purchasing-power gain or loss for that period.

Actually, the ideal situation seldom, if ever, exists. There are often artificial controls on exchange rates as well as restrictions on goods and services which can be bought and sold. Foreign monetary items can be translated into current U. S. dollars with the use of an exchange rate at which a transfer of funds could take place, but this will not necessarily provide a basis for the calculation of the purchasing-power gain or loss. Some procedure will have to be adopted for each case, the results of which correspond as closely as possible to the ideal conditions.

If funds in a foreign country cannot be repatriated because of exchange restrictions, it would be best to treat them as nonmonetary assets and value them at their market value in the United States.

Reporting Purchasing-power Gains and Losses

149

Whenever a set of adjusted financial statements is prepared, the net purchasing-power loss or gain on monetary items during a period of time results in a corresponding decrease or increase in the stockholders' or other residual proprietary equity. There are, however, differences of opinion as to whether any or all of the losses or gains should appear in the income statement and be included in the calculation of net income for the period.

Ralph C. Jones[9] considered the problem at some length and concluded that:

> If some reasonable basis could be found for allocating monetary capital to various functions such as expansion, debt retirement, and operation, gains and losses on the operating portion would certainly be worthy of a place in an income account purporting to show net business income in real terms. Since no comparable item is found on conventional income statements and since the separation of current (operating) monetary capital from other monetary accounts is difficult and uncertain, managements generally may prefer to treat purchasing power changes in all monetary accounts as a separate category.

---

[9] *Effects of Price Level Changes on Business Income, Capital, and Taxes,* p. 23. American Accounting Association. 1956.

In each of the four cases included in the American Accounting Association study made under the direction of Professor Jones,[10] the net gains and losses on monetary items were shown only in the analysis of the changes in the stockholders' equity in the sets of adjusted financial statements. In the report on the Armstrong Cork Company, the earnings per share of common stock were computed by different methods (p. 81), and Professor Jones commented that (1) the exclusion of all purchasing-power gains and losses on monetary items "has the practical advantage of making a minimum departure from customary methods and at the same time marking the furthest limit to which governmental bodies are ever likely to go in recognizing changes in the value of the dollar," (2) the rationale of the inclusion of the gains and losses on the net monetary assets and the exclusion of the gains and losses on the preferred stock (there were no bonds in this case) is "that purchasing power gains and losses on net monetary assets have to be recognized to get a reasonable picture of operating results but that changes in the purchasing power of senior securities represent shifts in the real equities of various classes of permanent investors and as such should not be allowed to affect the income account of the corporation itself," and (3) the inclusion of all purchasing power gains and losses "probably gives the most realistic measure of the total effect of inflation or deflation on the common stock."

150

The report of the Study Group on Business Income,[11] while lending support to the presentation of "information that will facilitate the determination of income measured in units of approximately equal purchasing power," did not mention purchasing-power losses and gains on monetary items as a component of such calculations. That this was intentional seems to be indicated by a consideration of a report of the Committee on Concepts and Standards Underlying Corporate Financial Statements of the American Accounting Association[12] in the supplementary comments of George O. May and Oswald Knauth (pp. 135-139):

> A more important difference of opinion is presented by the statement of the association's committee: "The measurement of price

---

[10] *Price Level Changes and Financial Statements—Case Studies of Four Companies.* American Accounting Association. 1955.

[11] *Changing Concepts of Business Income.* The Macmillan Company. 1952.

[12] "Price Level Changes and Financial Statements. Supplementary Statement No. 2." *Accounting Review,* Oct. 1951, pp. 468-474.

level changes should be all-inclusive; all statement items affected should be adjusted in a consistent manner." This would mean, we take it, that unless changes in the value of the dollar are to be taken into account in respect of purely monetary transactions they should not be taken into account in determining charges against revenues in respect of consumption of physical property. ... Such a proposal seems to us to confuse two distinct objects and to be tantamount to rejection of the proposal of which the committee approves.

An "all-inclusive" adjustment would result, *inter alia*, in showing a loss rather than income as being derived from the maturing of a savings bond of $100 which had been purchased ten years earlier for $75 if the purchasing power of the dollar had fallen more than 25 per cent in the interval. Such a view is, we believe, politically impracticable. It is not, in our opinion, a natural or logical corollary of the proposition that dispositions and consumptions of *physical properties* in the course of business activities should be measured in units of the same purchasing power as the revenues in measuring income derived from those activities. This income itself would still be expressed in monetary units comparable with those in which other forms of income are measured.

151

In the study made by the manufacturer in the aircraft industry, to which previous reference was made, the gains and losses on net current monetary assets were shown on the adjusted income statement after "Earnings Before Purchasing Power Gains (Losses) on Net Current Monetary Assets." In this case, the gain on the debentures, "Decrease in purchasing power of debentures," was shown in a schedule entitled "Statement of Consolidated Stockholders' Equity—Adjusted."

Eldon S. Hendriksen, in his case study of two public utility companies,[13] concluded that the "gains and losses from the holding of monetary assets and monetary current liabilities should be included in the computation of net income to the enterprise," but that gains and losses on long-term debt would ordinarily be included only in the net income to stockholders, as distinct from the "enterprise." He believes that the gains and losses on long-term debt represent a gain or loss to one group of equity holders, offset by a loss or gain to another group, that these gains and losses should appear in the income statement but after a showing of net operating income, and that showing them as

---

[13] *Price-Level Adjustments of Financial Statements.* Washington State University. 1961.

capital adjustments in the analysis of the change in the common stockholders' equity does not constitute proper disclosure.

Only one company has come to our attention which has published statements for which the purchasing-power gain or loss on monetary items has been computed. N. V. Philips' Gloeilampenfabrieken (Philips Industries) of Eindhoven, the Netherlands, charges losses of purchasing power on capital invested in net monetary assets to income. Gains from this source are credited to income to the extent that losses have been previously recognized. That is, when purchasing-power losses occur, income is charged and a special "Reserve for diminishing purchasing power of capital invested in monetary assets" is credited. When purchasing-power gains occur, the "reserve" is charged and income is credited until the reserve is exhausted. Further gains are not recorded unless preceded by losses.[14]

152

---

[14] A. Goudeket, "An Application of Replacement Value Theory," *The Journal of Accountancy*, July 1960, p. 41-4.

Accounting for Gains and Losses in Purchasing Power of Monetary Items[1]

By Marvin M. Deupree

Considerable progress has been made in recent years in analyzing the deficiencies in accounting and reporting that result from inflation and in developing the underlying theory and the procedures for adjusting financial statements to a common-dollar basis. However, there is one important unresolved area in the theory that is of sufficient importance to serve as a barrier to satisfactory general application of price-level adjustments. The question at issue is the treatment of changes in the purchasing-power equivalent of the monetary items in the financial statements. Such changes are commonly referred to as gains and losses on monetary items.

153

The purpose of this memorandum is to explore the nature of changes in the purchasing-power equivalent of the monetary items and to propose accounting treatment that is believed to be appropriate. The conclusion reached is that (1) reductions in the purchasing-power equivalent of receivables, cash and other monetary assets required by the enterprise are additional current costs of the business; and (2) reductions in the purchasing power equivalent of liabilities (net of monetary assets that are in excess of operating needs) represent a

---

[1] This Addendum presents a different view of the disposition of net monetary gains and losses. It was prepared at the request of the Director of Accounting Research in order to have all substantive points of view adequately presented in this research study.

credit element in the cost of the operating assets that should be taken into income as the assets are depreciated, sold or otherwise spent in the operations of the business. In the event of deflation, increases in the purchasing-power equivalent of the monetary items would be reflected similarly as a credit to current income or as a debit element in the cost of the operating assets.

Illustration of the Common-dollar Approach to Price-level Adjustments

Columns 1 through 4 of Exhibits I and II, pages 161-162, illustrate the common-dollar approach to price-level adjustments. In this illustration each item in the financial statements has been aged and translated to 1962 year-end dollars by use of a general price-level index, which is assumed to show that the general price level was 10 per cent higher at the end of 1962 than at the beginning of that year. To simplify the illustration, it is assumed that the company commenced business on January 1, 1961, that there was no change in the price level during 1961, and that there were no peaks or valleys in sales, expenses or other transactions during 1962. Column 4 shows the results of translating historical dollar amounts appearing in the accounts to 1962 year-end dollars, before taking into account the fact that the resulting amounts for the monetary items are in excess of actual. Charges or credits existing in the account balances throughout the entire year have been translated by application of the full inflation factor for the year, i.e., 10 per cent. Transactions during the year have been translated by use of the average factor for the year (5 per cent), which is appropriate since the transactions and the price-level rise were assumed to have taken place throughout 1962 at constant rates. The inventory balance in Column 4 of the balance sheet, for example, was determined in the manner shown on p. 155.

At this point the monetary assets are overstated by $120 and the liabilities by $460 (see Column 5 of Exhibit I). It is the disposition of these amounts that is under consideration.

Changes in Purchasing Power of the Monetary Items Should Be Reflected in Income in Appropriate Periods

Inflation has existed in the United States for more than twenty years, and it seems clear that it is a part of the environment in which business operates. Inflation has become a normal element in the cost

154

		Historical Dollars			Year-End Dollars
Balance 1/1/62		$1,000	1,000 × 110% =		$1,100
Purchases		1,400	1,400 × 105% =		1,470
		2,400			
Sold (Fifo):					
Balance 1/1/62	$1,000			$1,100	
Purchases during first 1/7 of 1962	200	1,200		219°	1,319
Balance 12/31/62		$1,200			$1,251

° The inventory sold during the year included the first purchases of the year amounting to 200 historical dollars. Purchases during the year amounted to $1,400, and the $200 of inventory purchased and sold represented the purchases during the first 1/7 of the year. Translation of transactions during the first 1/7 of the year from historical to year-end dollars would require the application of 6.5/7 (the mean for the first 1/7 of the year) of the inflation factor for the full year. Therefore, the inventory purchased and sold during the year in terms of year-end dollars amounted to (6.5/7 × 10% × 200) + 200 = $218.57.

structure of business that must be properly recognized in the income account in the appropriate periods if the amounts reported as net income are to be meaningful.

There are other costs now recognized in the income account that in many ways are similar to the costs of inflation. Income taxes levied to cover the cost of national defense, for example, arise from the political environment in which business functions at the present time. Social security taxes arise from the public consciousness of the need to provide for the unemployed and the aged. Similar explanations could be given for all taxes; they arise with regularity from the environment in which business operates, and it is well established that they should be included in the income account. All costs, including inflation and taxes, must be recovered in the sales price of the product before any profit can be realized.

It does not follow from this, however, that changes in the purchasing-power equivalent of the monetary items should be recognized in their entirety in the income account for the year in which the change in price level occurs. The concepts of accrual accounting support recognition of such changes in the accounts at the time the price-level change takes place, but the assignment of such changes to accounting periods as charges or credits to income is a separate problem. The accounting followed should be based on facts as to the nature of monetary gains and losses and their relationships to operations and costs.

The Functions of the Monetary Items

The monetary items ordinarily include cash (or cash equivalents), receivables, accounts payable and other fixed current liabilities, long-term debt and preferred stock. They differ from the other items in the balance sheet in that they are fixed in dollar amount.

The nonmonetary items in the balance sheet—inventories, property, investments, etc.—generally are carried at cost. Nonmonetary items represent investments that are realized in the course of operations through sales of products. They are essential to the operations of the business, and their function in the business is to serve as the basis for revenue. The first step in the determination of net income is to match revenues with the costs of the nonmonetary items that expired in the process of realizing the revenues.

Monetary items serve one of two business functions. They provide sales or other operating services to the business, or they provide general funds. Receivable and cash balances required to service customers or to maintain banking contacts, etc., provide operating services. Liabilities, less cash in excess of minimum balances required by operations (i.e., cash available to apply in reduction of liabilities), serve only to provide general funds.

Inflation costs relating to receivables (i.e., losses in purchasing power of amounts tied up in receivables) are necessary costs of selling on credit. The benefits against which these costs are matched in the determination of net income is the gross profit on the sales that are over and above the volume of sales that would be made if sales were made on a cash basis only. Such inflation costs may be avoided by discounting accounts receivable, but only to the extent that the funds received are invested in nonmonetary items. An additional interest expense, of course, would come into the picture. In countries where the rate of inflation is much greater than it is in the United States, such as in Brazil, business managements are well aware of the inflation cost of selling on credit, and many companies in these countries sell only for cash and immediately invest all available funds in inventories or other nonmonetary assets, or they levy a carrying charge against the customer to cover the inflation costs with respect to the receivables. Inflation losses on monetary assets devoted to operating services appear clearly to be chargeable to income for the period.

The second business function served by the monetary items is to provide general funds. Liabilities and preferred stock perform that business function. Cash on hand in excess of minimum balances perform no operating function as to receivables and minimum cash

156

balances. To the extent that such excess balances are not committed to any particular purpose, they are available to apply to reduction of liabilities. Together these items represent a *net monetary liability* serving solely to finance the operating items, including receivables, minimum cash balances, inventories, property, etc.

Common-dollar Price vs. Common-dollar Cost

The cost of an asset or service is generally understood to be equivalent to the total economic sacrifice made by the enterprise to acquire it. It is the amount, which when matched with the economic benefits accrued upon sale of the asset will result in a profit or loss amount that will measure the net economic benefit realized in acquiring and selling the asset. In conventional accounting, where "money" (historical dollars) is accounted for, cost is equal to the purchase price; it is merely the total of the dollars paid and the dollars yet to be paid to discharge the liability incurred in the purchase. The determination of cost for common-dollar accounting, where purchasing power is accounted for, is more difficult because the sacrifice in purchasing power necessary to discharge the liability is not known at the time the purchase is made. Inflation during the period in which the liability is outstanding causes the purchasing-power equivalent of the liability, and the sacrifice required to discharge the liability, to decline.

157

Let us consider the case of the X Company having a common-dollar balance sheet at the beginning of the year showing only cash of $500 and capital stock of the same amount. The general price level increased 10 per cent during the year. Now let us assume that the X Company purchased inventory at the beginning of the year priced at $1,000 and held it through the year-end. This transaction would exhaust the cash entirely and create an obligation to pay $500. The cost of the inventory at the year-end would be determined as follows:

	Historical Dollars	Year-end Common Dollars
Paid	$ 500	$ 550
To be paid	500	500
Historical dollar cost	$1,000	
Common-dollar cost		$1,050

The portion of the cost represented by the liability is fixed by contract with the seller at $500, and it is the same under both conventional accounting and common-dollar accounting. The portion of the price paid at the time of the purchase ($500) was equivalent to $550

($110% x $500) year-end dollars. The common-dollar price of the inventory was $1,100 (110% x $1,000), but the sacrifice to acquire it (the cost) was only $1,050 in terms of year-end dollars.

If the Company had borrowed $500 from a bank for the purpose of making the purchase and had paid the supplier the full $1,000 price immediately, the fact that the liability related to the inventory would not have been altered. And, similarly, that fact would have existed if the payment had been made with funds previously borrowed for general purposes.

The proposition that changes in liabilities are an element of the costs to which the liabilities relate is not new. Conventional accounting practice has long recognized that major adjustments in liabilities for prior-year income taxes, for example, should be recorded directly in surplus or shown as a special item after net income, and that upon restatement of income for prior years, such adjustments should be reflected in the income-tax costs for the prior years involved. Similarly, major adjustments of accounts payable resulting from credits from suppliers are recognized as adjustments of related inventory costs.

158 Liabilities are not directly productive of income; they are related to income only through the assets in which the funds derived from the liabilities are invested. Therefore, a fair matching of costs and revenues in the determination of net income will be effected by reflecting the changes in liabilities from inflation in the costs of the assets.

It seems appropriate to conclude that decreases in the net liability of a company from inflation represent reductions in costs, and that it is not appropriate to treat them as gains or as income for the period. To apply this conclusion in the usual accounting situation where specific costs are not identifiable with specific liabilities requires further discussion.

Assignment of Changes in the Net Monetary Liability to the Assets

The liability structure of a company has little or no significance as far as operations are concerned. To a large degree it is a result of financial decisions by management, and ordinarily it can be drastically modified without affecting operations. Cash can be applied to reduce current liabilities or long-term debt, long-term debt can be replaced by preferred stock or bank loans, funds can be borrowed and held as cash, etc., without affecting the net monetary liability of the company or the operations. An item is classified in the balance sheet as current or noncurrent on the basis of its due date, which has nothing to do with costs or the accounting for changes in the purchasing-power equivalents of the monetary items.

It has been shown that increases or decreases in liabilities arising from changes in the general price level represent adjustments of costs to which the liabilities relate. It is ordinarily inappropriate, however, to attempt to trace or relate individual liabilities to individual operating items (assets). The liability structure of a company is a result, principally, of the relative interest costs of obtaining funds from the various creditor sources available. Management will, to the greatest extent practicable, minimize the company's total outlay for interest by obtaining the maximum amount of credit from the sources demanding the lowest interest rates. Suppliers in the United States customarily provide a limited amount of credit at no interest cost, and for this reason accounts payable to suppliers usually exist. If suppliers demanded a high rate of interest on outstanding balances, undoubtedly companies would pay suppliers promptly upon delivery with funds obtained from banks or other sources.

The fact that accounts payable to suppliers exist does not mean that reductions in the purchasing power equivalents of these obligations from inflation are applicable solely to inventories; it means merely that suppliers provide an economical source for a part of the company's total general fund requirements. The company's total general-fund needs are fixed by the operating assets, which are not immediately realized. The choice of sources of credit is a financial problem.

159

The net monetary liability of a company is a permanent source of general funds, as is capital stock and surplus. It can be concluded, therefore, that the net monetary liability serves to support all operating assets that are not immediately realized, and that reductions in the net monetary liability caused by inflation should be assigned to all such assets proportionately on the basis of the needs of the various assets for funds. The cost of each such asset sold or consumed and entering into the determination of net income contains a liability element, and to the extent that changes in the price level cause the purchasing power equivalent of that element to change, common-dollar costs of the assets are affected.

Exhibit III, page 163, illustrates the application of this conclusion. The total funds required by operations amounted to $6,505 on an annual basis. In this particular instance, it was appropriate to determine this amount by averaging the beginning-of-year and end-of-year balances, since there were no peaks or valleys in the volume of transactions during the year. Of the $6,505 of funds required, $753 was used to finance operating assets (costs) that were taken into the income account before the end of the year, and the remainder was used to finance nonmonetary assets that remained in the balance sheet or monetary assets held during the year. The decrease in net liability to be accounted for amounted to $460. Of this amount, $142 related to the income account and the remainder applied to balance sheet items. The disposition of these amounts are shown in Column 5 of Exhibits I and II.

Conclusion

The majority of companies that do not have substantial amounts of long-term debt outstanding will probably find that they have no net monetary liability, as defined in the foregoing paragraphs, and that they are not particularly concerned with the problem being dealt with here. But this problem is of great importance to companies with large amounts of debt outstanding. If the practice is adopted of recognizing price-level gains on liabilities in the income statement currently, as has been recommended by some sources, it can be expected that in some instances such gains will exceed the increase in charges to income from restatement of assets to a common-dollar basis, and net income will be overstated to a greater extent than it would be under historical-dollar accounting. On the other hand, if the practice of reporting price-level gains on liabilities as direct credits to an equity account (which has also been recommended) is adopted, net income in many instances will be understated.

The labeling of changes in the purchasing-power equivalents of monetary assets and liabilities as "losses" or "gains" seems to have encouraged the conclusion that such changes should be reflected in their entirety in an equity account immediately (either directly or through the income account) in accordance with customary accounting practices for gains and losses. When such gains and losses are viewed in the light of the business functions served by the monetary items, it seems apparent that such a general conclusion is unwarranted. The above discussion has attempted to draw out and analyze the facts that should be considered in this question. This discussion is believed to have shown that inflation losses on monetary assets required by the business should be charged to current income, and that inflation gains on the net monetary liability (total liabilities less monetary assets in excess of operating requirements) should be associated with the operating assets and taken into income as those assets are charged to operations.

Exhibit I

XYZ Company
Balance Sheet

	(1) Historical Dollars 1961	(2) Historical Dollars 1962	(3) 1961(a)(d)	(4) December 31, 1962 Dollars — Before Adjustment of monetary Items (b)	(5) Adjustment of Monetary Items to Actual (c) 1962	(6) After Adjustment (d)
Cash	500	400	550	445	(45)	400
Accounts receivable	700	800	770	875	(75)	800
Total monetary assets	1,200	1,200	1,320	1,320	(x)(120)	1,200
Inventories (Fifo)	1,000	1,200	1,100	1,251	(y)(38)	1,213
Fixed assets:						
Cost	4,000	4,000	4,400	4,400	(311)	4,089
Accumulated depreciation	(200)	(400)	(220)	(440)	31	(409)
	3,800	3,600	4,180	3,960	(y)(280)	3,680
	6,000	6,000	6,600	6,531	(438)	6,093
Current liabilities	1,200	1,000	1,320	1,110	(110)	1,000
Bonds payable	3,500	3,500	3,850	3,850	(350)	3,500
Total monetary liabilities	4,700	4,500	5,170	4,960	(y)(460)	4,500
Capital stock	1,000	1,000	1,100	1,220	(x)(120)	1,100
Earned surplus	300	500	330	351	(y) 142	493
	1,300	1,500	1,430	1,571	22	1,593
	6,000	6,000	6,600	6,531	(438)	6,093

Explanatory Notes:

(a) 110% × 12/31/61 dollar balances. Inflation rate for 1962 was 10%.

(b) Arrived at, as explained on page 154 by applying appropriate inflation index factors to historical dollars; 10% for items existing during the entire year and 5% for items arising during the year. As a further example, cash was translated as follows:

	Historical Dollars	12/31/62 Dollars
Balance 12/31/61	500	500 × 110% = 550
Receipts	2,100	2,100 × 105% = 2,205
	2,600	2,755
Payments	2,200	2,200 × 105% = 2,310
Balance 12/31/62	400	445

(c) In this column (5) the decrease in monetary assets of $120 and the decrease in liabilities of $460 are accounted for. The explanations for entries (x) and (y) are contained in Note (b) to Exhibit II and in Exhibit III.

(d) In practice, it would be desirable to show in the financial statements, or in footnotes, the historical dollar amounts of certain accounts. It is not the purpose of this paper to explore the question of what historical dollar data should be disclosed.

161

Exhibit II

XYZ Company
Income Statement

	(1)	(2)	(3)	(4)	(5)	(6)
	Historical Dollars			December 31, 1962 Dollars 1962		
	1961	1962	1961(a)	Before Adjustment of Monetary Items (a)	Adjustment of Costs for Decreases in Monetary Items (b)	After Adjustment
Sales	2,000	2,200	2,200	2,310		2,310
Cost of goods sold	900	1,200	990	1,319	(y)(45)	1,274
Depreciation	200	200	220	220	(y)(8)	212
Other expenses	300	400	330	420		420
Inflation loss on monetary assets					(x) 120 (y)(89)	31
	1,400	1,800	1,540	1,959		1,937
Income before income taxes	600	400	660	351		373
Provision for income taxes	300	200	330	210		210
Net income	300	200	330	141		163
Earned surplus balance at beginning of year	—	300	—			330
Earned surplus balance at end of year	300	500	330			493

Explanatory Notes:

(a) See Note (b) of Exhibit I for explanation of method of translating to December 31, 1962 dollars. It is assumed that income taxes were paid at regular intervals throughout the year, as were other expenses, and accordingly it is appropriate to apply a translation factor of 105% to the historical dollar provision for income taxes for 1962.

(b) The full amount of the monetary assets is required in this instance to service operations, i.e., there were no excess funds on hand available for payment of liabilities. Accordingly, the entire decline of $120 in purchasing power of the monetary assets is reflected in the income account for the period (entry x). Entry (y) is explained by Exhibit III.

Exhibit III

XYZ Company
Determination of Costs to Which Decrease in
Purchasing Power Equivalent of Liabilities Applies

	(1) Funds (Annual Basis) Required, in Terms of 12/31/62 Dollars		(3)	(4)	(5) Costs to Which Decrease Applies	(6)
	Total	(2) Expired During Year	Deferred at December 31, 1962	Per Cent of Total Funds of $6,505	Income Account	Balance Sheet
Monetary Assets, total (1,320 + 1,200) ÷ 2 =	$1,260	$ —	$1,260	19.4%	$ 89	$ —
Inventories:						
Funds required during year for inventories sold	$ 643	643	—	9.8	45	—
Funds required for inventories on hand at December 31, 1962 (1,100 + 1,251) ÷ 2 =	532	—	532	8.2	—	38
Total	$1,175					
Fixed Assets:						
Funds required for property depreciated during year	$ 110	110	—	1.7	8	—
Funds required for undepreciated balances at December 31, 1962 (4,180 + 3,960) ÷ 2 =	3,960	—	3,960	60.9	—	(b) 280
Total	$4,070					
	$6,505	$753	$5,752	100.0%	$142	$318
Total Decrease in Purchasing Power Equivalent of Liabilities						142
						$460

See accompanying explanatory notes.

Explanatory Notes

(a) The decrease of $460 year-end dollars in the purchasing power equivalent of liabilities applies to each of the several operating assets proportionately, in relation to the amount of funds required by each such asset on an annual basis. In this worksheet the funds required in terms of year-dollars are indicated in column (1). There were no peaks or valleys in transactions during the year, and therefore the total amounts in column (1) have been determined by averaging the beginning-of-year and end-of-year balances, in 12/31/62 dollars taken from Exhibit I.

The funds required to finance the costs that expired during the period are shown in column (2) and the remainder are shown in column (3). The amounts relating to inventories were determined by analysis of the inventory account maintained on a Fifo basis. The beginning inventory of $1,100 (1,000 historical dollars) was sold at the rate of $110 (100 historical dollars) per month, January through October. This inventory was held, on the average $5/12$ of a year, and the funds required to carry it until it was sold amounted to $5/12 \times$ $1,100 = 458 year-end dollars. The inventory sold in November and December represented the purchases during the first $1/7$ of the year and amounted to $219 (200 historical dollars) as shown on page 155. This inventory was (on the average) purchased $\cdot 5/7$ of a year after the beginning of the year and sold $1/12$ of a year before the year-end. Therefore, it was held, on the average, $6 \cdot 5/7$ less $1/12$ of a year, and the funds needed to carry it until it was sold amounted to $71/84 \times$ $219 = 185 year-end dollars. The total amount of funds required during the year for inventories sold was $643 ($458 + $185), and the funds applied to inventories on hand at the year-end amounted to $532 ($1,175–$643).

The undepreciated balance of fixed assets at the year-end was $3,960; and since there were no retirements or additions during the year that figure accurately represents the amount of funds required by the fixed assets that were deferred at the year-end. Depreciation for the period was $220. Since this amount accumulated throughout the year at a constant rate, on an annual basis funds of 110 year-end dollars were needed to finance this portion of the fixed assets ($220) during the time that it remained on the balance sheet as an asset.

The percentages in column (4) have been applied to the $460 decrease in liabilities to arrive at the figures in columns (5) and (6).

164

(b) The amount applicable to 90 per cent of the cost of the property—the property is 10 per cent depreciated—is $280 (column (6)). Therefore, the credit applicable to the full cost of the property in the balance sheet is $311 ($\frac{100}{90} \times \$280$), and the amount (a debit) applicable to the reserve for depreciation is $31.

165

Disclosing Effects of Price-level Changes

Table of Contents

Examples From Annual Reports

A number of companies throughout the world have made it a regular practice to take into consideration the effects of price-level changes in reporting to the public. Many others have experimented from time to time with measuring the effects of price-level changes and have commented on these experiments in their annual reports or have revalued assets as a result of the studies.

This appendix consists of examples of methods which have been used in disclosing various effects of price-level changes in the annual reports of corporations. Inasmuch as this appendix is part of a study dealing with methods of reporting on the effects of changes in the value of the monetary unit, (as compared with changes in market prices of goods and services), it should be noted that few of the examples fall into this category. In the larger number of instances the financial statements reflect current or reproduction costs instead of "common-dollar" restatements of original dollar costs. The forms of statement presentation, however, are similar in both types of adjustment.

169

The examples are grouped in four main categories. The following outline presents the organization of the examples and highlights interesting and important features of the various presentations:

A. Companies presenting statements adjusted for the effects of changes in the price level.

We know of no case in recent years in which statements which have been completely adjusted for changes in the general price level have been presented in an annual report. Two companies have come to our attention, however, which have made significant steps in this direction.

1. The Reece Corporation (United States) has for a number of years completely adjusted its financial statements for internal purposes to reflect price-level changes and has presented certain significant adjusted items in the annual report.

2. Philips Industries (The Netherlands) adjusts monetary items for general price-level changes and adjusts fixed assets and inventories for replacement value changes.

B. Companies presenting unadjusted statements supplemented by price-level information.

1. Indiana Telephone Corporation (U.S.) presents complete supplementary financial statements with fixed assets and depreciation charges adjusted on the basis of a detailed current-cost study by a Registered Professional Engineer.

2. Hercules Powder Company (U.S.) presents three adjusted items, including net income.

3. Eastman Kodak Company (U.S.) presents its sales in "constant dollars."

All of the companies in these first two groups use broad-based price indexes for at least some items.

C. Companies adjusting depreciation charges as a result of recorded revaluations of fixed assets.

First Group—Revaluation under government revalorization provisions:

1. Simca (France)

2. Montecatini Mining and Chemical Company (Italy)

3. Nippon Telegraph & Telephone Public Corporation (Japan)

4. Tokyo Shibaura Electric Co., Ltd. (Japan)

5. Yawata Iron and Steel Co., Ltd. (Japan)

Revaluation under revalorization provisions is carried out in the three countries from which examples are taken (France, Italy, and Japan) by means of government-prepared "coefficients of revaluation" (indexes) which attempt to compensate for the effects of inflation on asset values. These statutes often provide that a company may use current or replacement values as long as the revaluations remain within the limits set by the government coefficients. Nippon Telegraph and Telephone has chosen this option.

Second Group—Revaluation on the basis of appraisals by outside experts:

6. Creole Petroleum Corporation (Venezuela)

7. Compañia Minera Aguilar, S.A. (Argentina), a subsidiary of St. Joseph Lead Company

8. The Bowater Paper Corporation Limited (England)

9. Electric and Musical Industries Limited (England)

10. Selfridges Limited (England)

11. Other English companies which have followed similar practices but for which examples are not given are: Fisons Limited; The Associated Portland Cement Manufacturers Limited; F. W. Woolworth and Co., Limited; Imperial Chemical Industries, Ltd.; Spillers Limited; and Unilever Limited

171

All of the companies in this group have used replacement cost determined by independent appraisal. Revaluations of this type are, of course, carried out infrequently; several of the companies mention only one revaluation.

Third Group—Revaluations based on appraisals but with unusual features:

12. Imperial Tobacco Company of Canada, Limited (Canda) revalued assets on the basis of appraisals in 1960 and 1961 and plans to restate asset values each year.

13. The Broken Hill Proprietary Co., Ltd. (Australia) charges depreciation on the basis of replacement value but has recorded less than replacement value on the books even though a revaluation was carried out.

D. Companies adjusting depreciation only.

1. Ayrshire Collieries Corporation (U.S.)

2. Iowa-Illinois Gas and Electric Company (U.S.)

3. Sacramento Municipal Utility District (U.S.)

4. John Summers and Sons Limited (England)

5. Joseph Lucas (Industries) Limited (England)

6. Algemene Kunstzijde Unie N.V. (The Netherlands)

7. Wm. H. Muller and Co. (The Netherlands)

The basis for the depreciation charge is not always clear in these cases. "Price-level depreciation," "replacement-value depreciation," and "fair value depreciation" are mentioned by various companies.

Companies which have attempted to adjust depreciation for changes in prices have used such a multiplicity of methods that no attempt has been made to classify the companies by method. Adjustment practices have been made up of combinations of the following variations:

1. Debit to depreciation account: (a) adjusted amount used, usually when the asset accounts have also been restated, or (b) unadjusted amount used, with the amount of the adjustment being charged to a special account.

172 2. Treatment of depreciable asset accounts: (a) at unadjusted original cost, or (b) adjusted to common-dollar or current cost basis.

3. Treatment of the credit for the difference between adjusted and unadjusted depreciation: (a) credited to a special stockholders' equity account, or (b) credited to the regular accumulated depreciation account, usually when the depreciable assets are adjusted.

4. Treatment on the operating statement of the difference between adjusted and unadjusted depreciation: (a) addition to unadjusted depreciation, (b) special item before showing of net profit, or (c) special item after showing of net profit.

5. Treatment of unrecorded cumulative adjustment of past depreciation: (a) usually ignored, or (b) set up by a charge to retained earnings.

6. Determination of amount of unrecorded adjustment: (a) based on adjusted amounts that would have been charged in past periods if adjustments had been made, or (b) brought up to date in terms of the current dollar.

7. Disposition of the special stockholders' equity account which in some cases is credited for the difference between the adjusted and unadjusted depreciation: (a) as a special item in the stockholders'

equity section, or (b) converted to legal or stated capital by means of a stock dividend or a transfer.

Examples

A. COMPANIES PRESENTING STATEMENTS ADJUSTED FOR CHANGES IN THE PRICE LEVEL.

A-1. *The Reece Corporation (U.S.)*

The Reece Corporation was one of the four companies included in the American Accounting Association study conducted by Ralph C. Jones.[1] Ever since the completion of this study, The Reece Corporation has included in its annual report a special section in which comments and charts have kept the reader up to date as to the effect of price-level changes upon certain selected phases of its operations. As far as we know, this is the only case where presentations have been based upon completely adjusted financial statements. It should be noted that the net income figures do not include gains and losses on monetary items since, under the method adopted in the original study, these 173 gains and losses were shown in an analysis of the changes in the stockholders' equity rather than in the income statement.

Because of the importance of this case, the entire section from the 1953 annual report is reproduced below, followed by excerpts from similar sections in subsequent annual reports, and by the entire section from the 1961 report.

From the 1953 report:

The Price Level Study
Including a Review of Earlier Remarks

For more than twenty years, it has been my responsibility to report to you annually and my effort has been always to report the real economic position of the Company. This has necessitated going behind the figures presented in traditional accounting procedure, and it has also required some fairly frank opinions of the attitude and practices of government officials affecting manufacturing industry.

---

[1] *Price Level Changes and Financial Statements—Case Studies of Four Companies.* American Accounting Association. 1955.

Although we have anticipated the results of the study in a general way, we appreciate having specific figures proving the principal point we have been stressing so long—the inadequacy of depreciation allowances to provide for plant and equipment replacements. To keep the sequence of events in order, it appears that a brief review of the general points mentioned should precede a summary of Professor Jones' Price Level Study. Therefore, quoting from our past reports to stockholders, we said:

1934 "Inflation is a continuous threat and makes it impossible for thoughtful men to be anything but uncertain, and rightly so, as all steps possible must be taken to guard against this eventuality."

"Taxes continue to be an increasing burden." (They were then 28.8% of net earnings before taxes!)

1942 "The Treasury Department is reluctant to allow adequate depreciation charges. This is a serious matter when tax rates are high. It inflates profits thereby increasing taxes which rapidly drains off cash necessary for the purchase of new equipment. . . .

"Your Company paid and reserved for taxes for the year 1942 $425,081.97. The corresponding charge for 1939 was $73,838.38."

1943 "We have charged depreciation to the extent through experience we believe the Treasury Department will allow. In your management's opinion this charge is inadequate."

"Your Company's taxes for the year amounted to $860,-562.73 or almost five times the dividend."

1944 "It is also now obvious that depreciation charges on capital goods will not provide for replacement due to increased costs. Inadequate depreciation inflates earnings with the result that the present high tax rates drain off cash at an alarming speed when ordinary prudent foresight dictates that it should be set aside for high cost replacement to insure efficient production and jobs. . . ."

1947 "A 1947 profit dollar behaves approximately like a 1939 fifty cent piece. Therefore, when profits in dollars in 1947 are compared with dollar profits of previous years the comparison is misleading."

1948 "Industry's profits in several respects are overstated. In the first place, the government allows deduction for depreciation to replace buildings and machinery on the basis of original cost, and cost in almost all cases is far below present prices."

1950   "Wages are reviewed and adjusted to the decreasing value
of the dollar whereas profits are almost universally viewed
and compared as dollars without regard to their decreased
value. The present value of a dollar profit to industry is
about forty cents as compared to its value in 1939."

1951   "The less depreciation charged the greater the apparent
earnings and the larger the actual tax. The result is that
earnings are stated fictitiously high and the government
takes in taxes most of what should have been set aside for
replacement of equipment. . . . It will show up sometime
in less efficient production, in higher costs than necessary,
and consequently in a lower standard of living for all."

The indefiniteness of these remarks can now be given real
values through analysis of the Price Level Study, which shows the
effects of inflation on this Company during the twelve years 1940
through 1951.

Basis of the Price Level Study

By means of index numbers based on the Consumer Price
Index, our financial statements for the years 1940 through 1951
have been restated to express each amount in terms of a uniform
measuring unit which we shall call a *Uniform Dollar.* Our financial statements have been expressed in terms of the actual dollar
in use at the time, and which has had a rapidly diminishing value
during this period. This dollar we shall call the *Historical Dollar.*

The study compares the reported results of operations as previously prepared by traditional accounting procedures in Historical
Dollars with the same results expressed in Uniform Dollars.

175

What the Charts Show

The charts show graphically how inflation distorts the apparent
results of business operations.

Chart 1 [page 176] demonstrates the distortion occurring between 1940 and 1951 on Invested Capital items; Physical (Uniform Dollars) increase in inventories is only 35% as compared to
the Historical Dollar increase of 156%; Plant has increased 50%
actually, whereas in Historical Dollars it has increased 145%;
Stockholders equity in 1951 (Historical) dollars increased 122%,
but in purchasing power only 30%; Common dividends while apparently 60% greater than in 1940, have, in 1951, 12% less purchasing power; and, finally, Working Capital available in 1951
was only 58% as useful as the 1940 working capital, in spite of
the apparent increase of 20% when stated in Historical Dollars.

Chart 2, Gross Income, [page 176] shows that while there was

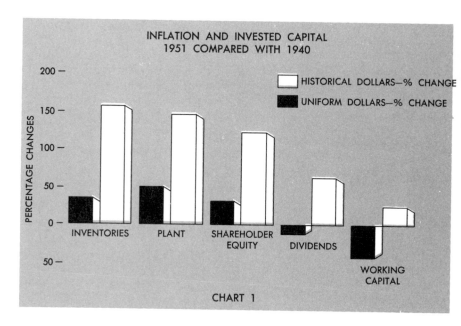

INFLATION AND INVESTED CAPITAL
1951 COMPARED WITH 1940

□ HISTORICAL DOLLARS—% CHANGE
■ UNIFORM DOLLARS—% CHANGE

CHART 1

176

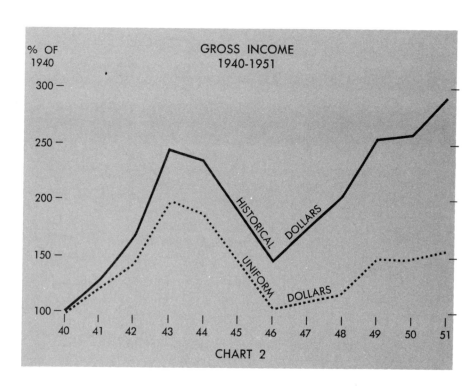

% OF
1940

GROSS INCOME
1940-1951

HISTORICAL DOLLARS

UNIFORM DOLLARS

CHART 2

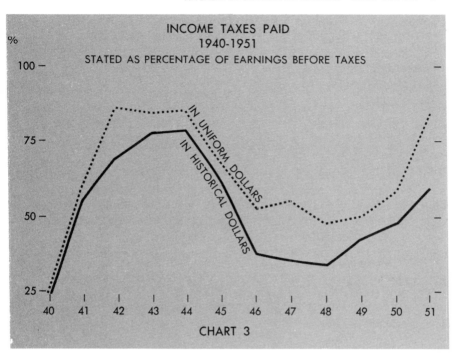

INCOME TAXES PAID
1940-1951
STATED AS PERCENTAGE OF EARNINGS BEFORE TAXES

CHART 3

177

a gratifying increase in business, 187%, on an Historical Dollar basis, the real increase measured in Uniform Dollars is only 55%. On the Historical Dollar basis, the war peak of 1943 was exceeded in 1949 and subsequent years, but on the Uniform Dollar basis 1943 is still the year of greatest volume.

In Chart 3 [this page] it is effectively shown how the legal requirement to use traditional accounting procedure in the computation of income taxes affects the Company most seriously. Inflation rapidly increases cash requirements for replacement reserves, plant expansion, and working capital, not to mention dividends to the owners. However, taxes must be computed using depreciation based on the original cost of fixed assets in Historical Dollars. Therefore, due to rapidly increasing costs of replacements, the permissible allowances for depreciation become completely inadequate to maintain plant and equipment. The chart of Taxes Paid as a Percentage of Earnings Before Taxes discloses our effective tax rate, using 1951 as an example, to have been slightly greater than 59% on the Historical Dollar basis, and over 83% on the Uniform Dollar basis.

Had we been permitted to use a Uniform Dollar as a basis for tax computation over the twelve year period, there would have been approximately $1,000,000 more cash available for reinvestment in plant and equipment and for distribution to stockholders.

Chart 4 [this page] compares the net income as reported in Historical Dollars with the spendable net income when all accounting figures are adjusted to the Uniform Dollar. The astonishing result is self-evident.

Concluding Remarks

This study points out specifically the extent to which inflation has plagued our capitalistic system and indicates the direction our thinking must follow.

It took the country little or no time to realize that wages should be viewed in the light of purchasing power. The fact that profits and dividends should also be viewed in that light is not yet generally recognized. For the overall good of our economy this must also be accepted.

Inflation destroys capital, but when the importance of capital is so overlooked that depreciation reserves to maintain plant and equipment cannot be created, capital destruction is accelerated. For when depreciation is understated, profit must be overstated, and the tax paid on such fictitious profit constitutes a direct tax on capital.

178

Reports on industrial expansion and modernization are misleading because they create the public impression that all industry is rapidly expanding and modernizing. This is far from the case. It has been true of fast-growing industries like television

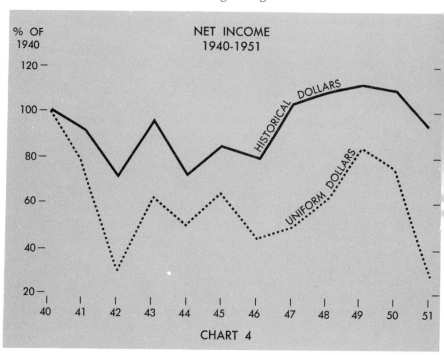

and is true of Public Utilities and basic industry like Steel, but is not true of manufacturing industry generally, most of which experienced its period of rapid growth years ago. As the company is a reasonable example of the latter group, the study will apply to the majority of manufacturing companies.

The American Machinist magazine states that the average age of machine tools must be reduced if American industry is to achieve low-cost production, yet in 1945 38% of the machine tools in use were over 10 years old, in 1949 43% were over 10 years old, and in 1953 55% were over 10 years old including 19% over 20 years old. I believe that the country's average age of basic machine tools, the tools used to manufacture things, should be six to eight years if we wish to obtain our potential in quality and low-cost production.

If this were accepted it would accomplish two of the most important things in our industrial economy. First it would maintain our basic machine tool industry on a production schedule sufficient for civilian and defense manufacturing needs and go a long way towards eliminating its traditional ups and downs and the scarcity of machine tools in times of emergency. Secondly it would allow our manufacturing facilities to be kept up-to-date with the most modern equipment for efficient, low-cost production.

179

The problem is acute. An industrial economy can operate on free competitive capitalism or on socialistic principles where Government controls all means of production. Strong, sound Capitalism can exist only in a climate where Government's fiscal policy prevents inflation and its taxation policies do not discourage investment and expansion. Our present Administration is making a bold return to Capitalism, but far more remains to be done.

F. A. REECE

From the 1954 report:

The continuing inadequacy of depreciation reserves based on original cost is borne out by an analysis of this Company's 1954 financial statements. In converting this Company's financial statements for 1954 from Historical Dollars to Uniform Dollars, we find that the effects of inflation are still very much with us. The depreciation taken in 1954 was $62,000 or 15% too little, and the cost of sales was understated by $7,000. Thus our profits were overstated by $69,000 and the Federal Income Tax thereon of $36,000 was in fact a capital levy and not an income tax at all!

For a single year, the discrepancies between figures reported in Historical Dollars and Uniform Dollars may not appear to be of great significance. On the other hand, the cumulative effect since . . . 1948, is very great indeed. Earned Surplus, which represents retained earnings since . . . [1948], is stated to be $1,143,000 on our Balance Sheet. However, upon conversion of the Balance Sheet to 1954 Uniform Dollars, we find that only $544,000 of earnings have been retained since 1948. Thus conventional accounting methods have overstated the retained earnings in a period of only six and one third years by 110%!

From the 1957 report:

This Price Level Study is a very useful tool to your management, particularly since this Company has relatively large investments in manufacturing facilities and in machines leased to customers. By publishing the results of the Study, we hope to present to you more fairly the progress of the Company and to keep you informed of the damaging effect of inflation not only on your company but on the economy generally. . . .

From the 1958 report:

	In Historical Dollars	In Uniform Dollars
Gross Income	$4,914,000	$4,914,000
Depreciation	$ 593,000	$ 669,000
Federal and Foreign taxes as a % of net income before taxes	49%	56%
Net Income	$ 505,000	$ 371,000
Earnings per common share after preferred dividends	$ 2.54	$ 1.84
Earnings retained after payment of dividends	$ 276,000	$ 142,000

From the 1959 report:

The chart on page 181 compares changes over the past ten years in certain significant balance sheet items:

From the 1961 report:

Price Level Study

1961 was a year of relative price stability during which the Consumer Price Index rose 1.1%. On figures adjusted for Price Level changes, even a moderate rise in prices within a year has some effect on inventory valuation, which is reflected in cost of sales. Coupled with past periods of ever increasing prices, the effect on required depreciation charges is substantial.

In this study, the Company's unconsolidated figures have been converted, by means of index numbers based on the Consumer

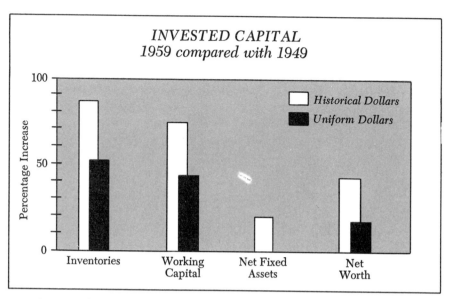

INVESTED CAPITAL
1959 compared with 1949

Price Index, from Historical Dollars (those used in conventional accounting and in our reported figures) to Uniform Dollars (defined as uniform measuring units whose purchasing power is equal to 1961 dollars) so that the Company's figures as reported may be compared with statements prepared on a uniform basis.

In 1961, the Company's unconsolidated net profit was $93,000 greater when expressed by conventional means than in Uniform Dollars. Conversion to Uniform Dollars required increases in depreciation and cost of sales of $52,000 and $35,000 respectively and a reduction in income of $6,000 caused by the sale of certain assets.

The accompanying charts compare on a percentage basis income and profit figures over the past 18 years expressed in Historical and in Uniform Dollars.

During the past five years, in which price levels increased 10.1%, a very significant difference in growth appears when Historical Dollar increases are compared with growth expressed in dollars of uniform purchasing power. For ease of comparison, increases in Historical and Uniform Dollars for certain Balance Sheet items are expressed in percentages below:

181

	Five-year % Increase	
	Historical Dollars	Uniform Dollars
Inventories	39.6	26.8
Working capital	55.8	32.2
Fixed assets	9.0	(.4)
Net worth	34.4	24.4

W. D. Brooks, Jr., *Treasurer*

Net Income
Before & After Taxes
1943-1961

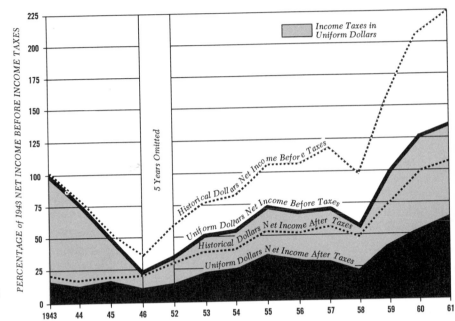

182

Gross Income
1943-1961

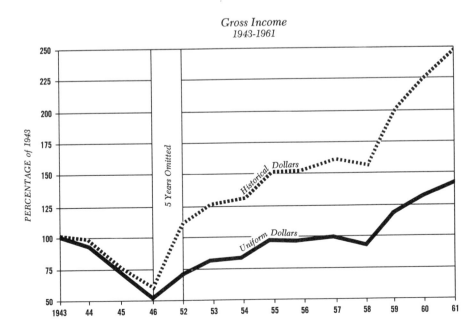

A point of special interest in the charts, page 182, is that the figures plotted on the curves are the percentages of 1943 amounts, rather than the dollar amounts. This practice has several advantages. It permits the showing of more than one type of information on the same scale, the percentages are shown in the same proportionate relationships as the dollar amounts, and it may avoid the psychological handicap of comparative dollar data which have to be revised each time a schedule or chart is prepared in terms of current dollars.

A-2. *N. V. Philips Gloeilampenfabrieken* (The Netherlands)
This company, which is known in the English-speaking world as Philips Industries or Philips Incandescent Lamp Works Co., has used replacement costs in its accounts and statements for many years. It maintains a special department to watch trends in prices, and adjustments are made in the accounts when price changes have been significant, not necessarily each year. Two types of adjustments are made. With respect to inventories and fixed assets, *specific* commodity or group price indexes are applied to each category. When prices increase, the offsetting credit is to the appropriate revaluation surplus account (i.e., revaluation surplus from property, plant and equipment or revaluation surplus from inventories). When prices decrease, the adjustments are charged to revaluation surplus until that account is exhausted. Any further decreases are charged to income. Depreciation expense and cost of sales are calculated on the basis of these replacement costs.

183

With respect to the monetary items, a general price-level index is applied to the amount of the net monetary items at the beginning of the period. When the price level increases, income is charged and a "reserve for diminishing purchasing power of capital invested in monetary items" is credited. When the price level decreases, the entries are reversed until the "reserve" is exhausted, after which no recognition is given to this type of "gain."[2]

The following examples of the financial statements and notes of Philips Industries are taken from a prospectus filed with the SEC and dated May 29, 1962. The excerpts are from the combined statements of Philips Industries and the United States Philips Trust:

---

[2] See "An application of replacement value theory," by A. Goudeket, *The Journal of Accountancy*, July 1960, pp. 37-47, for a more complete description of the procedures followed by this company.

Combined Summary of Earnings of Philips

The following summary of earnings of Philips Industries and United States Philips Trust, combined in order to show the interest of the Common Shareholders of Philips N. V. in Philips Industries and the United States Philips Trust, has been examined by Messrs. Klynveld, Kraayenhof & Co., independent public accountants, whose report appears hereinafter. The opinion of Messrs. Klynveld, Kraayenhof & Co., is based in part upon the report of Messrs. Smith and Harder, independent public accountants, whose report is included in the Registration Statement. The summary should be read in conjunction with the financial statements and the related notes in this Prospectus.

| | *(In Thousands of Neth.* | | |
	1961	*1960*	*1959*
Net sales (Note 2) Nfl.4,	935,998	Nfl.4,762,164	Nfl.4,182,000
Cost of goods sold (Note 3)	3,063,141	2,871,012	2,547,913
Selling, general and administrative expenses	1,141,688	1,029,131	894,451
	731,169	862,021	739,636
Other income:			
From non-consolidatd companies	14,639	15,141	9,511
Miscellaneous (Note 4) ...	27,620	32,909	47,671
Other deductions:			
Interest on bonds, mortgages and other debt	90,886	65,949	57,312
Miscellaneous	29,292	30,688	13,922
	653,250	813,434	725,584
Provision for taxes on income..	312,968	407,155	366,962
	340,282	406,279	358,622
Minority interest in consolidated subsidiaries	14,040	9,433	7,935
Net income (on basis of accounting principles customarily followed by Philips Industries and the United States Philips Trust) (Note 5)	326,242	396,846	350,687
Deduct:			
Profit-sharing with Supervisory Board, Board of Management and employees..	25,109	24,137	22,922
Cash dividends to Participating Preferred Shares..	11,520	11,520	11,520
Balance of net income	289,613	361,189	316,245
Estimated adjustment to state the aforementioned balance of net income on basis of accounting principles generally accepted in the United States (Note 1)	7,916	8,205	3,298
Adjusted balance of net income	Nfl.297,529	Nfl.369,394	Nfl.319,543
Per Common Share of Philips N. V. (par value Nfl. 25) (Notes 6 and 7):			
Adjusted net income ..	Nfl. 10.34	Nfl. 12.86	Nfl. 11.14
Cash dividends in respect of year	Nfl. 3.81	Nfl. 3.63	Nfl. 3.45
Number of Common Shares (par value Nfl. 25) of Philips N. V. outstanding at the end of each year as adjusted (Note 6)	28,778,180	28,720,260	28,661,300

Industries and United States Philips Trust

The summary, insofar as it relates to the determination of net income of Philips Industries, has been prepared on the basis of the accounting principles customarily followed by Philips Industries and generally accepted in The Netherlands. These principles differ in a number of respects from those generally accepted in the United States. However, the only differences which would have materially affected the determination of net income are those described in Note 1 following the summary.

Guilders)			⌐ *(Translated into Thousands of U. S. Dollars)* ⌐			
1958	*1957*	*1961*	*1960*	*1959*	*1958*	*1957*
Nfl.3,595,000	Nfl.3,177,000	$1,371,110	$1,253,201	$1,100,527	$946,053	$836,053
2,255,915	2,052,848	850,872	755,529	670,504	593,662	540,224
781,792	682,237	317,136	270,824	235,382	205,735	179,536
557,293	441,915	203,102	226,848	194,641	146,656	116,293
4,335	5,639	4,066	3,984	2,503	1,141	1,484
30,372	14,594	7,673	8,660	12,545	7,993	3,842
55,812	52,275	25,246	17,355	15,082	14,688	13,757
10,938	11,296	8,137	8,076	3,664	2,878	2,973
525,250	398,577	181,458	214,061	190,943	138,224	104,889
275,058	206,768	86,935	107,146	96,569	72,384	54,413
250,192	191,809	94,523	106,915	94,374	65,840	50,476
6,380	4,945	3,900	2,482	2,088	1,679	1,301
243,812	186,864	90,623	104,433	92,286	64,161	49,175
16,156	14,877	6,974	6,352	6,032	4,251	3,915
10,944	10,944	3,200	3,032	3,032	2,880	2,880
216,712	161,043	80,449	95,049	83,222	57,030	42,380
19,944	10,682	2,199	2,159	868	5,248	2,811
Nfl.236,656	Nfl.171,725	$ 82,648	$ 97,208	$ 84,090	$ 62,278	$ 45,191
Nfl. 8.37	Nfl. 6.14	$2.87	$3.38	$2.93	$2.20	$1.62
Nfl. 2.63	Nfl. 2.42	$1.06	$0.96	$0.91	$0.69	$0.64
28,603,180	28,602,660	28,778,180	28,720,260	28,661,300	28,603,180	28,602,660

185

The 1961 combined net income figures reflect a reduction in unit sales of television picture tubes in 1961 as compared with 1960, lower market prices for transistors, the conversion of net income earned outside The Netherlands and Western Germany into guilders at a lower exchange rate as a result of the revaluation of the guilder and the Deutsche mark on March 6, 1961 and increasing costs of labor.

Net sales for the first quarter of 1962 aggregated Nfl. 1,197 million *($333 million)* as compared with net sales of Nfl. 1,069 million *($297 million)* for the corresponding quarter of 1961. Net income (on the basis of the accounting principles customarily followed by Philips Industries and the United States Philips Trust) in the first quarter of 1962 was Nfl. 79 million *($21.9 million)* as compared with Nfl. 77 million *($21.4 million)* in the corresponding quarter of 1961. These amounts have not been audited by independent public accountants, but, in the opinion of the Company, they include all adjustments necessary for a fair statement of operations. There were no adjustments other than those of a normal recurring nature.

Notes to Combined Summary of Earnings

186 1. The accounting principles customarily followed by Philips Industries differ in the following respects from those generally accepted in the United States:

A. Provision for depreciation of fixed assets is based on their replacement value; see Note B to the Financial Statements.

B. Fully depreciated fixed assets, if they are still in use, continue to be depreciated on the basis of their replacement value; see Note I to the Financial Statements.

C. Inventories are stated on the basis of replacement value and such amounts are used in determining cost of goods sold.

D. Gain on sale of shares of the parent company (Philips N. V.) is included in income.

E. Profit-sharing with management and employees is shown as a deduction after net income.

Philips Industries has attempted to estimate what adjustment, in addition to the deduction for profit sharing, would have been required if Philips Industries had employed accounting principles generally accepted in the United States in lieu of the principles set forth above, that is, computing depreciation on the basis of historical cost, computing inventories on a cost basis, eliminating depreciation on fully depreciated assets and eliminating the gain on sale of shares of the parent company. In the opinion of Philips Industries, this would have required the estimated adjustment shown in the summary. There are other respects in which the accounting principles followed by Philips Industries differ from those generally accepted in the United States, but they would not have materially affected net income.

3. Provisions for depreciation and amortization of fixed assets based on replacement value were as follows:

	1961	1960	1959	1958	1957
Thousands of guilders	Nfl.208,920	Nfl.179,134	Nfl.158,319	Nfl.139,596	Nfl.117,906
Translated into thousands of U. S. dollars	$ 58,033	$ 47,141	$ 41,663	$ 36,736	$ 31,028

Inventories are on the basis of replacement value and are after deduction of allowance for possible obsolescence. Changes in the replacement value are credited or charged to Revaluation Surplus. 187

The amounts of the opening and closing inventories for the three years ended December 31, 1961, computed on the foregoing basis, were as follows:

	December 31			
	1961	1960	1959	1958
Thousands of guilders	Nfl.1,962,031	Nfl.1,580,609	Nfl.1,271,319	Nfl.1,249,704
Translated into thousands of U. S. dollars	$ 545,008	$ 415,950	$ 334,558	$ 328,869

5. Includes net income of the United States Philips Trust, after adjustments to conform with certain accounting principles of Philips Industries (See Note J to the Financial Statements) in the following respective amounts:

	1961	1960	1959	1958	1957
Thousands of guilders	Nfl.19,409	Nfl.15,699	Nfl.22,283	Nfl.11,885	Nfl.7,130
Translated into thousands of U. S. dollars	$ 5,392	$ 4,132	$ 5,864	$ 3,128	$ 1,876

Combined Statement of Financial Position of Philips

AS AT DECEMBER 31, 1961

ASSETS

	In Thousands of Neth. Guilders		(Translated into Thousands of U. S. Dollars)	
CURRENT ASSETS				
Cash on hand and demand deposits	Nfl.496,550		$137,931	
Time deposits	314	Nfl.496,864	87	$138,018
Marketable securities (at lower of cost or market) (Note E)		47,627		13,230
Notes receivable trade	323,811		89,948	
Accounts receivable trade (less allowances for doubtful accounts and doubtful notes) (Note F) ..	1,120,892		311,359	
	1,444,703		401,307	
Discounted notes	Cr. 181,084		Cr. 50,301	
	1,263,619		351,006	
Other receivables (less allowances)	149,511	1,413,130	41,530	392,536
Inventories: (Note G)				
Factory inventories	1,006,331		279,536	
Commercial inventories	955,700		265,472	
	1,962,031		545,008	
Less: prepayments from customers	81,798	1,880,233	22,721	522,287
Other current assets:				
Due from unconsolidated subsidiaries	29,495		8,193	
Prepaid expenses	104,924	134,419	29,146	37,339
Total current assets		3,972,273		1,103,410
INVESTMENTS				
Securities of affiliates (substantially at equity in their net assets)	131,476		36,521	
Indebtedness of unconsolidated subsidiaries not current	16,323		4,534	
Security investments (at cost or less)	9,876		2,743	
Other investments (at cost or less) (Note S)	86,273	243,948	23,965	67,763
PROPERTY, PLANT AND EQUIPMENT				
At replacement value (Note H)	3,414,337		948,427	
Less: depreciation based upon replacement value (Note I)	1,379,188	2,035,149	383,108	565,319
INTANGIBLE ASSETS (Note J)		—		—
		Nfl.6,251,370		$1,736,492

188

Industries and United States Philips Trust

LIABILITIES AND CAPITAL

	In Thousands of Neth. Guilders		(Translated into Thousands of U. S. Dollars)	
CURRENT LIABILITIES				
Payable to banks:				
Notes	Nfl.175,246		$ 48,679	
Accounts	436,340	Nfl.611,586	121,206	$ 169,885
Accounts payable, trade		313,039		86,955
Accrued liabilities:				
Provision for tax on income ..	267,804		74,390	
Accrued expenses:				
Interest	19,025		5,285	
Salaries and wages	30,677		8,522	
Other	177,385		49,273	
Deferred income	3,510		975	
Various specific provisions ...	120,517	618,918	33,477	171,922
Other current liabilities:				
Profit to be distributed (Note K)	146,298		40,638	
Other current liabilities	342,866		95,240	
Long-term liabilities, due within one year	47,508	536,672	13,197	149,075
Total current liabilities		2,080,215		577,837
LONG-TERM LIABILITIES (see COMBINED CAPITAL STRUCTURE OF PHILIPS INDUSTRIES AND UNITED STATES PHILIPS TRUST)				
Debentures (due 1962-1979)	186,185		51,718	
Mortgages	58,453		16,237	
Other long-term liabilities:				
Due to banks	38,763		10,768	
Due to others (Note L)	766,193		212,831	
	1,049,594		291,554	
Less: due within one year (Note M)	47,508	1,002,086	13,197	278,357
MINORITY INTERESTS IN CONSOLIDATED SUBSIDIARIES				
Capital	45,314		12,587	
Earned surplus	39,787		11,052	
▶Revaluation surplus	5,488	90,589	1,525	25,164
PROVISIONS				
Provision for deferred taxation (Note N)	199,542		55,428	
Other specific provisions	190,180	389,722	52,828	108,256
CONTINGENT LIABILITY (Note F)	—		—	
CAPITAL (see COMBINED CAPITAL STRUCTURE OF PHILIPS INDUSTRIES AND UNITED STATES PHILIPS TRUST)				
6% Cumulative Participating Preferred Shares, par value 25 Neth. guilders per share				
Authorized 10,000,000 shares				
Issued 5,760,000 shares	144,000		40,000	
Common Shares, par value 25 Neth. guilders per share				
Authorized 110,000,000 shares				
Issued 27,417,280 shares	685,432		190,398	
Paid-in surplus (Note R)	87,635		24,343	
Retained earnings (Notes O and R)	1,412,103		392,251	
	2,329,170		646,992	
▶Revaluation surplus	359,588	2,688,758	99,886	746,878
		Nfl.6,251,370		$1,736,492

189

Combined Statements of Surplus of Philips

	In Thousands of Neth. Guilders				
	1961	*1960*	*1959*	*1958*	*1957*
RETAINED EARNINGS (NOTE R)					
Balance at the beginning of period	Nfl.1,232,159	Nfl. 975,197	Nfl.757,997	Nfl.616,471	Nfl.524,73
Add, net income on the basis of accounting principles customarily followed by the companies	326,242	396,846	350,687	243,812	186,86
Deduct, dividends:					
In cash:					
on 6% Cumulative Participating Preferred Shares	11,520	11,520	11,520	10,944	10,94
on Common Shares	109,669	104,227	99,045	75,186	69,30
Profit sharing with management and employees	25,109	24,137	22,922	16,156	14,87
Balance at the end of period	Nfl.1,412,103	Nfl.1,232,159	Nfl.975,197	Nfl.757,997	Nfl.616,47
PAID-IN SURPLUS (NOTE R)					
Balance at the beginning of period	Nfl. 121,646	Nfl. 154,037	Nfl.118,245	Nfl. 63,622	Nfl. 54,62
Add, paid-in surplus from conversion of 5% Convertible Debentures, less related expenses	—	—	66,641	54,623	8,99
Deduct, dividends in Common Shares:					
on 6% Cumulative Participating Preferred Shares (1% in 1961, 1960 and 1959)	1,440	1,440	1,440	—	—
on Common Shares (5% in 1961, 1960 and 1959)	32,571	30,951	29,409	—	—
Balance at the end of period	Nfl. 87,635	Nfl. 121,646	Nfl.154,037	Nfl.118,245	Nfl. 63,62
REVALUATION SURPLUS					
Balance at the beginning of period	Nfl. 376,845	Nfl. 373,795	Nfl.365,074	Nfl.345,624	Nfl.323,13
Add (deduct), revaluation (Note T)	(17,257)	3,050	8,721	19,450	22,49
Balance at the end of period	Nfl. 359,588	Nfl. 376,845	Nfl.373,795	Nfl.365,074	Nfl.345,62

190

Notes to Financial Statements

Note B. Application of the Principle of Valuation at Replacement Value.
Fixed assets and inventories of Philips Industries are shown at replacement value; changes in this value are either credited or charged to Revaluation Surplus, which is shown under "Capital" in the COMBINED STATEMENT OF FINANCIAL POSITION. In the calculation of the replacement value the efficiency of the assets concerned is taken into account. This means that the calculation takes into account not only the mathematical change in value in relation to the price level but also a lower degree of efficiency of the asset in relation to a replacing asset.

Replacement value is determined on the basis of the price trends of the various assets in the countries where they are located. In making such determinations price indexes are employed.

In the calculation of net income, the cost of the goods sold which includes depreciation of property, plant and equipment, is computed on the basis of replacement value. In times of rising price levels, as in recent years, the use of replacement values results in a lower net income than would be the case if the items concerned were charged to the Profit and Loss Account at historical cost prices.

Industries and United States Philips Trust

	(Translated into Thousands of U. S. Dollars)				
RETAINED EARNINGS (NOTE R)	1961	1960	1959	1958	1957
Balance at the beginning of period	$342,266	$256,631	$199,473	$162,229	$138,088
Add, net income on the basis of accounting principles customarily followed by companies	90,623	104,433	92,286	64,162	49,174
Deduct, dividends:					
In cash:					
on 6% Cumulative Participating Preferred Shares	3,200	3,032	3,032	2,880	2,880
on Common Shares	30,464	27,428	26,064	19,786	18,238
Profit sharing with management and employees	6,974	6,352	6,032	4,252	3,915
Balance at the end of period	$392,251	$324,252	$256,631	$199,473	$162,229
PAID-IN SURPLUS (NOTE R)					
Balance at the beginning of period	$ 33,791	$ 40,536	$ 31,117	$ 16,743	$ 14,375
Add, paid-in surplus from conversion of 5% Convertible Debentures, less related expenses	—	—	17,537	14,374	2,368
Deduct, dividends in Common Shares:					
on 6% Cumulative Participating Preferred Shares (1% in 1961, 1960 and 1959)	400	379	379	—	—
on Common Shares (5% in 1961, 1960 and 1959)	9,048	8,145	7,739	—	—
Balance at the end of period	$ 24,343	$ 32,012	$ 40,536	$ 31,117	$ 16,743
REVALUATION SURPLUS					
Balance at the beginning of period	$104,679	$ 98,367	$ 96,072	$ 90,954	$ 85,035
Add (deduct) revaluation (Note T)	(4,793)	803	2,295	5,118	5,919
Balance at the end of period	$ 99,886	$ 99,170	$ 98,367	$ 96,072	$ 90,954

191

Note: The balances in U. S. dollars at the beginning of 1961 differ from the balances at the end of 1960 due to the revaluation of the Neth. guilder.

For the convenience of American readers, Philips Industries has estimated what its consolidated net income would have been if Philips Industries had employed accounting principles generally accepted in the United States, including computing depreciation on the basis of historical cost rather than replacement value. The estimated adjustment this would require is set forth in the COMBINED SUMMARY OF EARNINGS OF PHILIPS INDUSTRIES AND UNITED STATES PHILIPS TRUST.

If the method of historical cost had been applied in the past, it is estimated that the Revaluation Surplus, as shown in the COMBINED STATEMENT OF FINANCIAL POSITION as at December 31, 1961 would have been eliminated as follows:

	In Thousands of Neth. Guilders	(Translated into Thousands of U. S. Dollars)
Added to Retained Earnings	Nfl. 279,788	$77,719
Deducted from Fixed Assets	79,800	22,167
Revaluation Surplus as at December 31, 1961	Nfl. 359,588	$99,886

Note G. Inventories. Inventories are on the basis of replacement value and are after deduction of allowance for possible obsolescence. Changes in the replacement value are credited or charged to Revaluation Surplus.

Note H. Property, Plant and Equipment. A summary of the combined property, plant and equipment accounts at December 31, 1961 follows:

	Thousands of Neth. Guilders			(Translated into Thousands of U.S. Dollars)		
	Replacement Value	Allowance for Depreciation	Net Amount	Replacement Value	Allowance for Depreciation	Net Amount
Land and buildings	Nfl.1,626,034	Nfl. 402,255	Nfl.1,223,779	$451,676	$111,737	$339,939
Machinery and equipment	1,585,171	953,066	632,105	440,325	264,741	175,584
Houses and land	140,086	23,867	116,219	38,913	6,630	32,283
Vacant sites	63,046	—	63,046	17,513	—	17,513
Totals	Nfl.3,414,337	Nfl.1,379,188	Nfl.2,035,149	$948,427	$383,108	$565,319

Increases in the revalued amounts of property, plant and equipment in the years 1957-1961 have been debited to these accounts as follows:

	Thousands of Neth. Guilders	(Translated into Thousands of U. S. Dollars)
1961	Nfl. 23,882	$6,634
1960	37,623	9,901
1959	8,412	2,214
1958	13,763	3,622
1957	8,996	2,367

These amounts have been credited to Revaluation Surplus after deduction of an amount for deferred taxation based on actual tax rates. This deduction is transferred from deferred taxation to Revaluation Surplus in accordance with depreciation of the assets revalued (see Note B). The allowance for depreciation at December 31, 1961 includes extra depreciation of Nfl. 148,284,000 (U. S. $41,190,000) applicable to fully depreciated assets still in use (see Note I).

Note I. Depreciation and Amortization Policy. Depreciation of physical assets of Philips Industries is provided over the estimated service lives of the various classes of property on the basis of their replacement values (see Note B) using the straight-line method. In view of the wide variety of properties within each major class or functional group, it is not practicable to list the individual rates of depreciation used.

With respect to assets which have become fully depreciated in the accounts but which are still in use, the companies continue to provide depreciation just as though the assets were not fully depreciated, but beginning in May 1957 with respect to companies in The Netherlands, and beginning May 1959 with respect to companies outside The Netherlands, the additional provisions for "extra depreciation" were reduced by 50%. These changes in policy applicable to "extra depreciation" had no material effect on income.

When fixed assets are retired, the asset and allowance for depreciation accounts are relieved of the applicable amounts. Profits or losses on retirements are credited or charged to the "extra depreciation" account. The depreciation on the balance sheet includes both the "normal" depreciation and the "extra" depreciation.

In general maintenance and repairs are charged to income as incurred. Cost of relining glass furnaces, maintenance of dwellings and other minor items are charged to reserves created out of income. Renewals, and betterments are capitalized if they extend the service life of the asset.

The depreciation and amortization policies followed by companies controlled by the United States Philips Trust are stated in the financial statements of the Trust included in the Registration Statement.

Note T. Revaluation Surplus. The reduction in revaluation surplus in 1961 is due to:

	In Thousands of Neth. Guilders	(Translated into Thousands of U. S. Dollars)
Deduction in connection with revaluation of the Neth. Guilder	Nfl. 71,271	$19,797
Revaluation increase in relation to price level	54,014	15,004
Net reduction	Nfl. 17,257	$ 4,793

The following is an excerpt from the Auditors' Report:

193

In our opinion, based upon our examination and upon the report of Messrs. Smith and Harder, the financial statements listed in the accompanying index present fairly (a) the financial position of Philips N. V. at December 31, 1961 and the results of its operations for the years 1957 through 1961 and (b) the combined financial position of Philips Industries and the United States Philips Trust at December 31, 1961 and the combined results of their operations for the years 1957 through 1961, all in conformity with generally accepted accounting principles in The Netherlands applied in all material respects on a consistent basis. Also in our opinion, the information under Combined Capital Structure of Philips Industries and the United States Philips Trust and Capital Structure of Philips N. V. is fairly presented.

There are certain differences between the accounting principles followed by the companies and those generally accepted in the United States of America. In our opinion, the differences which have a material effect on the computation of net income are set forth in the notes following the combined summary of earnings. The application of accounting principles generally accepted in the United States of America would, in our opinion, have required the adjustments in net income which have been estimated and are reflected in the aforementioned summary of earnings.

Eindhoven, The Netherlands,   Klynveld, Kraayenhof & Co.
March 12, 1962.

B. Companies Presenting Unadjusted Statements Supplemented by Price-Level Information.

B-1. *Indiana Telephone Corporation (U.S.)*

Beginning with its annual report for the year 1955, the Indiana Telephone Corporation has prepared its financial statements in two-column form, one column showing the results under conventional accounting methods and the other reflecting adjustments of depreciation and the related asset accounts. The following excerpts are taken from the report of the company for the year ended December 31, 1961. In the examples, Column A contains the conventional accounting statements of the corporation; Column B contains the supplementary price-level information.

Indiana Telephone Corporation
COMPARATIVE INCOME STATEMENTS

	Year 1960		Year 1961	
	Column A	*Column B*	*Column A*	*Column B*
REVENUES				
Local service	$2,393,183.76	$2,393,183.76	$2,517,535.04	$2,517,535.04
Toll service	1,245,447.11	1,245,447.11	1,324,400.63	1,324,400.63
Miscellaneous	133,458.52	133,458.52	134,874.69	134,874.69
Less—Provision for uncollectibles	14,168.49	14,168.49	15,650.54	15,650.54
Total revenues—Net	$3,757,920.90	$3,757,920.90	$3,961,159.82	$3,961,159.82
EXPENSES				
Estimated inroads on total plant result from current wear and tear, decay, obsolescence, etc. (Note 1)	$ 471,624.51	$ 593,798.84	$ 501,821.66	$ 656,318.47
Maintenance (Note 4)	430,676.23	430,676.23	525,196.33	525,196.33
Traffic	846,965.78	846,965.78	927,321.16	927,321.16
Commercial	224,250.40	224,250.40	255,645.54	255,645.54
General office salaries and expenses	127,833.79	127,833.79	194,460.22	194,460.22
Other operating expenses	100,853.48	100,853.48	134,370.52	134,370.52
Total	$2,202,204.19	$2,324,378.52	$2,538,815.43	$2,693,312.24
Taxes				
State and local property	$ 189,092.64	$ 189,092.64	$ 201,605.94	$ 201,605.94
Indiana gross income	48,940.44	48,940.44	51,459.82	51,459.82
Social security	55,272.51	55,272.51	61,662.32	61,662.32
Federal income	589,834.26	589,834.26	493,985.99	493,985.99
Total taxes	$ 883,139.85	$ 883,139.85	$ 808,714.07	$ 808,714.07
Total expenses	$3,085,344.04	$3,207,518.37	$3,347,529.50	$3,502,026.31
NET OPERATING INCOME (NOTE 2)	$ 672,576.86	$ 550,402.53	$ 613,630.32	$ 459,133.51
Add—Other income—Net	23,666.34	23,666.34	18,190.17	18,190.17
INCOME AVAILABLE FOR FIXED CHARGES	$ 696,243.20	$ 574,068.87	$ 631,820.49	$ 477,323.68
Deduct—Fixed charges				
Interest on funded debt	$ 141,312.49	$ 141,312.49	$ 148,770.88	$ 148,770.88
Other fixed charges	5,263.70	5,263.70	8,039.83	8,039.83
Total fixed charges	$ 146,576.19	$ 146,576.19	$ 156,810.71	$ 156,810.71
NET INCOME (NOTE 1)	$ 549,667.01	$ 427,492.68	$ 475,009.78	$ 320,512.97
Deduct—Preferred stock dividends	61,472.59	61,472.59	60,671.20	60,671.20
NET INCOME APPLICABLE TO COMMON STOCK	$ 488,194.42	$ 366,020.09	$ 414,338.58	$ 259,841.77
Deduct—Common stock dividends	—	—	328,329.71	328,329.71
NET INCOME AFTER DIVIDENDS	$ 488,194.42	$ 366,020.09	$ 86,008.87	($ 68,487.94)
Total number of stations in service at end of year	40,491	40,491	42,771	42,771

( ) denotes red figure.

The accompanying Notes to Financial Statements are an integral part of these Income Statements.

Indiana Telephone Corporation
BALANCE SHEETS
DECEMBER 31, 1961

ASSETS

	Column A	Column B
TELEPHONE PLANT including construction in progress (Note 1)	$11,661,053.53	$14,683,370.59
Less: Estimated inroads on total plant resulting from accumulated wear and tear, decay, obsolescence, etc.	3,618,897.28	4,809,533.85
	$ 8,042,156.25	$ 9,873,836.74
MATERIAL AND SUPPLIES	$ 164,941.54	$ 164,941.54
OTHER PHYSICAL PROPERTY AND INVESTMENTS	$ 61,128.15	$ 61,128.15
CURRENT ASSETS		
Cash and special deposits	$ 408,064.00	$ 408,064.00
Temporary cash investments—At cost plus accrued interest receivable	844,677.08	844,677.08
Accounts and notes receivable—Net	330,926.98	330,926.98
	$ 1,583,668.06	$ 1,583,668.06
PREPAYMENTS AND DEFERRED CHARGES	$ 94,054.84	$ 94,054.84
	$ 9,945,948.84	$11,777,629.33

STOCKHOLDERS' EQUITY AND LIABILITIES

	Column A	Column B
STOCKHOLDERS' EQUITY		
Common stock—No par value, stated value $10.00 per share, 250,000 shares authorized. 206,605 shares issued of which 1,818 shares are held in treasury	$ 2,047,870.00	$ 2,047,870.00
Capital surplus	514,369.20	514,369.20
Capital adjustment (resulting from conversion of historical cost to current dollars) charged to: (Note 1)		
Income, 1954 to 1961, inclusive	—	932,414.63
Telephone plant, to be charged to income in future periods	—	1,831.680.49
Earned surplus	1,040,085.77	107,671.14
Less: Stock discount and expense	75,582.48	75,582.48
	$ 3,526,742.49	$ 5,358,422.98
Cumulative Preferred Stock (Note 3)	1,198,500.00	1,198,500.00
	$ 4,725,242.49	$ 6,556,922.98
FIRST MORTGAGE SINKING FUND BONDS—Less current sinking fund payments (Note 3)	$ 4,244,000.00	$ 4,244,000.00
CURRENT LIABILITIES		
Sinking fund payments—Bonds and preferred stock	$ 54,000.00	$ 54,000.00
Accounts payable	167,891.37	167,891.37
Dividends payable	97,023.05	97,023.05
Federal income tax payable	277,985.99	277,985.99
Other	336,652.17	336,652.17
	$ 933,552.58	$ 933,552.58
OTHER DEFERRED CREDITS	$ 43,153.77	$ 43,153.77
	$ 9,945,948.84	$11,777,629.33

195·

The accompanying Notes to Financial Statements are an integral part of these Balance Sheets.

Indiana Telephone Corporation
STATEMENTS OF SURPLUS
FOR THE YEAR ENDED DECEMBER 31, 1961

CAPITAL SURPLUS

	Column A	Column B
BALANCE, December 31, 1960	$ 10,398.20	$ 10,398.20
Year 1961		
Add:		
Excess of market value over stated value of 29,493 shares of no par value common stock issued as a common stock dividend as of March 14, 1961	501,381.00	501,381.00
Excess of stated value over cost of 259 shares of no par value common stock received as a stock dividend	2,590.00	2,590.00
BALANCE, December 31, 1961	$ 514,369.20	$ 514,369.20

EARNED SURPLUS

	Column A	Column B
BALANCE, December 31, 1960	$1,751,157.15	$ 973,239.33
Year 1961		
Add—Net income, year 1961	475,009.78	320,512.97
Total	$2,226,166.93	$1,293,752.30
Deduct:		
Stock dividend		
Market value ($27.00 per share) of 29,493 shares of no par value common capital stock issued, as of March 14, 1961, as a common stock dividend	$ 796,311.00	$ 796,311.00
Cash—fractional shares	670.51	670.51
Cash dividends declared:		
On common stock	327,659.20	327,659.20
On preferred stock	60,671.20	60,671.20
Expense and premium on bonds retired through sinking fund—Net	380.32	380.32
Expense and discount on preferred stock retired through sinking fund—Net	388.93	388.93
Total deduction	$1,186,081.16	$1,186,081.16
BALANCE, December 31, 1961	$1,040,085.77	$ 107,671.14

The accompanying Notes to Financial Statements are an integral part of these Statements of Surplus.

Accountants' Opinion

To the Stockholders of
Indiana Telephone Corporation

We have examined the balance sheets of Indiana Telephone Corporation as of December 31, 1961, and the related statements of income and surplus for the year then ended. Our examination was made in accordance with generally accepted auditing standards, and accordingly included such tests of the accounting records and such other auditing procedures as we considered necessary in the circumstances. We previously made a similar examination for the year ended December 31, 1960.

In our opinion, the accompanying financial statements shown under Columns **A** present fairly the financial position of the Company as of December 31, 1961, and the results of its operations for the year then ended, in conformity with generally accepted accounting methods applied on a basis consistent with that of the preceding year.

    In our opinion, however, the accompanying financial statements shown under Columns B more fairly present the financial position of the Company and its results of operations since recognition has been given to variations in the purchasing power of the dollar, as more fully set forth in Note 1 of the financial statements.

Indianapolis, Indiana   HERDRICH, BOGGS AND CO.

March 1, 1962   Certified Public Accountants

Indiana Telephone Corporation

SOURCE AND DISPOSITION OF FUNDS

YEAR 1961

FUNDS PROVIDED:

Net income (per Column B) (Note 1)	$ 320,512.97
Expenses deducted in arriving at the above net income which did not require funds:	
Estimated inroads on total plant resulting from current wear and tear, decay, obsolescence, etc.	
Telephone plant	656,318.47
Vehicles and other work equipment	9,399.57
Miscellaneous physical property	439.23
Amortization of bond expense and premium—Net	1,208.28
Proceeds from sale of bonds	500,000.00
Salvage value of materials, etc., recovered from plant retired	62,955.55
Decrease in working capital	391,628.36
Total funds provided	$1,942,462.43

FUNDS APPLIED:

Gross additions to plant including construction in progress	$1,460,331.93
Dividends—Common stock	328,329.71
Dividends—Preferred stock	60,671.20
Sinking fund—Bonds and preferred stock	44,000.00
Cost of removal of plant retired	30,576.43
Prepaid current charges—Net	11,964.69
Cost of preferred stock reacquired	4,929.00
Miscellaneous	1,659.47
Total funds applied	$1,942,462.43

197

Notes to Financial Statements

Note (1). The historical cost of telephone plant is expressed in the dollar values current at the various dates of its acquisition or construction. Dollars are a means of expressing purchasing power at the time of their use. It is improper to deal with dollars of different purchasing power as mathematical likes. Unless they are converted to a common denominator they will not express the business or economic truth. We believe that the only sound basis for businessmen, commissions, taxing bodies, and others to proceed intelligently is to begin with accounting data which rests on a sound economic foundation.

What is commonly referred to as "depreciation" is referred to in this report as "Estimated inroads on total plant resulting from current wear and tear, decay, obsolescence, etc."

The inroads on total plant in connection with current operations must be ascertained from sound estimates of the wear, tear, decay and obsolescence occurring. Actually, all that is being done is to convert to current dollars the only significant item of expense which would not be so stated under current methods of accounting.

The amount shown on the balance sheets as "Estimated inroads on total plant resulting from accumulated wear and tear, decay, obsolescence, etc." is merely the accumulated total of the annual charges against income, however determined.

The problem of accounting for dollar value changes varies with the length of life of the plant, its various dates of installation, and the rate of change (generally a decline) in the purchasing power of the dollar. The problem created by the changing value of the dollar exists in varying degrees in all businesses which have fixed plant not consumed in one year.

To accomplish the foregoing objectives the historical cost of telephone plant, the estimated inroads on total plant resulting from wear and tear, decay, obsolescence, etc., and the current-year estimates of such costs have been converted into current dollars. The effects are shown in Column B of the income statement for 1960 and 1961, and in Column B of the balance sheets at December 31, 1961. This is not done in the financial statements presented under Column A, which are presented substantially in accordance with the accounting usually prescribed by regulatory authority. Such accounting requires that "depreciation" be based on the original cost of plant and gives no recognition to changes in the purchasing power of the dollar since the dates the plant was acquired or constructed.

We believe the information shown in Column B presents the accounting data on a sound economic basis. In order that comparisons may be made with other companies, however, we have furnished the conventional information under Column A. When other companies begin to show the information which we show in Column B, it will be possible to realistically compare our results with theirs.

The realistic net income for 1961 is $320,512.97 or $154,496.81 less than the amount shown in Column A. This reduction in net income results from repricing in current dollars the estimated current inroads on plant.

Since the present Internal Revenue Code does not recognize this increase of cost measured in current dollars it is not deductible for computing Federal income tax payments, and the Company in fact pays taxes on alleged earnings which economically do not exist. Therefore, the Federal income tax for 1961 is' stated in Column B in the same amount as in Column A. If this additional amount of $154,495.81 were deductible, as it should be, a reduction of $80,338.34 in Federal income tax for 1961 would result.

The repricing of the historical costs referred to above for 1960 was made on the basis of price-level information furnished by Earl L. Carter, a Registered Professional Engineer, in a detailed current-cost study dated January 1, 1961. The repricing of the historical costs has been brought forward through December 31, 1961, on the basis of information which Mr. Carter prepared from the index of wholesale prices, "All commodities other than farm and foods," issued by the Department of Labor, covering said period. Our experience in the past shows that the methods followed by the Company have been conservative.

➡️*Note (2).* Under the law of Indiana your Company is entitled to earn a fair return on the fair value of its property used and useful in the public service in addition to a return of such property. (Note (1) deals with a return of the property.) In determining whether a fair return is being earned on the fair value of the property, the figure entitled "Net Operating Income" in Column B may be considered to be substantially the "return" figure.

B-2. *Hercules Powder Company* (U.S.)

The Hercules Powder Company discloses the effect of cost and price-level changes in the "General Statistics" section of its annual report. Three selected items are restated—research expenditures, gross fixed assets, and net income. A recent example is shown below.

199

General Statistics

| | | | | | Restatement of Reported Data in Dollars of Constant Value ➡️ ⬅️ | | |
	Year	Number of Common Stock-holders	Average Number of Em-ployees*	Wage and Salary Costs*†	Research Expendi-tures	Research Expendi-tures (Adjusted to 1960 Costs)‡	Gross Fixed Assets (Revalued in Terms of Dec. 31, 1960 Con-struction Costs)§	Net Income (Adjusted to 1960 Con-sumers' Prices)‖
			Thousands of Dollars				
1951	9,148	11,160	53,103	5,433	7,900	280,000	15,600
1952	9,619	10,679	52,986	6,394	8,800	292,000	12,500
1953	9,703	10,689	58,325	7,905	10,300	298,000	12,900
1954	9,649	10,943	60,714	7,578	9,600	318,000	15,600
1955	9,883	11,259	67,005	7,903	9,600	326,000	21,000
1956	11,111	11,365	71,537	10,523	12,200	356,000	19,300
1957	12,555	11,497	76,719	10,172	11,200	369,000	19,100
1958	12,698	10,743	74,326	10,816	11,500	376,000	17,900
1959	13,546	11,221	84,302	11,602	12,000	389,000	23,800
1960¶	16,833	13,810	106,716	14,090	14,100	448,000	27,200

* Includes employes engaged in construction but excludes those at U. S. Government-owned ordnance plants.
† Includes provisions for pensions and other employe benefits.
‡ As measured by U. S. Bureau of Labor Statistics' index of hourly earnings in all manufacturing industries.
§ As measured by the Engineering News-Record construction cost index.
‖ As measured by the Consumer Price Index of the U. S. Bureau of Labor Statistics.
¶ 1960 includes Imperial, prior years have not been restated.

The corresponding unadjusted net income amounts were as follows:

1951	$13,656	1956	$17,703
1952	11,218	1957	18,116
1953	11,681	1958	17,509
1954	14,140	1959	23,397
1955	19,012	1960	27,165

It will be noted that the adjusted net income figures were computed merely by increasing the unadjusted amounts by a percentage equal to the percentage increase in the price-level index. No adjustment was made of depreciation or of other components of the net income.

B-3. *Eastman Kodak Company* (U.S.)

The Eastman Kodak Company, in the "Management Comments" of its annual report, presents a chart which compares the sales of the Company with the Gross National Product for a ten-year period, both sets of data having been expressed in "constant dollars." The following comment was made in the 1961 report:

> Over the past ten-year interval, the percentage gain in Kodak sales, adjusted for price changes, has been more than double the gain in the U. S. economy as measured by Gross National Product, also adjusted for price changes.

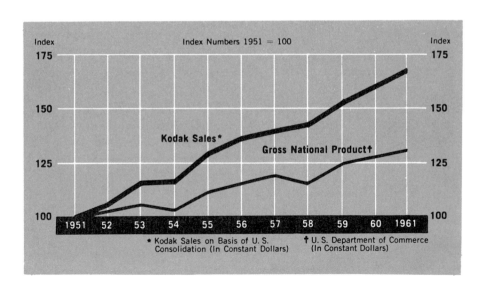

200

C. Companies Adjusting Depreciation Charges as a Result of Recorded Revaluations of Fixed Assets.

First Group—Revaluation Under Government Revalorization Provisions:

C-1. *Simca*—Prospectus dated April 17, 1959, containing financial statements for the year ended December 31, 1958. (France)

The following excerpts describe the procedures followed by the company:

From "Notes to Financial Statements," p. 32.

> *Note 4. Property, Plant and Equipment and Reserves for Depreciation.* Under French tax laws, companies may recognize the loss in purchasing power of the French franc by revaluing their fixed assets. The revaluation of physical properties may be based on estimates of current useful value with the limitation that the value thus found may not exceed the amount that would have been obtained by applying approved co-efficients to the original cost of the properties and to the recorded provisions for depreciation. These co-efficients which are published by the French Government are intended to give expression to the change in price level each year beginning with the year 1914. Upon recording such a revaluation, companies may subsequently deduct from taxable income depreciation computed on the basis of the higher amounts. The surplus resulting from revaluation is maintained in a special reserve for revaluation and may be used to increase the stated value of capital stock upon payment of a relatively small tax.

> The Company has revalued its properties on three separate occasions, at the end of 1945, 1949 and 1951, on the basis of co-efficients of revaluation authorized by the French Government as of those dates. See Note 9 to Financial Statements. Thereafter, the Company has charged against earnings depreciation on the higher amounts, as permitted by French tax law.

Fixed assets were carried in the accounts at these revalued amounts, and depreciation expense, based on these amounts, was deducted in the profit and loss statement in arriving at net operating income for the year. When assets were revalued, the credit was to "surplus from revaluation of fixed assets," which arose as follows:

From "Notes to Financial Statements," p. 35.

Note 9. Surplus from Revaluation of Fixed Assets. See Note 4 to Financial Statements. This surplus arose as follows:

201

Revaluation of assets:
Fixed assets:

	Amount	Reserve for Depreciation	Net
1945	Frs. 742,410	Frs. 388,260	Frs. 354,150
1949	2,107,968	1,253,245	854,723
1951	1,889,920	775,348	1,114,572
	4,740,298	2,416,853	2,323,445

Foreign currencies:

1945		35,727
		Frs. 2,359,172

Less: Stock dividends:

1947	Frs. 250,000	
1950	90,316	
1951	250,000	
1954	1,000,000	1,590,316
		Frs. 768,856

Excess of sales proceeds over book-value of machinery
sold to UNIC 447,797

Total .... Frs. 1,216,653

202

C-2. *Montecatini Mining and Chemical Company*—1960 Annual Report. (Italy)

The following excerpts from the notes to consolidated financial statements in the report describe the procedures followed by the company:

Note 1. Basis of Presenting Financial Statements. Under Italian monetary and Belgian tax laws, companies have been permitted to recognize, to some extent, loss in purchasing power of the respective country's currency through permission to restate assets (and related reserves) at amounts in excess of cost on the basis of co-efficients established under the law. The last revalorization enactment in Italy was in 1952 and related only to assets acquired in 1946 or earlier. As to the Belgian company, the last revalorization of assets was made in 1949. Depreciation has been charged against income based on the higher amounts.

Note 2. Inventories. The inventories are valued at the lower of the previous year's price (actual cost or historical cost as revalorized in accordance with legal co-efficients) or market to the extent that the quantities existed at the beginning of the year and at the lower of cost or market to the extent that quanties increased during the year.

Note 3. Investments in and Advances to Affiliated and Associated Companies. Investments in and advances to affiliated and associated companies are stated at cost or revalorized cost except that in certain instances where losses have been incurred the investment has been written down.

Note 4. Property, Plant and Equipment. Property, plant and equipment are stated at revalorized amounts as described in Note 1 with additions subsequent to the revalorization dates being stated at cost. . . .

The amount resulting from revalorization of the assets was included with capital surplus on the balance sheet.

C-3. *Nippon Telegraph & Telephone Public Corporation,* prospectus dated May 2, 1961, containing financial statements for the year ended March 31, 1960. (Japan)

The following excerpts from the prospectus indicate the procedures followed by the company:

From "Notes to Financial Statements," p. 23.

Note 2. Plant and Equipment. As provided for by regulations under the basic law relating to NTT, plant assets at April 1, 1954 were revalued upwards. Under the Assets Revaluation Law substantially all major Japanese companies revalued their fixed assets. The purpose of the revaluation law was to provide for depreciation charges adjusted for the substantial monetary inflation which occurred immediately after World War II. NTT adopted certain of the detailed indexes to be used for revaluation purposes, as set forth in the revaluation law, but for the most part used current purchase or reproduction costs. Corresponding adjustments in accumulated depreciation were made simultaneously. Accordingly, plant and equipment accounts were increased by approximately 285,000,000 thousand yen and related reserves for depreciation by approximately 145,000,000 thousand yen; the net amount of the revaluation, 140,754,740 thousand yen (390,985 thousand U.S. dollars), is included in surplus arising from revaluation of plant and equipment. The results of the revaluation were approved by the Minister of Posts and Telecommunications, with minor adjustments which have been reflected in the statement of earnings under "Other (charges) and credits."

203

Depreciation expense, based on the higher amounts, was deducted as an "operating expense" in the "statement of earnings."

C-4. *Tokyo Shibaura Electric Co., Ltd.*—Report for six months ended March 31, 1960. (Japan)

The report disclosed that a reappraisal was made of assets on April 1, 1954, the credit going to a capital reserve account. It was also indicated that the stockholders approved the capitalization of a portion of this reappraisal surplus by means of the issuance of new shares. The following additional information was received from the Company's Accounting Division Manager in a letter dated May 10, 1962:

1. Depreciation is calculated on the reappraised values.
2. The depreciation is deducted as an expense for the term.
3. The reappraisal amounts for assets were decided according to the Special Measure Law for Assets Reappraisal.

C-5. *Yawata Iron and Steel Co., Ltd.*—Annual Report for the year ended March 31, 1960. (Japan)

The Japanese Government placed into effect asset revaluation laws as needed to adjust for fluctuations in the price level. These laws stipulated criteria which determined the companies required to make the adjustments, and disclosed the procedures to be followed. The laws were passed for the following reasons:

(1) To adjust conspicuous differences between the book value and the actual value of fixed assets resulting from inflationary trends after the War

(2) To establish a fair distribution in the burden of taxation

(3) To provide a firm structure of corporate capital through the legal enforcement of adequate depreciation as provided by law

(4) To correct undue disparity between the old and new stockholders

In the case of the first law, the revaluation surplus was taxed at 6 per cent, whereas, with the third law, "special tax measures were passed . . . for reducing or exempting revaluation and fixed assets taxes." It was stated that "the surplus [arising from revaluation] was not to be used for any purpose except for charging the payment of the revaluation tax, absorbing of losses resulting from the sale of revalued fixed assets, and for transfers into paid-up capital."

Second Group—Revaluations on the Basis of Appraisals by Outside Experts:

C-6. *Creole Petroleum Corporation*—1961 Annual Report. (Venezuela)

The following excerpts from the Company's Annual Report indicate the techniques followed:

From "The President Reports," p. 5.

Property, Plant, and Equipment

Capital expenditures in 1961 totaled $34 million, compared with $44 million in 1960.

During the year, the company retained independent experts to appraise the current cost of reproducing its fixed assets, excluding concessions. For some time, it had been increasingly apparent that the unamortized portion of the company's investments in physical plant, as recorded on its books based on historical costs, failed to reflect the true value of such investments when compared with today's much higher costs for the labor, material and services required in drilling and construction. This condition caused depreciation to be understated in terms of present costs and at the same time reflected earnings as being disproportionately high in relation to net assets. To rectify this situation, the company revalued its physical plant as of December 31, 1961, in accordance with the findings of the independent appraisers. This resulted in the addition of $405,955,005 to the net investment in property, plant, and equipment at year end.

From "Review of Company Finances," p. 22.

205

As a result of the appraisal, $405,955,005 was added to the net investment in property, plant, and equipment as of December 31, 1961; a corresponding amount was added to shareholders' equity described as surplus arising from revaluation of plant and equipment. The addition to fixed assets will be subject to depreciation in the company's income statement starting January 1, 1962. It is estimated that the additional depreciation resulting from revaluation will amount to $14,000,000 in 1962.

In recording the results of the independent appraisal, $461,-839,026 was added to gross plant investment and $55,884,021 to depreciation reserves to indicate the economic remaining life of plant investment as estimated by the independent experts.

"Opinion of Independent Public Accountants," p. 28.

To the Shareholders of Creole Petroleum Corporation:

We have examined the consolidated statement of financial position of Creole Petroleum Corporation and its subsidiaries as of December 31, 1961, and the consolidated statement of income and earned surplus for the year then ended. Our examination was made in accordance with generally accepted auditing standards and accordingly included such tests of the accounting records and such other auditing procedures as we considered necessary in the circumstances.

→   As of December 31, 1961, an independent appraisal was made of the company's investment in physical plant, and the amount of such appraisal over unamortized cost, amounting to $405,955,-005, was added to net Property, Plant and Equipment. A corresponding amount is reflected under Surplus arising from revaluation of plant and equipment. Under generally accepted accounting principles such revaluations, although seldom now adopted by companies in the United States for statement purposes, are generally regarded as permissible when appraised current values are formally recorded for all productive facilities subject to depreciation.

    In our opinion, the accompanying financial statements with the foregoing explanation present fairly the consolidated financial position of Creole Petroleum Corporation and its subsidiaries at December 31, 1961, and the results of their operations for the year, in conformity with generally accepted accounting principles. These principles have been applied on a basis consistent with that of the preceding year except for the revaluation of physical plant referred to above and further explained in the Review → of Company Finances, under the heading "Fixed Assets," on page 21, which affected the statement of financial position at December 31, 1961, and which will affect net income for 1962 and subsequent years.

206

Caracas, Venezuela   PRICE WATERHOUSE & Co.
March 8, 1962

C-7. *St. Joseph Lead Company*—1960 Annual Report. Separate financial statements were presented in the report for Compañia Minera Aguilar, S. A., a nonconsolidated subsidiary in Argentina owned 99.9 per cent by St. Joseph Lead Company. The following extracts from the subsidiary's financial statements reflect the effects of price-level adjustments:

From Notes to Financial Statements, pp. 20-21.

* * * * *

    (2) As of January 1, 1960 capital assets were subject to a revaluation as permitted by Argentine Law No. 15,272. The total appreciation of pesos 393,738,090 was applied to mining properties and mineral rights (pesos 52,489,454) and to land, buildings, plant and equipment (pesos 341,248,636); concurrently an equal amount was credited to other capital—arising from revaluation. At their revalued amount, net capital assets are still considered to be stated at less than present values.

    Following the principle of Law No. 15,272, depletion of the original cost and of the 1936 valuation of mining properties and mineral rights, discontinued since 1950, has been recommenced. Depletion and depreciation of the amounts of 1936 and 1960 appreciation on revaluation charged against earnings in 1960 totaled pesos 32,256,045.

Application of the foregoing for tax purposes has resulted in a reduction of 1959 and 1960 income and extraordinary profits taxes of pesos 36,927,138, credited against the total of such taxes shown in the 1960 statement of earnings.

Following the practice of prior years, a special appropriation of pesos 46,679,556 for replacement of capital assets has been made out of earnings for the year 1960. Similar special appropriations were made out of earnings in the preceding nine years aggregating pesos 253,119,600.

* * * * *

From the Balance Sheet, pp. 20-21.

* * * * *

	December 31, 1959 Argentine Paper Pesos		December 31, 1960 Argentine Paper Pesos	
CAPITAL ASSETS (NOTES 2 AND 4):				
Mining properties and mineral rights:				
Cost, including exploration and development prior to the commencement of operations	4,401,217		4,401,217	
Less allowance for depletion	3,803,619	597,598	3,502,941	898,276
Appreciation arising from valuation in 1936 and revaluation in 1960	101,936,190		49,446,117	
Less allowance for depletion	43,356,416	58,579,774	39,700,779	9,745,338
Total mining properties and mineral rights, net		59,177,372		10,643,614
Land, buildings, plant and equipment:				
Cost	209,124,684		185,764,252	
Less allowance for depreciation	58,350,687	150,773,997	56,846,283	128,917,969
Appreciation arising from revaluation in 1960	341,248,636		—	
Less allowance for depreciation	28,600,408	312,648,228	—	—
Total land, buildings, plant and equipment, net		463,422,225		128,917,969
Total capital assets, net		522,599,597		139,561,583

* * * * *

RESERVES:				
Replacement of capital assets (Note 2)	317,217,498		270,537,942	
Employees' compensation under Argentine social laws	22,153,315		19,844,743	
Accidents	28,760,840		20,817,511	
Other	28,412,717	396,544,370	21,705,481	332,905,677
STOCKHOLDERS' EQUITY:				
Capital Stock—Nominal value of 80 Argentine paper pesos each: Authorized 2,500,000 shares Issued—1960, 2,375,000 shares; 1959, 1,375,000 shares		190,000,000		110,000,000
Other Capital (Note 2):				
Arising from 1936 valuation of mining properties and mineral rights (remainder after transfer of pesos 48,-000,000 to stated value of capital stock)	1,446,736		1,446,736	
Arising from 1960 revaluation of capital assets	393,738,090	395,184,826	—	1,446,736

* * * * *

207

From Statement of Earnings, p. 22.

* * * * *

	1960 Argentine Paper Pesos	1959 Argentine Paper Pesos
DEDUCT:		
Selling, general and administrative expenses	21,987,274	19,671,685
Taxes, other than taxes on income	30,464,216	6,246,191
Depreciation and depletion (Note 2)	34,841,170	13,701,994
Total Deductions	87,292,660	39,619,870
Earnings Before Taxes on Income and Special Appropriation	236,213,922	342,256,451
Provision for Argentine Income and Extraordinary Profits Taxes, Net (Note 2)	32,706,966	111,116,568
Earnings before Special Appropriation	203,506,956	231,139,883
Special Appropriation for Replacement of Capital Assets (Note 2)	46,679,556	65,246,200
Net Earnings for the Year (after special appropriation) (Note 4)	156,827,400	165,893,683

* * * * *

Accountants' Report, p. 23.

St. Joseph Lead Company:

208

We have examined the balance sheet of Compañia Minera Aguilar, S. A. (incorporated and doing business in Argentina) as of December 31, 1960 and the related statements of earnings and unappropriated retained earnings for the year then ended. Our examination was made in accordance with generally accepted auditing standards, and accordingly included such tests of the accounting records and such other auditing procedures as we considered necessary in the circumstances.

During the year 1960 a special appropriation of 46,679,556 Argentine paper pesos for replacement of capital assets was made out of net earnings for the year. Similar special appropriations were made annually out of earnings in the preceding nine years, aggregating 253,119,600 Argentine paper pesos. In our opinion, accepted accounting principles require that such appropriations be set aside not out of earnings for the year but out of retained earnings.

In our opinion, except as described in the preceding paragraph the accompanying balance sheet with the footnotes thereon, and statements of earnings and unappropriated retained earnings present fairly the financial position of Compañia Minera Aguilar, S. A. at December 31, 1960 and the results of its operations for the year then ended, in conformity with accounting principles generally accepted in Argentina and applied (except for the changes in the methods of accounting for capital assets and for inventories explained in Notes 2, 3 and 4 to the Balance Sheet) on a basis consistent with that of the preceding year.

The accounting for capital assets and related depletion and depreciation (including the charges to earnings of appropriations for replacement of capital assets) as described in Note 2 to the Balance Sheet differs from that normally accepted in the United States. However, in all other material respects the accompanying financial statements, in our opinion, have been prepared in conformity with accounting principles generally accepted in the United States.

February 28, 1961   HASKINS & SELLS

C-8. *The Bowater Paper Corporation Limited.* (England)

From the 1959 Annual Report.

> Fixed assets are taken at cost, with the exception of certain assets of the United Kingdom Mills Company which were revalued by the Directors at 31st December 1955 and hydro-electric assets and water power rights in Newfoundland which were independently valued at 15th April 1955.

In answer to a request for more specific information regarding these revaluations, the Company Treasurer stated the following in a letter dated April 12, 1962:

1. Depreciation is calculated on the revalued amounts.   209
2. Depreciation is deducted as an expense in arriving at net profit.
3. The revaluation was made by the Directors of the Corporation on the basis of independent appraisal by professional valuers.

C-9. *Electric & Musical Industries Limited.* (England)

From the Annual Report for the year ended June 30, 1960.

> The freehold land and buildings in the United Kingdom are as revalued in November 1959, at which date the book value was increased by £2,867,000 from £582,000 to £3,449,000. In certain overseas subsidiaries fixed assets have been revalued; the remaining fixed assets of the Group are at the net book value at June 30, 1948 with subsequent additions at cost. (Page 10.)
>
> ...the book value of £582,000 was written up to £3,449,000 (which was less than the amount of the revaluation). (Page 15.)

The following additional information was received from the Company's Treasurer in a letter dated April 2, 1962:

> *Re: Revaluation of Assets*
>
> In 1959 our Board decided to revalue the freehold land and buildings of this company situated in the United Kingdom. Many of our factories were built prior to 1939 and their written down book value was consequently far below their current market value.

Our plant and machinery has a much shorter life and in view of our replacement policy we did not feel the necessity to revalue our plant and machinery or fixtures and fittings in our published accounts.

With regard to the specific questions you have asked, the information is as follows:

(1) Depreciation is calculated on the revalued amounts.

(2) Depreciation is deducted as an expense in arriving at the net profit for the year. We regard depreciation on current valuations as an essential cost of the business and not as an appropriation of profit.

(3) The revaluation adopted by the Board was based on a study undertaken by independent valuers. We do not revalue each year, but utilizing price indices make an assessment of the amount of appreciation which has occurred since the last independent valuation in 1959. If and when there is a reasonable difference between our book value and current valuations we will again revalue, this time using price indices for the purpose.

C-10. *Selfridges Limited*—Annual Report for the year ended January 31, 1961. (England)

Freehold land and buildings were stated in the accounts at amounts determined by professional valuers in 1960. The surplus on revaluation was credited to a capital reserve account. The remaining assets were carried at cost or revaluation amounts determined in 1940. Depreciation expense, based on the revalued assets, was deducted in determining profit for the year.

Third Group—Revaluations Based on Appraisals but With Unusual Features.

C-11. *Imperial Tobacco Company of Canada, Limited*—1961 Annual Report.

Land is carried at current market value; all other fixed assets are carried at replacement cost. Real estate values are based on appraisals made by independent appraisers as of December 31, 1960 and 1961. Machinery and equipment were valued at replacement cost by company officials. The company proposes to restate fixed assets at current replacement cost every year and to establish annually the resulting increase in capital, which is reflected in the consolidated balance sheet in a "capital increment" account. Depreciation expense, based on these replacement costs, was deducted in determining "earnings from operations." As fixed assets were retired, a portion of the "capital increment" arising from appraisals was transferred into retained earnings.

C-12. *The Broken Hill Proprietary Co., Ltd.*—Annual Report for year ended May 31, 1961. (Australia)

Fixed assets were revalued and the related depreciation reserves were adjusted by amounts agreed to by the Board of Directors after considering valuations received, possible obsolescence, and the age and condition of various units of plant. These new values established in 1960 were less than the then estimated current replacement costs. The offsetting credit was to "assets revaluation reserve account." A portion of this reserve was permanently capitalized by means of a stock dividend. Depreciation expense was not based on the recorded revalued amounts for fixed assets. Instead, it was based on estimated replacement costs, which were higher than the new book values. The credit was to the "reserve for depreciation" account.

D. COMPANIES ADJUSTING DEPRECIATION ONLY.

D-1. *Ayrshire Collieries Corporation*—1961 Annual Report. (U.S.)

Following are those sections of the report dealing with price-level adjustments:

From Consolidated Balance Sheet, p. 3.

* * * * *

	June 30, 1961	June 30, 1960
STOCKHOLDERS' EQUITY:		
Common stock, par value $3 per share, authorized 800,000 shares; issued and outstanding—774,947 and 760,034 shares, respectively	2,324,841	2,280,102
Paid-in surplus	8,000,106	7,250,728
Capital maintained by recognition of price-level depreciation (see note on statement of income)	2,587,315	2,378,391
Earned surplus	21,137,040	24,855,977
	34,049,302	36,765,198

* * * * *

From Consolidated Income Statement, p. 4.

* * * * *

	June 30, 1961	June 30, 1960
NET INCOME	3,055,388	3,719,322
Provision for price-level depreciation (see note)	208,924	195,585
NET INCOME, after deducting provision for price-level depreciation	$ 2,846,464	$ 3,523,737

211

> NOTE: The provision for price-level depreciation represents the excess of depreciation cost measured by the current purchasing power of the dollar over depreciation cost measured by the purchasing power of the dollar at the dates of acquisition or construction of the companies' depreciable property. Reference is made to the opinion of Arthur Andersen & Co. for approval of this accounting.
>
> ❖   ❖   ❖   ❖   ❖

Auditors' Report, p. 5.

To the Stockholders and Board of Directors, Ayrshire Collieries Corporation:

We have examined the consolidated balance sheet of AYRSHIRE COLLIERIES CORPORATION (a Delaware corporation) and subsidiaries as of June 30, 1961, and the related statements of income and surplus for the year then ended. Our examination was made in accordance with generally accepted auditing standards, and accordingly included such tests of the accounting records and such other auditing procedures as we considered necessary in the circumstances.

In our opinion, the accompanying financial statements referred to above present fairly the consolidated financial position of Ayrshire Collieries Corporation and subsidiaries as of June 30, 1961, and their consolidated net income for the year then ended, and were prepared in conformity with generally accepted accounting principles applied on a basis consistent with that of the preceding year.

> Generally accepted principles of accounting for cost of property consumed in operations are based on historical costs and do not recognize the effect of changes in the purchasing power of the dollar since dates of acquisition or construction of the companies' depreciable property. In our opinion, therefore, the consolidated net income for the year is more fairly presented after deducting the provision for price-level depreciation because such provision does recognize the effect of changes in the purchasing power of the dollar.

August 21, 1961   Arthur Andersen & Co.

D-2. *Iowa-Illinois Gas and Electric Company*—1960 Annual Report.

Notes to Financial Statements, p. 19.

Fair Value Depreciation

The cost depreciation expense as shown in the accompanying statement of income is computed in accordance with the general practice in the utility industry and in accordance with presently generally accepted accounting principles. However, because of the continuing increase in price levels, depreciation based on cost is not an adequate measure of the property consumed in current operations.

A 1957 decision of the Iowa Supreme Court in the case of the City of Fort Dodge vs. Iowa-Illinois Gas and Electric Company gave recognition to the inadequacies of cost depreciation and permitted the recovery, through rates charged customers, of the fair value of the property used to serve customers. Rate increases which include an allowance for fair value depreciation have subsequently been obtained in certain Iowa districts.

In June 1958, the Company began charging fair value depreciation to operating expenses based on the fair value of the property in those districts where such depreciation had been allowed in the determination of rates. An amount equivalent to revenues collected to provide fair value depreciation ($720,000 annually), after reduction for the estimated income tax on such increased revenues, or a net amount of $337,200 annually, has been credited to an account for capital maintained by recovery of fair value depreciation. This accounting has the approval of Arthur Andersen & Co. as set forth in their certificate.

Statement of Income, p. 15.

213

* * * * *

	Year Ended December 31		
	1960	*1959*	*1958*
OPERATING EXPENSES:			
Operation—			
Gas purchased	$16,016,889	$15,065,557	$12,310,992
Production and transmission	4,937,454	4,771,963	3,773,252
Distribution	2,613,206	2,535,336	2,296,509
Commercial	1,844,769	1,744,476	1,612,428
Administrative and general	2,869,742	2,750,162	2,659,139
Total operation	$28,282,060	$26,867,494	$22,652,320
Maintenance	1,604,140	1,462,986	1,439,070
Depreciation—			
Cost	3,728,233	3,476,166	3,374,554
Fair value (see note)	720,000	720,000	420,000
State, local and miscellaneous Federal taxes	4,514,609	3,800,599	3,528,712
Iowa income tax	109,259	97,649	64,810
Federal income tax	5,409,208	6,174,631	5,132,318
Deferred income taxes—			
Accelerated depreciation	535,133	447,320	382,558
Accelerated amortization	119,400	119,400	117,314
Total operating expenses	$45,022,042	$43,166,245	$37,111,656
Operating income	$ 7,511,849	$ 7,393,559	$ 6,521,826

* * * * *

Balance Sheet, p. 17.

* * * * *

	December 31	
	1960	1959
SHAREHOLDERS' EQUITY AND LIABILITIES		
SHAREHOLDERS' EQUITY:		
Common shares—authorized 2,750,000 shares, $1 par value —outstanding 2,340,804 and 2,300,292 shares, respectively, stated at	$39,710,743	$38,312,849
Undistributed earnings	8,043,607	6,621,000
Capital maintained by recovery of fair value depreciation (see note)	873,200	536,000
Premium on $4.36 series preferred shares	32,394	32,394
Preferred shares—authorized 200,000 shares, $100 par value, cumulative—		
$4.36 Series, outstanding 60,000 shares	6,000,000	6,000,000
$4.22 Series, outstanding 40,000 shares	4,000,000	4,000,000
	$58,659,944	$55,502,243

* * * * *

Accountants' Certificate, p. 14.

214

To the Directors and Shareholders of Iowa-Illinois Gas and Electric Company:

We have examined the balance sheet of IOWA-ILLINOIS GAS AND ELECTRIC COMPANY (an Illinois corporation) as of December 31, 1960, and the related statements of income and undistributed earnings for the year then ended. Our examination was made in accordance with generally accepted auditing standards, and accordingly included such tests of the accounting records and such other auditing procedures as we considered necessary in the circumstances. We previously had made a similar examination for the years ended December 31, 1958 and 1959.

 In 1958, the Company commenced collecting increased revenues in certain of its operating areas in recognition of depreciation allowed in rate proceedings on the fair value of related property. To the extent recovered in increased rates, fair value depreciation has been recorded by the Company as set forth in the notes to the financial statements. Although generally accepted accounting principles presently provide that depreciation shall be based upon cost, it is our opinion that these principles should be changed with respect to depreciation to recognize increased price levels. We approve of the practice adopted by the Company, since it results, in our opinion, in a fairer statement of income than that resulting from the application of generally accepted accounting principles. In all other respects, in our opinion, the financial statements were prepared in conformity with generally accepted accounting principles.

In our opinion, the accompanying balance sheet and statements of income and undistributed earnings present fairly the financial position of Iowa-Illinois Gas and Electric Company as of December 31, 1960, and the results of its operations for the year then ended, and were prepared on a basis consistent with that of the preceding two years.

Chicago, Illinois,   ARTHUR ANDERSEN & CO.
February 7, 1961

D-3. *Sacramento Municipal Utility District*—1957 Annual Report.

From Body of Report, p. 23.

In 1957 the District adopted, with the full approval of its independent auditors, Arthur Andersen & Co., the principle of providing depreciation based on the fair value of its property. In periods of substantial inflation or deflation, because of changes in the purchasing power of the dollar, depreciation based on cost is not a fair measure of the property consumed in operations. This principle of accounting, sometimes referred to as "price-level depreciation", recognizes that a utility should collect in revenues an amount to cover the fair value of its property consumed in operations if the real capital dedicated to the business (which for the District is its customers' equity) is to be maintained. The effect of this change in principle on net revenue for 1957 is a reduction of $665,000, which is the amount by which fair-value depreciation exceeds cost depreciation. This amount charged against revenues is reflected in the accompanying balance sheet as a credit to "Accumulated Price-Level Depreciation", a part of the "Customers' Equity Employed in the Business".

215

* * * * *

From Balance Sheet, p. 27.

* * * * *

	December 31	
	1957	*1956*
CUSTOMERS' EQUITY EMPLOYED IN THE BUSINESS:		
Accumulated price-level depreciation (Note 1)	$ 665,000	$ —
Accumulated net revenue —		
Prior to 1957	26,289,197	26,289,197
Net revenue for the year 1957	4,747,914	—
	$31,702,111	$26,289,197
	$62,496,768	$55,049,822

* * * * *

From Income Statement, p. 28.

	Year Ended December 31	
	1957	1956
OPERATING EXPENSES:		
Operation—		
Purchased power	$ 4,590,667	$ 4,370,987
Other	2,850,448	2,622,715
Maintenance	465,155	439,553
Provision for depreciation—		
‖ Computed on historical cost	1,506,624	1,262,885
➤ ‖ Additional provision to reflect increase		
‖ in price level (Note 1)	665,000	—
Amortization of intangible plant costs	—	430,856
Total operating expenses	$10,077,894	$ 9,126,996
Net operating revenue	$ 4,886,388	$ 4,717,726

* * * * *

Accountants' Certificate, p. 29.

To the Board of Directors of
Sacramento Municipal Utility District:

216

We have examined the balance sheet of SACRAMENTO MUNICIPAL UTILITY DISTRICT as of December 31, 1957, and the related statement of net revenue for the year then ended. Our examination was made in accordance with generally accepted auditing standards, and accordingly included such tests of the accounting records and such other auditing procedures as we considered necessary in the circumstances. Power bonds outstanding at December 31, 1957 (for which there are no trustees) were confirmed by direct correspondence with the paying agent. We had made a similar examination for the year ended December 31, 1956.

As set forth in Note 1 to the accompanying financial statements, the statement of net revenue reflects an additional charge for depreciation of $665,000; this charge is equivalent to the amount by which depreciation computed on the cost of depreciable property adjusted to reflect current price levels exceeds depreciation computed on cost. Although this practice is not yet recognized as a generally accepted principle of accounting, it is our opinion that, for the District, it results in a fair statement of net revenue for the year, and we have approved its adoption. In other respects, the financial statements, in our opinion, were prepared in accordance with generally accepted accounting principles applied on a basis consistent with that of the preceding year.

In our opinion, the accompanying balance sheet and statement of net revenue present fairly the financial position of Sacramento

Municipal Utility District as of December 31, 1957, and the results of its operations for the year then ended.

San Francisco, California,   ARTHUR ANDERSEN & Co.
January 30, 1958.

* * * * *

D-4. *John Summers & Sons Limited*—Annual Report for the year ended October 1, 1960. (England)

In this case, fixed assets were carried at net book value as at December 31, 1947 with subsequent additions at cost. In determining profit for the period, however, a charge was made in addition to depreciation on cost determined by reference to current replacement costs of capital assets existing at that time. The corresponding credit was to a capital reserve account.

D-5. *Joseph Lucas (Industries) Limited*—Annual Report for the year ended July 31, 1961. (England)

Fixed assets were shown at net book value on July 1, 1948 with additions since at cost. In determining profit (surplus on trading), however, depreciation was charged on the basis of replacement cost. Depreciation in excess of that attributable to historical cost (totaling 500,000 pounds) was credited to a revenue reserve: "Replacement Reserve: Buildings, Plant, and Equipment."   **217**

D-6. *Algemene Kunstzijde Unie N.V.* (United Rayon Manufacturing Corporation)—Prospectus dated December 1953. (The Netherlands)

From "Notes to Financial Statements," p. 57.

The Company follows the policy of computing provisions for depreciation of plant buildings and machinery and equipment based on estimated current replacement value. The estimated replacement value for each asset is determined basically by multiplying the historical cost by a price factor which represents the relation between the current price level and the price level in the year of acquiring the asset. The provision applicable to a specific asset is continued as long as the asset is used for productive purposes. That part of the annual provision applicable to historical cost is added to the reserve for depreciation, until the asset becomes fully depreciated, and the balance of the provision to a reserve entitled "Reserve arising from excess of depreciation based on estimated replacement value over historical cost depreciation." In order to provide for current increases in the price level applicable to depreciation provided in prior years the Company further increases the latter reserve by transferring thereto as necessary additional amounts from unappropriated earned surplus.

Fixed assets and depreciation reserves were stated in the accounts on a cost basis. Depreciation expense was reflected in the combined statements of income (p. 54), as follows:

Algemene Kunstzijde Unie N. V. and Enkalon N. V.

COMBINED STATEMENTS OF INCOME

(In Dutch florins)

	For the Year			For the Twenty-eight Weeks Ended
	1950	1951	1952	July 11, 1953
				(Unaudited)
SALES, less returns and allowances	Hfl.119,941,013	Hfl.159,268,654	Hfl.150,001,196	Hfl.94,108,412
OPERATING CHARGES:				
Cost of sales	Hfl.70,850,572	Hfl.100,012,676	Hfl.100,617,131	Hfl.60,880,511
Depreciation on historical cost basis	6,570,224	7,787,323	9,822,900	6,453,847
Excess of depreciation based on estimated replacement value over historical cost depreciation	3,959,994	4,745,894	5,301,064	2,651,654
Selling, general and administrative expenses	7,386,730	8,234,606	9,469,242	5,332,055
Preparatory costs (exclusive of amounts included in depreciation)	—	—	2,357,328	330,683
	Hfl.88,767,520	Hfl.120,780,499	Hfl.127,567,665	Hfl.75,648,750
OPERATING INCOME	Hfl.31,173,493	Hfl.38,488,155	Hfl.22,433,531	Hfl.18,459,662

218

D-7. *Wm. H. Muller Co.*—1960 Annual Report. (The Netherlands)

Fixed assets and depreciation reserves were carried at initial cost less depreciation. The replacement-value method was adopted in 1960 for "the ascertainment of the annual depreciation on ships, cranes, and establishments," with the credit going to a "replacement reserve." Replacement-value depreciation expense is deducted in determining profit for the year.

Annotated Bibliography of Cases

Table of Contents

Page

Cases From Literature

Appendix D, "Disclosing Effects of Price-Level Changes," contains a number of illustrations taken from published annual reports of domestic and foreign corporations. The literature also contains a number of actual cases where price-level adjustments of one type or another have been carried out even though they were not adopted for annual report purposes. This annotated bibliography lists those which have come to our attention together with summaries of the results, notes as to procedures followed, etc.

I. W. T. Baxter, "Inflation and the accounts of steel companies," *Accountancy* (Eng.), May 1959, pp. 250-57, and June 1959, pp. 308-14.[1]

In this survey, three steel companies were analyzed for the period 1939-47, and seven steel companies (including the three) for the period 1949-57. Company names were not revealed. The indexes used for adjustment were:

(a) Index of consumers' expenditure, average value index, in *London and Cambridge Bulletins,* published quarterly in the *Times Review of Industry.*

---

[1] Reproduced with permission of W. T. Baxter and *Accountancy.*

(b) Raw materials price index (method 4) prepared by the British Iron and Steel Federation. Figures from 1939-45 are insertions based on index of wholesale prices of manufacturers, table 287, *Annual Abstract of Statistics, 1937-47.*

(c) Index of replacement cost of industrial assets, steelworks, prepared by the *Economist* Intelligence Unit. Figures for 1939-45 are insertions based on index of wholesale prices of building materials, table 287, *Annual Abstract of Statistics, 1937-47.*

All items in the financial statements were adjusted for changes in the general level of prices using (a) above. Further adjustments were then made to reflect gains resulting from price changes in specific assets by adjusting inventories and cost of goods sold using (b) above, and fixed assets and depreciation expense using (c) above. The principal effects of adjustment, as computed by W. T. Baxter, were as follows:

A. For the three steel companies—(stabilized profits and surplus in terms of December 31, 1947 pounds):

222

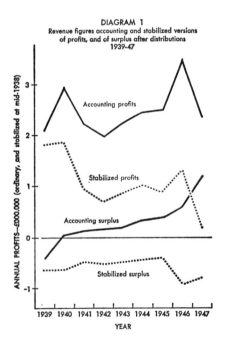

DIAGRAM 1
Revenue figures accounting and stabilized versions
of profits, and of surplus after distributions
1939-47

Accounting profits

Stabilized profits

Accounting surplus

Stabilized surplus

ANNUAL PROFITS—£000,000 (ordinary, and stabilized at mid-1938)

3

2

1

0

-1

1939 1940 1941 1942 1943 1944 1945 1946 1947

YEAR

(p. 255, May 1959 article)

B. Three versions of profits and surplus after distribution for the seven steel companies—(corrected versions in terms of September 30, 1957 pounds).

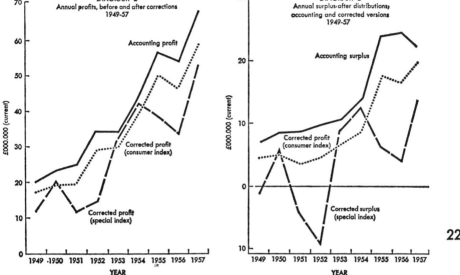

(p. 310, June 1959 article)

223

II. Bell, Albert L., "Fixed assets and current costs," *Accounting Review*, January 1953, pp. 44-53.[2]

Adjustments to Armstrong Cork Company items were for the years ended June 30, 1948, 1949, and 1950. The index used was computed as an arithmetic average of the Construction Cost Index and the Building Cost Index, both published by *Engineering News-Record*. Assets were converted to replacement values at the end of each of the three years. Depreciation expense was then based on these revised amounts. The principal effects of the adjustments (taken from the article with the figures rounded and placed in table form), as computed by Albert L. Bell, were:

---

[2] Reproduced with permission of *The Accounting Review*.

For the Year Ending June 30	Depreciation Expense		Unrecovered Value	
	Based on Cost	In Current Dollars	At Cost	In Current Dollars
1948	2,239,000	4,355,000	33,503,000	58,776,000
1949	2,628,000	4,736,000	37,792,000	62,864,000
1950	3,177,000	5,818,000	46,670,000	79,126,000

III. Bierman, Harold, Jr., "The effect of inflation on the computation of income of public utilities," *Accounting Review*, April 1956, pp. 258-62.[3]

Adjustments were made to fixed assets and depreciation expense for a group of utilities for the years 1940 and 1953 using the Wholesale Price Index of the U. S. Bureau of Labor Statistics. Items were converted into 1952 dollars for comparative purposes. The data, computed and presented by the author in the article, have been reorganized into the table on page 226.

IV. Cooper, Howard E., "Depreciation on current values is half as much again—an experimental determination," *N.A.C.A. Bulletin* (sec. 1), June 1950, pp. 1179-86.

In this study, a weighted average of two series of prices taken from the Wholesale Price Index were used: Building Materials, and Metals and Metal Products, in an attempt, primarily, to determine what the relative depreciation charge would have been had it been calculated on the basis of replacement value rather than original cost. The analysis can be broken down into the following two subdivisions:

Study of Aggregate Figures from Selected Annual Reports. The statements of thirty large industrial companies, each of whose total assets exceeded one hundred million dollars, were combined for the year 1947. For the year 1948, a group of fifty companies were similarly studied. Principal conclusion for the group was that profits for the two years would have been about 20 per cent lower had depreciation been calculated on replacement costs.

Study of an Individual Company. Fixed assets, the related reserves, and depreciation expense were converted to 1948 replacement costs. The author's major conclusions were as follows:

224

---

[3] *Ibid.*

1. Current (replacement) cost of all buildings was 69 per cent higher than original cost, while the depreciation reserve was 66 per cent higher than on original cost.

2. Current replacement cost of machinery and equipment was 42 per cent higher than original cost, while depreciation reserve was 43 per cent higher.

3. Current replacement cost of furniture and fixtures was 39 per cent higher than original cost; the depreciation reserve was also 39 per cent higher.

4. Current replacement cost of *all* fixed assets combined was 58 per cent higher than original cost, while accumulated depreciation was 49 per cent more than that based on cost.

V. Corbin, Donald A., "The impact of changing prices on a department store," *The Journal of Accountancy*, April 1954, pp. 430-40; and "A case study of price-level adjustments," *Accounting Review*, April 1955, pp. 268-81. (Both articles are concerned with the same department store, name not given.)

Adjustments covered all items of the department store's balance sheets of January 31, 1933 through January 31, 1953, and the income statements for the years ended January 31, 1934 through January 31, 1953. All items were converted into their equivalents of January 31, 1953 dollars.

Items were first adjusted using the Consumer Price Index of the U. S. Bureau of Labor Statistics. However, where the differences between these restated costs and current values of the specific items were significant, the asset values were adjusted to reflect these specific price changes. Various indexes and appraisals were used for this purpose.[4] The principal effects of adjustment, as determined by Donald A. Corbin and reported in one or the other of these two articles, follow on page 227.

---

[4] The indexes and appraisals used were
   a. Department Store Inventory Price Indexes of the U. S. Bureau of Labor Statistics.
   b. Regional Construction Cost Indexes of the American Appraisal Company.
   c. Personal property assessed valuations.
   d. An independent appraisal for insurance purposes.

226

Principal Effects of Adjustment (in $1,000)

Company	Income for Year 1953	Depreciation Charge for Year 1953	Adjustment to Depreciation	Adjusted Income for 1953	Unadjusted Income for 1953 as Per Cent of 1940 Income	Adjusted Income for 1953 as Per Cent of the Adjusted Income for 1940 converted into 1952 Dollars
1. Bangor Hydro-Electric Company	$ 1,228	$ 611	$ 313	$ 915	119.3%	40.9%
2. Carolina Telephone and Telegraph Company	2,431	1,623	90	2,341	623.2%	273.6%
3. Cleveland Electric Illuminating Company	16,897	8,509	3,589	13,308	172.6%	60.4%
4. General Telephone Company of Indiana	1,365	904	155	1,210	253.3%	95.4%
5. General Telephone Company of Pennsylvania	1,835	1,141	165	1,670	277.1%	114.9%
6. Kentucky Utilities Company	6,801	3,061	1,362	5,439	211.3%	79.2%
7. Michigan Bell Telephone Company	24,159	18,494	8,062	16,097	204.7%	59.8%
8. The Narragansett Electric Company	4,760	2,473	1,256	3,504	142.0%	70.9%
9. New Jersey Power and Light Company	2,105	1,004	367	1,738	115.1%	41.8%
10. The Peoples Gas, Light and Coke Company	8,906	4,034	2,016	6,890	174.5%	63.7%
11. Southern California Edison Company	29,800	14,900	5,800	24,000	156.8%	56.1%
12. Utah Power and Light Company	7,033	1,802	885	6,148	147.4%	57.3%
13. Wisconsin Public Service Corporation	5,767	2,623	1,162	4,605	186.2%	65.9%
14. X Power Company (a fictitious name)	31,033	13,650	5,695	25,338	197.1%	72.2%

1. The average difference over the twenty years between reported and adjusted income was 20 per cent of the reported income, with a standard deviation of 13 per cent, and a range of from 4 to 58 per cent.

2. The discrepancies in the rates of return on stockholders' equity, based on reported figures, averaged 29 per cent, with a standard deviation of 17 per cent.

3. Adjusted income tax rates exceeded reported rates by 3 to 11 per cent (averaging 7 per cent higher over the entire twenty-year period) in every postwar year except 1949, when prices fell slightly.

4. Over the twenty-year period, the dividend rate averaged 51 per cent of reported earnings and 61 per cent of adjusted earnings.

5. Through the years of rising prices, the gains from being a debtor and the losses from being a creditor amounted to several million dollars. In both 1947 and 1948 there were purchasing power losses of over a million dollars per year. The net loss for the entire twenty-year period was $1,653,000.

6. Unadjusted growth indicators, such as sales, plant, inventory and stockholders' equity overstated the company's expansion by from 50 to over 100 per cent.

VI. Dean, Joel, "Measurement of profits for executive decisions," *Accounting Review*, April 1951, pp. 185-96.[5]

Adjustments were applied to all assets on the balance sheets of General Electric Co., Radio Corporation of America, and Westinghouse Electric Corp. for the years 1935 through 1948. The assets were stated in terms of their 1935 prices by deflating each major group by means of specialized indexes;[6] the intention was to value all assets at their replacement cost in the base period. Changes in the total net assets from year-end to year-end, plus dividends, and minus new capital funds added (as adjusted for price changes), gave the "derived" adjusted net income for each year. The principal effects of adjustment (taken from a table in the article), as determined by Joel Dean, were as follows:

---

[5] Reproduced with permission of *The Accounting Review*.
[6] The indexes used were not disclosed by the author.

Total Earnings Available
For Interest and Dividends (in $1,000)

Year	General Electric Co. Per Books	General Electric Co. In Constant (1935) Dollars	Radio Corporation of America Per Books	Radio Corporation of America In Constant (1935) Dollars	Westinghouse Electric Corp. Per Books	Westinghouse Electric Corp. In Constant (1935) Dollars
1935	$ 31,020	$ 30,302	$ 5,518	$ 5,408	$ 10,802	$10,830
6	46,152	39,536	6,477	5,437	14,976	12,495
7	64,512	39,878	7,907	4,391	19,294	9,224
8	28,432	32,266	8,778	8,973	8,827	11,094
9	42,764	38,881	7,578	7,092	14,188	13,230
1940	58,539	45,630	9,253	7,437	17,709	13,441
1	60,167	32,541	10,466	5,714	21,797	8,408
2	51,637	23,660	12,094	2,010	17,912	2,567
3	50,865	30,953	16,181	5,811	25,299	11,670
4	57,544	27,764	9,747	3,576	25,701	12,024
5	58,666	22,031	11,812	5,942	28,188	10,203
6	42,385	5,604	11,216	2,485	6,896	(13,544)
7	102,681	(8,190)	19,300	(829)	51,988	(12,312)
8	201,534	58,868	24,583	5,060	53,907	2,769
Total 1935–1948	$896,898	$419,724	$160,910	$68,507	$317,484	$92,099

228 VII. Dean, Joel, "Measurement of real economic earnings of a machinery manufacturer," *Accounting Review*, April 1954, pp. 255-66.[7]

Adjustments were applied to all the assets of Machinery, Inc. (a fictitious name) for the years 1936 through 1950. The assets were stated in terms of their 1936-39 prices by adjusting each major group by means of various published price indexes;[8] the intention was to value all assets at their replacement cost in the base period. Changes in the total net assets from year-end to year-end, plus dividends and minus new capital funds added (as adjusted for price changes), gave the "derived" adjusted net income for the year.

The following charts reflect the principal effects of adjustment, as calculated and presented by Joel Dean:

[7] Reproduced with permission of *The Accounting Review*.
[8] The author did not disclose the indexes used.

Machinery, Inc. (a fictitious name)

BOOK EARNINGS VS. REAL EARNINGS

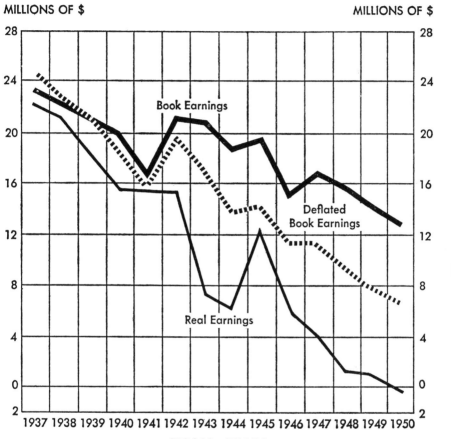

CHART 3

(p. 261)

DIVIDENDS vs. REAL EARNINGS

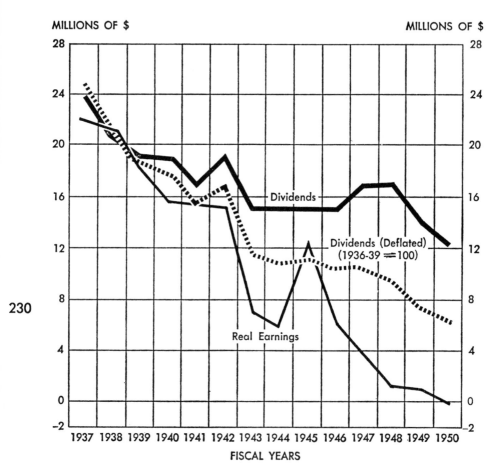

CHART 4

(p. 263)

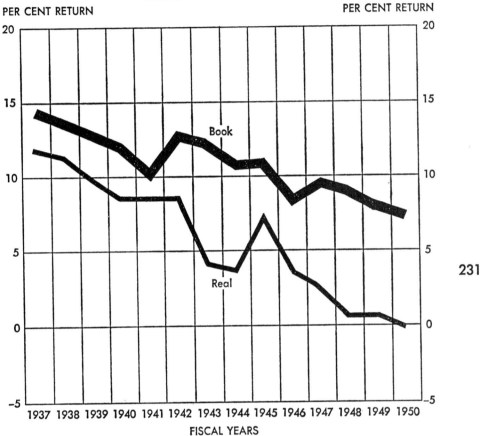

RETURN ON NET INVESTMENT
Book Return on Book Investment
vs.
Real Return on Real Investment

PER CENT RETURN

PER CENT RETURN

231

Book

Real

1937 1938 1939 1940 1941 1942 1943 1944 1945 1946 1947 1948 1949 1950

FISCAL YEARS

CHART 6

(p. 265)

VIII.   Gordon, Myron J., "The valuation of accounts at current cost," *Accounting Review*, July 1953, pp. 373-84.[9]

Adjustments were made to the XYZ Farm Equipment Corporation (a fictitious name) items for the years 1947 and 1948. The intention was to value fixed assets, inventories, cost of sales, and depreciation expenses on a replacement cost basis. The following subindexes of the Wholesale Price Index of the U. S. Bureau of Labor Statistics were used for this purpose:

1.   Agricultural Machinery and Equipment—for Inventory,

2.   A weighted average of the Building Materials, and Metals and Metal Products Indexes—for Plant and Equipment.

The principal effects of adjustment, as computed by Myron J. Gordon, have been compiled (from Exhibits 1 and 2 in the article) in the following table:

XYZ Farm Equipment Corporation
(a fictitious name)

232

	Historical Cost		Current Cost	
	1947	1948	1947	1948
Plant and Equipment, Cost	$ 90,700	$106,700	$127,300	$157,900
Allowance for Depreciation	$ 38,600	$ 42,800	$ 54,200	$ 66,400
Retained Earnings	$ 98,500	$115,300	$ 73,500	$ 81,000
Aggregate Capital Gain	—	—	$ 46,000	$ 61,900
Cost of Goods Sold (Labor and Material)	$155,100	$229,700	$168,100	$237,100
Depreciation Expense	$ 3,200	$ 4,600	$ 4,600	$ 6,500
Net Income After Taxes	$ 16,400	$ 27,100	$ 2,000	$ 17,800
Current Capital Gains: Inventory Capital Gain	—	—	$ 13,000	$ 7,400
Plant and Equipment Capital Gain	—	—	$ 10,800	$ 8,500

The author then pointed out that additional adjustments must be made to reflect the change in the purchasing power of the dollar in order to reflect real income for the period. To accomplish this, the beginning and ending net worths were adjusted, using the Consumer Price Index of the U. S. Bureau of Labor Statistics, with the following results:

---

[9] Reproduced with permission of *The Accounting Review*.

Real Income of XYZ Corporation
in Current Dollars

Account	1947	1948
(1) Net worth at start of period in prior period dollars	$162,800	$180,400
(2) General price index for current period relative to prior period*	114.3	107.5
(3) Net worth at start of period in current period dollars (1)×(2)	$186,800	$193,900
(4) Net worth at close of period plus dividends in current period dollars	$188,600	$214,100
(5) Income during period in current period dollars (4)−(3)	$ 1,800	$ 20,200

* With cost of living index for 1935-39 equal to 100, 1946 = 139.3, 1947 = 159.2, 1948 = 171.2. The index numbers used are derived from these figures.

(p. 382)

IX. Hendriksen, Eldon S., *Price-Level Adjustments of Financial Statements*, Washington State University Press. Pullman, Washington, 1961.[10]

233

In this study, fluctuations in the purchasing power of the dollar were removed by stating financial statement items in terms of December 1956 dollars in order to make inter-period comparisons possible. Adjustments were made to the balance sheets of two public utilities for the years December 31, 1936 through December 31, 1956 and to the income statements for the years 1937 through 1956. Professor Hendriksen experimented with six different indexes. Four of the tables from the study, together with brief excerpts of the discussion relating to them, are reproduced here. They are taken from Chapter 3, "The Choice of a Price Index":

> In order to compare the results of using different price indexes, the statements of Washington Water Power Company and Portland General Electric Company were adjusted on the basis of six indexes. These indexes were: (1) the Consumer Price Index (CPI), (2) the BLS Wholesale Price Index (BLS-Wholesale), (3) the GNP Implicit Price Deflator using the 1929 conversion factor for all years prior to 1929 (GNP-Constant), (4) the GNP Implicit Price Deflator using the relative change in the CPI to

---

[10] Reproduced with permission of Eldon S. Hendricksen, Washington State University.

estimate the conversion factors prior to 1929 (GNP-CPI, (5) the composite of the GNP price deflators for "other new construction" and "producers' durable equipment" (GNP-Investment), and (6) the composite of the Handy-Whitman Construction Cost Index for Electric Light and Power and the Marshall-Stevens Equipment Cost Index for Public Utilities (Public Utility Composite). The statement data used in the comparison include net income, net plant and equipment, the rate of return on total investment, the rate of return on stockholders' investment, and the dividend payout ratio.

Net Income

The average net incomes for the 20 years from 1937 to 1956 for Washington Water Power Company (WWP) and Portland General Electric Company (PGE) are summarized in Table 3.1. The unadjusted net income figures are the averages of the annual net incomes based on historical cost and converted into constant December, 1956, dollars by the appropriate index. The adjusted figures represent the averages of the net incomes adjusted for price-level changes expressed in December, 1956, dollars. The differences in the six adjusted average net incomes, therefore, are a result of two factors: (1) the adjustment of depreciation expense for price-level changes prior to the balance-sheet date and (2) the dispersions in the indexes from the balance-sheet dates to December, 1956. The averages of the ratios of the unadjusted to the adjusted figures, therefore, isolate the effect of the depreciation adjustment in the given year.

(pp. 58-9)

234

Table 3.1

Average Net Incomes for Years 1937-1956
(in thousands of December, 1956, dollars)

	Washington Water Power Company			Portland General Electric Company		
Index	*Unadjusted*	*Adjusted*	*Average Ratio Unadjusted to Adjusted*	*Unadjusted*	*Adjusted*	*Average Ratio Unadjusted to Adjusted*
(1) CPI	$4,509	$3,935	116.5%	$3,439	$2,538	136.3%
(2) BLS-Wholesale	4,767	4,222	116.8	3,582	2,671	138.6
(3) GNP-Constant prior to 1929	4,740	4,363	110.9	3,589	3,015	119.5
(4) GNP-CPI	4,740	4,003	120.8	3,589	2,430	150.6
(5) GNP-Investment Composite	5,209	4,601	116.5	3,923	3,003	133.5
(6) Public Utility Composite	5,619	4,732	123.4	4,213	2,813	159.1

(p. 60)

Net Plant and Equipment

The investment in net plant and equipment is the original cost of all plant and equipment in use, less the accumulated depreciation. When these items are adjusted for price-level changes, they reflect the purchasing power of the original investment in fixed assets and the purchasing power of the portion of this investment allocated to expense. While the residual net plant valuation does not represent the current value of the assets, it is an important item in the presentation of financial statements and in the computation of the rate of return and other ratios.

The choice of an appropriate price index is an important consideration in the computation of net plant and equipment in adjusted constant dollars. Table 3.3 presents a comparison of the average net plant in constant 1956 dollars as adjusted and unadjusted and the average ratios of the unadjusted to the adjusted figures for the six price indexes.

(pp. 65-7)

Table 3.3

Average Net Utility Plant for Years 1937-1956
(amounts expressed in millions of 1956 dollars)

Index	Washington Water Power Company			Portland General Electric Company		
	Un- adjusted	Adjusted	Average Ratio Un- adjusted to Adjusted	Un- adjusted	Adjusted	Average Ratio Un- adjusted to Adjusted
(1) CPI	$102.8	$136.6	75.0%	$ 88.9	$111.5	80.1%
(2) BLS-Wholesale	108.4	140.0	77.4	93.8	118.1	79.8
(3) GNP-Constant	108.3	128.0	85.4	93.6	110.0	86.0
(4) GNP-CPI	108.3	152.1	70.8	93.6	123.1	75.8
(5) GNP-Investment	118.2	152.1	78.1	102.4	129.7	79.7
(6) Public Utility Composite	127.1	180.2	70.6	110.0	147.9	75.0

(p. 66)

The Rate of Return

The rates of return for total equity and for stockholders' equity are dependent, in large part, on the valuation of the plant and equipment and on net income. It is not surprising, then, that the rankings of the average rates of return by the use of the several price indexes for the adjustment process should be similar to the rankings for net income and net plant. The Public Utility Composite index, which resulted in the lowest net income and the highest net plant valuation, obtained, as one would expect, the lowest average rate of return on total equity—3.6 per cent for WWP and 3.8 per cent for PGE compared with average unadjusted ratios of 6.0 and 6.2 per cent, respectively. The highest

236

Table 3.5
Average Rates of Return on Total Equity and Stockholders' Equity, 1937-1956

| | Washington Water Power Company | | | | Portland General Electric Company | | | |
| | Total Equity | | Stockholders' Equity | | Total Equity | | Stockholders' Equity | |
Index	Average Rate	Average Ratio Unadjusted to Adjusted	Average Rate	Average Ratio Unadjusted to Adjusted	Average Rate	Average Ratio Unadjusted to Adjusted	Average Rate	Average Ratio Unadjusted to Adjusted
CPI	4.0%	157%	4.2%	197%	4.1%	161%	4.2%	282%
BLS-Wholesale	4.1	159	4.4	198	4.2	165	4.7	295
GNP-Constant	4.7	137	5.2	164	4.9	135	7.3	196
GNP-CPI	3.7	174	3.8	224	3.9	170	3.7	318
GNP-INV	4.2	155	4.5	196	4.4	166	5.2	267
PU	3.6	179	3.7	240	3.8	186	3.6	375
Unadjusted	6.0	—	7.8	—	6.2	—	10.7	—

(p. 69)

average rate of return on total equity is provided by the GNP-Constant index—4.7 per cent for WWP and 4.9 per cent for PGE. These average rates for total equity and stockholders' equity are summarized in Table 3.5 for WWP and PGE.

(pp. 68-70)

Dividend Payout Ratios

The average dividend payout ratios computed from unadjusted figures and those computed by using the six conversion indexes are presented in Table 3.6 for WWP and PGE. Because consistent dividends were paid by PGE only since 1948, the averages for PGE are presented for the period 1948 to 1956 only.

Dividends are monetary in character so that the differences in payout ratios result from differences in the computation of income only. However, the net income transferred to retained earnings rather than net operating income was used in this computation. Nevertheless, the rankings of the payout ratios are very similar to the rankings of the net operating incomes of the two firms.

(p. 71)

Table 3.6

Average Dividend Payout Ratios

Index	Washington Water Power Company 1937-1956	Portland General Electric Company 1948-1956
Unadjusted	77.6%	69.0%
CPI	90.2	109.7
BLS-Wholesale	90.2	116.7
GNP-Constant	85.8	96.0
GNP-CPI	94.0	124.0
GNP-Investment	90.2	113.1
PU-Composite	95.5	144.4

(p. 71)

X.   Jones, Ralph C., *Price Level Changes and Financial Statements—Case Studies of Four Companies*, American Accounting Association, 1955.[11]

The objectives of the study were listed on Page 2:

(1) To develop and test techniques and methods for the preparation of supplementary financial statements expressed in

---

[11] Reproduced with permission of the American Accounting Association.

constant-value units, that is, in dollars of uniform purchasing power measured by a general index of prices.

(2) To compare the supplementary statements expressed in uniform dollars with the conventional statements expressed in historical dollars in order to measure the effect of inflation on companies of various types and sizes, and to determine the extent to which the conventional financial statements have been affected by the use of an unstable unit of measurement.

(3) To present quantitative data which will give business managements, individual accountants, committees of accounting associations, and governmental bodies some basis for judging the need for and the usefulness of figures and statements in dollars of uniform purchasing power.

Items for the four companies were stated in terms of December 1951 dollars to make the results comparable, using the Consumer Price Index of the U. S. Bureau of Labor Statistics. The principal effects of adjustment, as determined by Ralph C. Jones, were as follows:

238

1. *Armstrong Cork Company*, pp. 66-107; adjustments were made to the balance sheets of December 31, 1940 through December 31, 1951; and to the income statements for the years 1941 through 1951.

Résumé of Results

1941-1951	Published Statements	Adjusted Statements
Earning rate on average equity of stockholders	8.8%	4.5%
Net earnings	$92 million	$59 million
Retained earnings	$39½ million	$6½ million
Income taxes	47% of net income	58% of net income
Dividends	56% of net earnings	89% of net earnings
1951		
Total equity of stockholders, December 31, 1951	$110 million	$137 million
Working capital in 1951	59% greater than in 1941	3% less than in 1941

(p. 67)

2. *New York Telephone Company*, pp. 12-63; adjustments were made to the balance sheets of December 31, 1939, 1940 and 1945 through 1952; and to the income statements for the years 1940 and 1946 through 1952.

Results in Brief

Return on investment:

	1940	1946-1952
Book figures	6.6%	6%
Adjusted figures	7.5%	3%

	1940-1946	1947-1952
Excess of book income over adjusted income	7%	50%
Excess of real capital investment over book investment, 1946-1952		37%

Income taxes, 1946-1952:

Nominal or statutory tax rate	40.6%
Real tax rate	52.3%
Excess of the actual tax over a tax on real earnings at the nominal rate	$50 million

Depreciation deficiency, 1946-1952:

Amount	$108 million
As percentage of charges booked	35%

Earnings, dividends, and equity per share:

	Per Cent of 1940	
	Book	Adjusted
Earnings, 1952	110	34
Dividends, 1952	100	53
Equity, Dec. 31, 1952	98	51

Dividend increase required to yield 8% on real investment in common stock:

1940-1946	51%
1947-1952	78%

(p. 13)

3. *The Reece Corporation.* (See Appendix D)

4. *Sargent & Company,* pp. 145-75; adjustments were made to the balance sheets of December 31, 1928 through December 31, 1952; and to the income statements for the years 1929 through 1952.

Contrasts
Deflation—Inflation

	1929-1940	1941-1952
When computed in dollars of uniform purchasing power:	The net loss was only half as large as that computed in historical dollars	The net income was less than a third as large as that computed in historical dollars
Depreciation actually charged was:	Approximately equal to depreciation measured in uniform dollars	Lower by nearly $1,000,000 than depreciation measured in uniform dollars
Cost of goods sold (exclusive of depreciation) was:	Higher by nearly $900,000 in historical dollars than in uniform dollars	Lower by nearly $1,700,000 in historical dollars than in uniform dollars

	1929–1940	*1941–1952*
Total expenses and losses measured in uniform dollars were:	Lower than book figures by approximately $100,000 a year, or 1% of the capital employed	Higher than book figures by approximately $250,000 a year, or 3.5% of the capital employed
The average investment of stockholders, measured in uniform dollars, was:	About $400,000 higher than book figures	About $1,100,000 higher than book figures
The effective rate of income tax during profitable years only was:	Approximately the same as the nominal or statutory rate	Approximately 50% higher than the nominal or statutory rate
The difference between net income and dividends measured in uniform dollars was:	More favorable by about $1,000,000 than the difference in historical dollars	Less favorable by about $3,000,000 than the difference in historical dollars
The conventional statements did not recognize changes in the purchasing power of net monetary assets which resulted in:	A gain of nearly half a million dollars	A loss of half a million dollars

240

(p. 146)

XI.   Jones, Ralph C., "Effect of inflation on capital and profits: the record of nine steel companies." *The Journal of Accountancy*, January 1949, pp. 9-27.

The objective of the study was to eliminate the effects of changes in the purchasing power of the dollar by stating financial statement items in terms of 1935-39 dollars. Names of the companies were not given, although it was stated that they were "doing 80% of the nation's steel business." The adjustments covered balance sheets for the years ended December 31, 1940-1947; and the funds and income statements for the years 1941 through 1947. As determined by Ralph C. Jones:

Highlights and Contrasts

The Company Statements Show in Current Dollars:	*While the Purchasing-Power Statements Show in 1935-1939 Dollars:*
Dividends *earned* by a substantial margin every year.	Dividends *not earned* in any year since 1941.
Income retained to provide additional capital, $543,000,000.	Dividends, interest, and income taxes *paid out of capital*, $409,000,000.

Reported *income* for 1946 before transfers from reserves, $200,000,000.

Net income available to investors in 1947, $356,000,000.

Working capital increased 51% during seven-year period.

Working capital decreased $219,000,000 during 1946 and 1947.

Fixed assets decreased 6% during seven years.

Preferred stock decreased 12% during seven years.

Excess of depreciation cost over additions to plant, 1940-1947, $46,000,000.*

Real *loss* for 1946 before transfers from reserves, $88,000,000. (Equivalent to $123,000,000 in terms of 1946 dollars.)

Net income available to investors in 1947, $91,000,000. (Equivalent to $145,000,000 in terms of 1947 dollars.)

Working capital increased 2% during seven-year period.

Working capital decreased $394,000,000 during 1946 and 1947.

Fixed assets decreased 19% during seven years.

Preferred stock decreased 48% during seven years.

Excess of depreciation cost over additions to plant, 1940-1947, $400,000,000.*

---

* Due primarily to amortization of emergency facilities during the war period.   **241**

(p. 13)

XII.   Kennedy, Ralph D. and McMullen, Stewart Y., *Financial Statements—Form, Analysis, and Interpretation* (third edition), Richard D. Irwin, Inc., 1957, pp. 370-400.[12]

Adjustments were made to Caterpillar Tractor Company's income statements for the years 1941 through 1950 and to its balance sheets for the year ended December 31, 1950. Items were adjusted to their equivalents in terms of December 31, 1950 dollars. In commenting on the following table, the authors stated:

> In column 3, all items except fixed-dollar items have been revised, using the wholesale commodities index.[13] In column 4, inventories were adjusted, using the agricultural implements index,[14] and depreciable fixed assets were adjusted, using the Department of Commerce cost-of-construction index; all other items except fixed-dollar items were adjusted, using the wholesale commodities index. . . . In both columns 3 and 4, the ad-

---

[12] Reproduced with permission of Richard D. Irwin, Inc.
[13] U. S. Bureau of Labor Statistics.
[14] U. S. Bureau of Labor Statistics.

Caterpillar Tractor Company
Statement of Financial Position*
As of December 31, 1950
(In Millions)

			Price Indexes Applied	
	Reported Data (Un-adjusted)	Inventories Adjusted to FIFO	Wholesale Com-modities	Various
Items				
Current Assets:				
Cash	$ 6.9	$ 6.9	$ 6.9	$ 6.9
U.S. Government Securities	35.2	35.2	35.2	35.2
Receivables	34.1	34.1	34.1	34.1
Inventories:				
LIFO Basis	73.0			
FIFO Basis		78.3	80.6	80.4
Total Current Assets	$149.2	$154.5	$156.8	$156.6
Deduct: Current Liabilities:				
Payables	$ 29.4	$ 29.4	$ 29.4	$ 29.4
Federal Income Taxes	33.1	35.9	35.9	35.9
Total Current Liabilities	$ 62.5	$ 65.3	$ 65.3	$ 65.3
Net Current Assets	$ 86.7	$ 89.2	$ 91.5	$ 91.3
Prepayments	.2	.2	.2	.2
Buildings, Machinery, and Equipment	$ 84.1	$ 84.1	$106.4	$106.2
Deduct: Accumulated Depreciation	18.1	18.1	25.5	25.4
Net Book Value	$ 66.0	$ 66.0	$ 80.9	$ 80.8
Land	3.2	3.2	5.2	5.2
British Subsidiary	.3	.3	.3	.3
	$156.4	$158.9	$178.1	$177.8
Deduct: Ten-Year 2% Debentures	18.1	18.1	18.1	18.1
Net Assets	$138.3	$140.8	$160.0	$159.7
Preferred Stock	$ 25.0	$ 25.0	$ 25.0	$ 25.0
Common Stock:				
Paid in	23.2	23.2	51.3	51.3
1949 Stock Dividend	14.5	14.5 ⎫	83.7	83.4
Profit Employed in the Business	75.6	78.1 ⎭		
	$138.3	$140.8	$160.0	$159.7

242

(°Notes are not reproduced)
(p. 373)

justed common stock item represents only amounts paid in; the common stock issued as a stock dividend in 1949 has been restored to profit employed in the business. The wholesale commodities index has been applied in both cases. . . . The amounts shown as profit employed in the business were determined by ascertaining the amounts needed to balance the adjusted statements of financial position (columns 3 and 4).

With regard to the income statement, cost of goods sold is an average obtained by using the wholesale commodities index and the agricultural implements index. Depreciation expense was adjusted using the wholesale commodities index. The following results were obtained:

Caterpillar Tractor Company
Net Income, as Reported and as Adjusted
(In Millions)

Year	Reported Profits	Understatements Cost of Goods Sold	Understatements Depreci- ation	Adjusted Profits	Reported Sales Adjusted(for Com- parison)	Profits Expressed as a Percentage of Sales Adjusted	Profits Expressed as a Percentage of Sales Reported
1941	$ 7.7	$ 2.4	$ .4	$ 4.9	$ 102.0	4.8%	7.5%
1942	7.0	1.6	1.0	4.4	142.2	3.1	4.9
1943	7.6	.5	1.3	5.8	171.4	3.4	4.4
1944	7.3	.3	1.4	5.6	242.2	2.3	3.0
1945	6.5	.4	.9	5.2	230.6	2.3	2.8
1946	6.1	7.0	.3	(1.2)	128.4	(.9)	4.7
1947	13.5	6.6	.8	6.1	189.1	3.2	7.2
1948	17.5	4.6	1.2	11.7	218.0	5.4	8.0
1949	17.9	(2.2)	.8	19.3	254.9	7.6	7.0
1950	31.8	6.8	.8	24.2	337.2	7.1	9.4
	$122.9	$28.0	$8.9	$86.0	$2,016.1		
	6.1%				4.3%	100.0%	

(p. 383)

XIII. Kunkler, David L., "Fixed depreciation and flexible dollars," *N.A.A. Bulletin* (sec. 1), Aug. 1961, pp. 25-33.[15]

The depreciation expense of ABC Hosiery Mills, Inc. (a fictitious name) was adjusted to the price level of each particular year using the Consumer Price Index of the Bureau of Labor Statistics. The objec-

---

[15] Reproduced with permission of the National Association of Accountants.

tive was to adjust depreciation expense for changes in the general purchasing power of the dollar. The results, as computed by David L. Kunkler, were as follows:

ABC Hosiery Mills, Inc.
Depreciation Adjustments—1949-1959

Depreciation Provision

Year	Common-dollar	Historical Cost	Income Overstatement
1949	$ 158,513	$ 123,946	$ 34,567
1950	162,421	130,348	32,073
1951	178,438	139,375	39,063
1952	145,792	116,891	28,901
1953	117,059	97,720	19,339
1954	120,706	103,998	16,708
1955	133,146	119,942	13,204
1956	153,559	139,256	14,303
1957	158,395	140,019	18,376
1958	164,827	143,050	21,777
1959	191,728	169,891	21,837
	$1,684,584	$1,424,436	$260,148

244

The income overstatements and their effect on reported income, before Federal and state income taxes, are shown below:

ABC Hosiery Mills, Inc.
Income Adjustments—1949-1959

Year	Reported Income (Before Taxes)	Income Overstatement	Adjusted Income
1949	$ 308,732	$ (34,567)	$ 274,165
1950	540,477	(32,073)	508,404
1951	439,057	(39,063)	399,994
1952	392,007	(28,901)	363,106
1953	201,997	(19,339)	182,658
1954	222,364	(16,708)	205,656
1955	95,536	(13,204)	82,332
1956	204,799	(14,303)	190,496
1957	249,466	(18,376)	231,090
1958	233,029	(21,777)	211,252
1959	289,209	(21,837)	267,372
	$3,176,673	$(260,148)	$2,916,525

The cumulative effect of the income overstatements for the eleven-year period is 8.19 per cent of reported income before taxes or 16.38 per cent after taxes, assuming an average tax rate of 50 per cent for the period.

(p. 30)

XIV. *Large Industrial Corporation* (an unpublished study made by the company).

The purpose of the study was to remove the effects of the changing value of the dollar by stating financial statement items in terms of December 1957 dollars. Adjustments were made to the balance sheets of December 31, 1950 through December 29, 1957; and to the income statements for the years 1951 through 1957. The following table of the principal effects of adjustment was compiled from data determined and presented by the company in the report:

1951-57	As Reported	Adjusted
Consolidated Earnings	$100,273,000	$ 94,837,000
Return on Stockholders' Equity	17.8%	14.7%
Taxes	$116,184,000	$122,476,000
Provision for Depreciation and Amortization	$ 37,732,000	$ 41,607,000
Taxes, as a Per Cent of Net Income Before Taxes	54%	56% *
Net Gains on Net Current Monetary Assets 1951-57	–	$ 17,894,000
Gains on Debentures 1951-57	–	$ 3,520,000

* After purchasing power gains (losses) on net current monetary assets.

XV. McNichols, Thomas J., and Boyd, F. Virgil, "Adjustment of fixed assets to reflect price level changes," *Accounting Review*, January 1954, pp. 106-13.

Fixed assets and depreciation expense for International Harvester Company were adjusted for the years 1902-1951 using the Wholesale Commodity Price Index of the U. S. Bureau of Labor Statistics. The goal was to remove the effects of changes in the value of the dollar on these items. They were stated in terms of 1951 dollars so that cumulative results could be obtained. Additional adjustments were then made in order to show the effects of general price-level changes for the year 1951 alone. The principal results as computed by the authors were as follows:

1. The difference between the historical cost of the fixed assets and the cost adjusted to reflect price-level changes for the period 1902-1951

amounted to $181.3 million, representing a 49.2 per cent increase over the historical cost of the fixed assets at October 31, 1951.

2. The adjustment of the depreciation reserve to reflect price-level changes showed an understatement of depreciation charges of $105.6 million, representing an increase of 73.9 per cent in the adjusted reserve for depreciation over the reserve for depreciation based on historical cost.

3. The increase in fixed assets due to price-level changes for the period of October 31, 1950 to October 31, 1951 amounted to $54.9 million, an increase of 14.9 per cent over historical cost at October 31, 1950.

4. The adjusted depreciation charge for the year 1951 was $9.5 million greater, or 44.8 per cent more than the depreciation charge based on historical cost. This understatement of depreciation charges amounted to 15 per cent of the net profit figure after taxes. Using a tax rate of 52 per cent and ignoring the excess profits tax, the taxes paid on this unrealized income amounted to $4.9 million, approximately 8 per cent of the reported net income figure.

246

XVI. Ross, Clarence H., "Compensating for dollar inflation in rate regulation," *Public Utilities Fortnightly*, May 24, 1951, pp. 663-73.[16]

Adjustments were made to net telephone plant, materials and supplies, and working capital of Middle States Telephone Company of Illinois. These items were stated in terms of 1935-39 dollars using the Consumer Price Index of the U. S. Bureau of Labor Statistics, and in terms of 1939 dollars using "the price index used by the office of business economics of the U. S. Department of Commerce in 'Estimates of Gross National Product in Constant Dollars, 1929-49.' "[17] The earnings required for a 10 per cent return on present book value of the Company's common stock were also adjusted to 1935-39 and 1939 dollars using these same two indexes. The goal was to compare this return on the book value of net tangible assets with the return when the figures were stated in comparable dollars. The following table, computed and presented by the author, reflects the effects of these adjustments:

---

[16] Reproduced with permission of Public Utilities Reports, Inc.

[17] Department of Commerce, *Survey of Current Business*, Jan. 1951.

	Per Books	1935-39 Dollars	1939 Dollars
Net Telephone Plant in Service 10/31/50	$5,942,405.21	$3,955,350.16	$3,777,531.69
Materials and Supplies	231,866.60	134,026.94	126,703.06
Working Capital	111,118.90	64,230.58	60,720.71
Total	$6,285,390.71	$4,153,607.68	$3,964,955.46
Earnings Requirement	$ 363,035.95	$ 209,847.37	$ 198,380.03
Per Cent Return	5.78%	5.05%	5.00%

XVII. Sweeney, H. W., *Stabilized Accounting*, Harper & Row (formerly Harper & Brothers) 1939, pp. 54-168.[18]

The study was basically concerned with removing the effects of fluctuations in the general purchasing power of the dollar, using a price index compiled under the auspices of the Federal Reserve Bank of New York. The following tables reflecting the principal effects of adjustment were compiled from data determined and presented by the author:

1. *Mill Agents, Inc.* (a fictitious name)—adjustments were made to the balance sheets of September 30, 1929 through September 30, 1931; and to the income and funds statements for the years ended September 30, 1930 and 1931. All items were converted to dollars of uniform **247** purchasing power as of the close of the particular year involved.

	Unadjusted	Adjusted
Net Income (Loss), Including Gains and Losses on Monetary Items:		
Year Ended: 9/30/30	$ 70,020.80	$ 191,850.90
9/30/31	($ 112,049.70)	38,363.35
Stockholders' Equity:		
At: 9/30/29	$1,354,655.43	$1,355,788.21
9/30/30	$1,324,676.23	$1,323,963.88
9/30/31	$1,162,626.53	$1,160,378.25
Dividends as a Percentage of Net Income:		
Year Ended 9/30/30 only	143%	51%
Net Income (Loss), Including Gains and Losses on Monetary Items, as a Percentage of Average Total Assets:		
Year Ended: 9/30/30	3.4%	9.9%
9/30/31	(7.2%)	2.6%

---

[18] Reproduced with permission of Henry W. Sweeney and Harper & Row, Publishers.

2. *Prairie Water Works* (a fictitious name)—adjustments were made to the balance sheets of October 31, 1928 and 1929; and to the income and funds statements for the year ended October 31, 1929. Items were converted to dollars of uniform purchasing power as of the close of the particular year involved.

	Unadjusted	Adjusted
Net Income, Including Gains and Losses on Monetary Items	$ 5,070.66	$ 3,548.53
Stockholders' Equity at:		
10/31/28	$129,570.63	$142,852.70
10/31/29	$129,257.51	$141,105.00
Dividends as a percentage of Net Income:		
Year Ended 10/31/29 only	130%	183%
Net Loss, Including Gains and Losses on Monetary Items, as a Percentage of Average Total Assets:		
Year Ended 10/31/29 Only	3.9%	2.5%

248

3. *The Williams Mills* (a fictitious name)—adjustments were made to the balance sheets of July 31, 1928 and 1929; and to the income and funds statement for the year ended July 31, 1929. Items were converted to dollars of uniform purchasing power as of the close of the particular year involved.

	Unadjusted	Adjusted
Net Loss, Including Gains and Losses on Monetary Items	$ 82,746.41	$ 70,065.72
Stockholders' Equity at:		
7/31/28	$300,739.16	$322,854.67
7/31/29	205,003.21	249,701.01
Dividends (Including Preferred) as a Percentage of Net Loss:		
Year Ended 7/31/29 only	17%	20%
Net Loss, Including Gains and Losses on Monetary Items, as a Percentage of Average Total Assets:		
Year Ended 7/31/29 Only	9.7%	7.8%

XVIII. Warner, George H., "Depreciation on a current basis," *Accounting Review*, Oct. 1954, pp. 628-33.[19]

Adjustments were made for five diversified companies for the years 1938 through 1951, using the Consumer Price Index of the Bureau of Labor Statistics. Items were stated in terms of current dollars for each particular year. The goal was to restate the depreciation charge in terms of current dollars of equal purchasing power. The percentage reductions (increases) in each year's income after taxes, as computed by George H. Warner, were:

Percentage Reduction (*Increase) in Net Income After Taxes Depreciation Adjusted to Reflect Changes in Price Levels

	Consolidated Gas, Electric, Light, and Power Company of Baltimore, Md.	United States Steel Corporation	California Packing Company	Chrysler Corporation	Sears Roebuck and Company
1938	1*	12[1]	1[1]	1*	0
1939	1*	5*	2*	1*	1*
1940	1*	2*	1*	1*	1*
1941	2	2	1	1	1
1942	9	22	5	6	3
1943	17	37	7	6	5
1944	20	23	8	6	5
1945	23	22	10	4	5
1946	23	20	5	6	6
1947	37	26	9	7	5
1948	41	51	14	6	4
1949	33	40	14	4	3
1950	31	25	8	4	2
1951	37	32	22	9	2

249

[1] Experienced net operating loss for the year.

(p. 633)

---

[19] Reproduced with permission of *The Accounting Review*.

Comments of Herbert E. Miller

Mr. Miller does not favor reporting the net gain or loss on monetary items, "as a component part of the calculation of net income for the period," as permitted by the study. He concurs that the net gain or loss on monetary items should not be "buried" in the owners' equity, but questions the wisdon of recommending that the disclosure should be located on the face of the income statement "either as the last element in or immediately following the calculation of net income."

250

Comments of Russell Morrison

I concur in this research report except in one respect—the treatment of inflation gains on long-term debt, a monetary liability. The report recognizes that there may be differences of opinion as to the method of reporting inflation gains or losses on monetary items, but appears to favor showing them at the bottom of the income statement as special credits below net profit for the year (Appendix B, pages 126 and 128), with the last line described as "Net profit *and* net inflation gain (loss)." This, in effect, treats these items as direct credits or charges to retained earnings, with the result that no portion of the inflation gains or losses ever enters into the determination of net profit.

The purchasing power of the monetary unit is constantly changing, and where accounting recognition is given to the changes (as I believe is essential to fair financial reporting, where the effect is significant), the gain or loss on short-term monetary items is a current-period factor that should enter into the determination of net profit for the period. For instance, assume that a monetary asset of $100,000 cash was held at the beginning and at the end of the year, and that there was a 10 per cent rise in price level during the year. Clearly there was a purchasing power loss of $10,000 that should be deducted in arriving at net profit for the year.

However, the inflation gain on long-term debt in a period of rising price levels calls for different treatment. Ordinarily, the funds obtained by long-term borrowings are invested largely in long-term nonmonetary assets, and to that extent the inflation gain is an adjustment of cost that should be deferred and taken into income on some reasonable basis over the useful life of the related assets in order to obtain a proper matching of costs and revenues. Suppose that a piece of equipment with an estimated useful life of ten years was purchased for $100,000 and financed entirely with long-term debt maturing $10,000 a year, which is equivalent to the depreciation of $10,000 a year, thus providing a full hedge against the effect of inflation. Then suppose that in the first year the price-level doubled, resulting in an inflation gain of $100,000 on the long-term debt (a monetary liability). Would it be appropriate to take the $100,000 inflation gain into retained earnings at once, while spreading the $100,000 price-level increase applicable to the equipment over the remaining ten years at $10,000 a year as increased depreciation? Clearly not! The common-sense treatment would be to defer the inflation gain on the long-term debt and take it into income over the ten years to offset the increased depreciation that would arise from the price-level increase in the equipment. While this may be an oversimplified illustration, it does point up the practical relation between the inflation gain on debt and the assets financed thereby.

In the above comments, I have dealt with (a) short-term monetary items (both assets and liabilities), and (b) long-term debt, since the research report considers them in these two categories. However, all of the liabilities, both current and long-term together, constitute the total pool of borrowed funds used in the business. Therefore, it would be more appropriate (as developed in the memorandum, "Accounting for Gains and Losses in Purchasing Power of Monetary Items," appearing on pages 153 to 165) to deal with the inflation gain on all of the liabilities in relation to assets financed thereby. The inflation gain on that portion of the liabilities invested in monetary assets would go to current income as a reduction of the inflation loss on such assets; and the gain on the portion invested in nonmonetary assets (mainly inventories and property) would be absorbed into income as the cost of these assets flowed into operations.

Comments of Robert C. Tyson

Although I have no aversion to the conduct of "fundamental" research, I believe that research documents widely distributed to the members of the practicing accounting profession and to industry should be directed toward "applied" research. In other words, I feel that an academic approach, such as the subject study, will contribute toward a growing image of the profession as divided within itself with impractical and complex tendencies. Since I believe no amount of disclaimers can divorce research studies from the American Institute of Certified Public Accountants in the public mind, I do not recommend publication in its present form.

It is stated that "The purpose of price-level adjustments . . . is to express each item on the financial statements in terms of . . . a dollar of the same general purchasing power. Such figures can logically be compared and meaningful conclusions can be drawn from them."

I am not opposed to issuance of supplemental income statements giving effect to price-level changes on the basis I shall briefly outline below. In fact, on that basis I would favor moving toward inclusion of such adjustment in the formal income statement. However, restatement of the balance sheet, supplementally or otherwise, may be of doubtful usefulness. Current dollar values are not realizable even in liquidation of the company. They represent added costs as they flow through earnings, so that a fantastically increased "equity" value in the balance sheet may indeed be misleading to the enthusiastic investor.

Further, I believe that the adoption of an all inclusive restatement, as set forth in the study, will result in confusion.

The main items entering into the determination of income are:

1. Sales of Products and Services

2. Employment Costs

3. Products and Services Bought

4. Depreciation

5. Interest

6. Taxes

For any practical purpose, all such items are expressed in the current dollars received or spent therefor with the only exceptions being any effects of inventory valuation and the write-off of depreciation. Why then unduly complicate everything. Let's examine practical means of adjusting for those two important cost elements.

Again, as stated before, needless confusion will be introduced if the proposed restatement of all items of the balance sheet is adopted. The balance sheet shows, in current dollars, the proper figures at the balance-sheet date for cash, receivables, and debts. The only material items which may not be so reflected are inventories, investments and properties (and related long-term deferred items). If such restatement is desirable at all, why not concentrate on determining what adjustments should be made to those items. Any changes in the values of such items are an automatic revision of the stated equity.

If logical treatment of those few items is made, the accounting profession will progress toward the stated objective of accurate measurement of the results of operation and of the financial condition rather than further confusing the practical world of investors.

Selected Bibliography

(The following items were selected primarily for their relevance to this research project. No attempt has been made to trace ideas to their sources or to compile a definitive bibliography on the topics covered in the report. With a few exceptions, general reference works, including textbooks and handbooks, have been omitted.)

AMERICAN ACCOUNTING ASSOCIATION COMMITTEE ON CONCEPTS AND STANDARDS. *Supplementary Statement No. 2*, "Price level changes and financial statements," Aug. 1, 1951. Also in *Accounting Review*, Oct. 1951, pp. 468-74; and *Journal of Accountancy*, Oct. 1951, pp. 461-65.

AMERICAN INSTITUTE OF CERTIFIED PUBLIC ACCOUNTANTS, TECHNICAL SERVICES DEPARTMENT. "Opinion survey on price-level adjustment of depreciation," *Journal of Accountancy*, Apr. 1958, pp. 36-43.

ARTHUR ANDERSEN & CO., *Accounting and Reporting Problems of the Accounting Profession*, "Price-level depreciation." (Privately printed.) Sept. 1960.

ASSOCIATION OF CERTIFIED AND CORPORATE ACCOUNTANTS. *Observations on Recommendation XV of the Institute of Chartered Accountants in England and Wales on Accounting in Relation to Changes in the Purchasing Power of Money*. London: Association of Certified and Corporate Accountants. Dec. 1953. Also in *Accountants Journal* (Eng.), Jan. 1954, pp. 3-5; and *Accountant* (Eng.), Jan. 16, 1954, pp. 76-78.

ASSOCIATION OF CERTIFIED AND CORPORATE ACCOUNTANTS, TAXATION AND RESEARCH COMMITTEE. *Accounting for Inflation; a Study of Techniques Under Conditions of Changing Price Levels*. London: Gee and Co., Ltd., June 1952.

BAILEY, GEORGE D., "Economic restrictions on earnings determined under present accounting conventions," *Journal of Accountancy*, Jan. 1949, pp. 77-80.

BAXTER, W. T., "Accountants and the inflation," *Accountant* (Eng.), June 4, 1949, pp. 456-61.

BAXTER, W. T., "Inflation and the accounts of steel companies," *Accountancy* (Eng.), May 1959, pp. 250-57; and June 1959, pp. 308-14.

BEDFORD, NORTON M., "Accounting measurements of economic concepts," *Journal of Accountancy*, May 1957, pp. 56-62.

BIERMAN, HAROLD, JR., "Effect of inflation on the computation of income of public utilities," *Accounting Review*, Apr. 1956, pp. 258-62.

BLACKIE, WILLIAM, "What is accounting accounting for—now?" *N.A.C.A. Bulletin*, sec. 1, July 1, 1948, pp. 1349-78.

BLOUGH, CARMAN G., editor, Accounting and Auditing Problems, "Depreciation not a provision for replacements," *Journal of Accountancy*, July 1958, pp. 78-79.

BLOUGH, CARMAN G., editor, Accounting and Auditing Problems, "Dutch deal with U.S. depreciation," *Journal of Accountancy*, Aug. 1958, pp. 77-78.

BLOUGH, CARMAN G., "Depreciation—to measure income or to provide funds for replacement?" *N.A.A. Bulletin*, sec. 3, Aug. 1959, pp. 47-55.

BLOUGH, CARMAN G., editor, Accounting and Auditing Problems, "More about depreciation not a provision for replacements," *Journal of Accountancy*, Dec. 1958, pp. 73-74.

BLOUGH, CARMAN G., *Practical Applications of Accounting Standards*. American Institute of Certified Public Accountants. 1957.

"BLS consumer price index," ¶ 56,100 of *Labor Law Reporter, Union Contracts Arbitration 1*. Commerce Clearing House, Inc. 1960.

BONBRIGHT, JAMES C., "Public utility rate control in a period of price inflation," *Land Economics*, Feb. 1951, pp. 16-23.

BOULDING, KENNETH E., *Economic Analysis*, third edition. Harper & Row. 1955. Especially Chapter 38.

BOWERS, RUSSELL, "Business profit and the price level," *Accounting Review*, Apr. 1951, pp. 167-78.

BOWERS, RUSSELL, "Objections to index number accounting," *Accounting Review*, Apr. 1950, pp. 149-55.

BOWS, ALBERT J., "The urgent need for accounting reforms," *N.A.A. Bulletin*, sec. 1, Sept. 1960, pp. 43-52.

BRAY, F. SEWELL, "English accountant agrees with proposal to state current costs," (excerpts from the Accountant (Eng.), Sept. 11, 1948), *Journal of Accountancy*, Dec. 1948, pp. 478-81.

BRAY, F. SEWELL, *The Measurement of Profit*. Oxford University Press. 1949.

BRENNAN, MICHAEL J., *Preface to Econometrics*. South-Western Publishing Company. 1960.

BROAD, SAMUEL J., "Cost: Is it a binding principle or just a means to an end?" *Journal of Accountancy*, May 1954, pp. 582-86.

BROAD, SAMUEL J., "Development of accounting standards to meet changing economic conditions," *Journal of Accountancy*, May 1949, pp. 378-89.

BROAD, SAMUEL J., "Effects of price level changes on financial statements," *N.A.C.A. Bulletin*, sec. 1, July 1, 1948, pp. 1329-48.

BROWN, E. CARY, *Effects of Taxation—Depreciation Adjustments for Price Changes.* Harvard University. 1952.

BRUMBAUGH, MARTIN A., KELLOGG, LESTER S., and GRAHAM, IRENE J., *Business Statistics,* Chapter XIX, "Index numbers." Richard D. Irwin, Inc. 1949.

CANNING, JOHN B., *The Economics of Accountancy; a Critical Analysis of Accounting Theory.* Ronald Press Co. 1929.

CARMAN, LEWIS A., "Profits and the elastic dollar," *Journal of Accountancy,* June 1934, pp. 432-39.

CARSON, A. B., "Fund-change-statement approach to the calculation of inflationary distortion in conventional income measurements," *Accounting Review,* July 1954, pp. 373-82.

CASTENHOLZ, WILLIAM B., "Accountant and changing monetary values," *Accounting Review,* Dec. 1931, pp. 282-88.

CHAMBERS, R. J.,"Accounting and inflation," *Australian Accountant,* Jan. 1952, pp. 14-23.

CHAMBERS, R. J., "Accounting and shifting price levels," *Australian Accountant,* Sept. 1949, pp. 313-20.

CLAGUE, EWAN, "Comment" on "Food prices and the Bureau of Labor Statistics" by William H. Kruskal and Lester G. Telser, *Journal of Business,* July 1960, pp. 280-84.

COOPER, W. W., "Index-number adjustments of financial statements," *Illinois Certified Public Accountant,* Sept. 1950, pp. 15-23.

CORBIN, DONALD A., "Accounting and rising prices in a student cooperative," *Accounting Review,* Oct. 1951, pp. 568-72.

CORBIN, DONALD A., "Analysis of financial statements during inflation," *Analysts Journal,* Nov. 1956, pp. 73-79.

CORBIN, DONALD A., "Case study of price-level adjustments," *Accounting Review,* Apr. 1955, pp. 268-81.

CORBIN, DONALD A., "Current replacement costs," (corresp.), *Journal of Accountancy,* Dec. 1960, pp. 27-29.

CORBIN, DONALD A., "Impact of changing prices on a department store," *Journal of Accountancy,* Apr. 1954, pp. 430-40.

COUGHLAN, JOHN W., "Accounting and changing prices," *Accounting Review,* Oct. 1956, pp. 646-47.

COUGHLAN, JOHN W., "Applicability of the realization principle to money claims in common dollar accounting," *Accounting Review,* Jan. 1955, pp. 103-13.

COUGHLAN, JOHN W., "Two approaches to the problem of changing prices," *Journal of Accountancy,* Aug. 1957, pp. 42-47.

COUTTS, W. B., "Accounting for price level changes; appraisal of theoretical techniques," *Canadian Chartered Accountant,* Jan. 1961, pp. 60-65.

DAVIDSON, SIDNEY, and YASUBA, YASUKICHI, "Asset revaluation and income taxation in Japan," *National Tax Journal,* Mar. 1960, pp. 45-58.

DEAN, ARTHUR H., "Impact of changing price levels on rate making," *Public Utilities Fortnightly,* Dec. 3, 1953, pp. 817-36.

DEAN, ARTHUR H., "Inquiry into the nature of business income under present price levels." Revision of a paper read before the Study Group on Business Income. Feb. 1949.

DEAN, ARTHUR H., "Provision for capital exhaustion under changing price levels," *Harvard Law Review,* June 1952, pp. 1339-60.

DEAN, ARTHUR H., "Relation of law and economics to the measurement of income," *Accounting Review,* July 1953, pp. 328-42.

DEAN, JOEL, "Measurement of profits for executive decisions," *Accounting Review,* Apr. 1951, pp. 185-96.

DEAN, JOEL, "Measurement of real economic earnings of a machinery manufacturer," *Accounting Review,* Apr. 1954, pp. 255-66.

DEAN, JOEL, "Method of measuring real economic earnings and net investment," published separately by Council for Technological Advancement, Chicago, Ill., Jan. 1953, 15 p.

DEIN, RAYMOND C., "Price-level adjustments: fetish in accounting," *Accounting Review,* Jan. 1955, pp. 3-24.

DEIN, RAYMOND C., "Price level adjustments: rejoinder to Professor Husband," *Accounting Review,* Jan. 1956, pp. 58-63.

DE JANOSI, PETER E., "A note on provisional estimate of the gross national product and its major components," *Journal of Business,* Oct. 1961, pp. 495-99.

Depreciation Policy and the Postwar Price Level. Machinery and Allied Products Institute. Apr. 1947.

"Depreciation and the price level"; a symposium, by JAMES L. DOHR, W. A. PATON, MAURICE E. PELOUBET, WILLIAM H. BELL, HOWARD C. GREER, and ERIC L. KOHLER. *Accounting Review,* Apr. 1948, pp. 115-36.

DOHR, JAMES L., "Cost and value," *Journal of Accountancy,* Mar. 1944, pp. 193-96.

DOHR, JAMES L., "Limitations on the usefulness of price level adjustments," *Accounting Review,* Apr. 1955, pp. 198-205.

DOHR, JAMES L., "The next step in depreciation accounting," *Journal of Accountancy,* Feb. 1950, pp. 114-19.

DOHR, JAMES L., "Price and cost," *Journal of Accountancy,* Jan. 1947, pp. 11-15.

EDWARDS, EDGAR O., "Depreciation policy under changing price levels," *Accounting Review,* Apr. 1954, pp. 267-80.

EDWARDS, EDGAR O., and BELL, PHILIP W., *The Theory and Measurement of Business Income.* University of California Press. 1961.

Effects of Depreciation Policy, Studies in Business Economics Number Twenty-two, pp. 9-14, "Economic vs. accounting income." National Industrial Conference Board, Inc. 1950.

ENGELMANN, KONRAD, "Realization basis of determining income would eliminate distortions caused by inflation," *Journal of Accountancy*, Oct. 1950, pp. 321-23.

EPPS, MAX I., "Realistic accounting under South American inflation," *Journal of Accountancy*, Jan. 1961, pp. 67-73.

EPPS, MAX I., "Realistic accounting with changing money values." Talk given before Abacus Society, Sao Paulo, Brazil, Apr. 1957.

FERGUSSON, D. A., "Accounting and the price level," *Accounting Review*, Oct. 1954, pp. 639-42.

FISHER, IRVING, *The Making of Index Numbers*, third edition, revised. Houghton Mifflin Company. 1927.

FISHER, IRVING, *The Money Illusion*. Adelphi Company. 1928.

FISHER, IRVING, *The Nature of Capital and Income*. Macmillan Company. 1906.

FITZGERALD, A. A., "Accounting and price level changes," *Australian Accountant*, Apr. 1950, pp. 129-47.

FITZGERALD, A. A., *Current Accounting Trends*, Chapter 4, "Accounting and price-level changes," Butterworth & Co. (Australia) Ltd. 1952.

FRISBEE, IRA N., "The determination of net income," *New York Certified Public Accountant*, July 1958, pp. 475-85.

GARCIA, LEVERNE W., "What are CPA's doing about the effect of price level changes on financial statements?" *California Certified Public Accountant*, Nov. 1952, pp. 8-12.

GILBERT, MILTON, "The problem of quality changes and index numbers," *Monthly Labor Review*, Sept. 1961, pp. 992-97.

GILBERT, MILTON, "Quality change and index numbers: the reply," *Monthly Labor Review*, May 1962, pp. 544-45.

GILMAN, STEPHEN, *Accounting Concepts of Profit*. Ronald Press Co. 1939.

GORDON, MYRON J., "Valuation of accounts at current cost," *Accounting Review*, July 1953, pp. 373-84.

GORDON, R. A., "Differential changes in the prices of consumers' and capital goods," *American Economic Review*, Dec. 1961, pp. 937-57.

GOUDEKET, A., "Application of replacement value theory," *Journal of Accountancy*, July 1960, pp. 37-47.

GOUDEKET, A., "How inflation is being recognized in financial statements in the Netherlands," *Journal of Accountancy*, Oct. 1952, pp. 448-52.

Government Price Statistics, part I. Hearings before the Subcommittee on Economic Statistics of the Joint Economic Committee, Eighty-Seventh Congress, first session. Jan. 24, 1961.

GRADY, PAUL, "Accounting developments relating to price-level changes," *Proceedings, National Conference of Electric and Gas Utility Accountants*, pp. 354-73. 1952.

GRADY, PAUL, "Conservation of productive capital through recognition of current cost of depreciation," *Accounting Review*, Oct. 1955, pp. 617-22.

GRADY, PAUL, "Depreciation—to measure income or to provide funds for replacement," *N.A.A. Bulletin*, sec. 3, Aug. 1959, pp. 56-63.

GRADY, PAUL, "Economic depreciation in income taxation and in accounting," *Journal of Accountancy*, Apr. 1959, pp. 54-60.

GRADY, PAUL, "Proposal for the adoption of standards of disclosure for changing price levels," *Journal of Accountancy*, Nov. 1952, pp. 565-69.

GRADY, PAUL, "Replacement value theory," (corresp.), *Journal of Accountancy*, Aug. 1960, p. 27.

GRAHAM, ROBERT F., "Valuation for profit determination," *Accounting Review*, June 1940, pp. 145-65.

GRAHAM, WILLARD J., "Defining income," (corresp.), *Journal of Accountancy*, Aug. 1960, pp. 28-31.

GRAHAM, WILLARD J., "Effect of changing price levels upon the determination, reporting, and interpretation of income," *Accounting Review*, Jan. 1949, pp. 15-26.

GRAHAM, WILLARD J., *Public Utility Valuation—Reproduction Cost as a Basis for Depreciation and Rate-Base Determination*. Studies in Business Administration. University of Chicago. 1934.

GREER, HOWARD C., and WILCOX, EDWARD B., "Case against price-level adjustments in income determination," *Illinois Certified Public Accountant*, Sept. 1950, pp. 1-14.

GRIFFITH, DONALD K., "Weaknesses of index-number accounting," *Accounting Review*, June 1937, pp. 123-32.

GRILICHES, ZVI, "Quality change and index numbers: a critique," *Monthly Labor Review*, May 1962, pp. 542-44.

GYNTHER, R. S., "Accounting for price-level changes," *Accountancy* (Eng.), July 1962, pp. 560-4.

HENDRIKSEN, ELDON S., *Price-Level Adjustments of Financial Statements; an Evaluation and Case Study of Two Public Utility Firms*. Washington State University Press. 1961.

HENKEL, GEORGE E., "Replacement value theory," (corresp.), *Journal of Accountancy*, Sept. 1960, p. 33.

HERRICK, ANSON, "Inflation in accounting," *Journal of Accountancy*, Sept. 1960, pp. 51-56.

HERRICK, ANSON, "Procedures to avoid the noncomparability of comparative income statements," *Arthur Young Journal*, Apr. 1959, pp. 1-9.

HIGGINS, THOMAS G., "Financial statements and inflation," *New York Certified Public Accountant*, Mar. 1960, pp. 169-79; and *Ohio CPA*, Autumn 1960, pp. 153-62.

HIGGINS, THOMAS G., "New look at historical costs vs. current costs," *Arthur Young Journal*, Oct. 1954, pp. 1-17.

HIGGINS, THOMAS G., "Why is there still reluctance to adjust financial statements for the effects of inflation?" *Arthur Young Journal*, Oct. 1959, pp. 1-14.

Hill, Thomas M., "Analysis of supplementary statement no. 2," *Accounting Review*, Jan. 1952, pp. 16-24.

Hofsten, Erland v., *Price Indexes and Quality Changes*. London: George Allen & Unwin Ltd. 1952.

Hoover, Ethel D., "The CPI and problems of quality change," *Monthly Labor Review*, Nov. 1961, pp. 1175-85.

Horngren, Charles T., "Depreciation, flow of funds and the price level," *Analysts Journal*, Aug. 1957, pp. 45-47.

Horngren, Charles T., "Security analysts and the price level," *Accounting Review*, Oct. 1955, pp. 575-81.

Husband, George R., *Accounting—Its Nature and Functions*, pp. 205-35, "Changing monetary-measurement significance and the accounting statements." Chilton Co. 1959.

Husband, George R., "Professor Dein, Mr. Alexander and supplementary statement no. 2," *Accounting Review*, July 1955, pp. 383-99.

Institute of Chartered Accountants in England and Wales, *Recommendations on Accounting Principles: XV—Accounting in Relation to the Changes in the Purchasing Power of Money*. London: Gee and Co., publishers) Ltd., May 30, 1952. Also in *Accountant* (Eng.), May 31, 1952, pp. 577-82; and *Journal of Accountancy*, Aug. 1952, pp. 220-25, under title "Accounting principles regarding changes in purchasing power issued by British chartered accountants."

Institute of Chartered Accountants in England and Wales, "Rising prices and accounts," *Accountancy* (Eng.), Feb. 1949, p. 37.

Institute of Cost and Works Accountants. *Accountancy of Changing Price Levels*. London: Institute of Cost and Works Accountants. Mar. 1952.

Jones, Ralph C., "Effect of inflation on capital and profits: the record of nine steel companies," *Journal of Accountancy*, Jan. 1949, pp. 9-27.

Jones, Ralph C., *Effects of Price Level Changes on Business Income, Capital, and Taxes*. American Accounting Association. 1956.

Jones, Ralph C., "Financial statements and the uncertain dollar," *Journal of Accountancy*, Sept. 1935, pp. 171-97.

Jones, Ralph C., *Price Level Changes and Financial Statements—Case Studies of Four Companies*. American Accounting Association. 1955.

Kane, John E., "Relationship between depreciation allowance and maintenance of capital during inflation," *Journal of Accountancy*, Dec. 1952, pp. 697-701.

Kane, John E., "Structural changes and general changes in the price level in relation to financial reporting," *Accounting Review*, Oct. 1951, pp. 496-502.

Kennedy, Ralph D., and McMullen, Stewart Y., *Financial Statements— Form, Analysis, and Interpretation*, third edition, chapters XVII-XXI. Richard D. Irwin, Inc. 1957.

KOLLARITSCH, FELIX P., "Austria's answer to inflationary profits and taxation," *Accounting Review*, July 1961, pp. 439-45.

KOLLARITSCH, FELIX P., "Replacement values in practice—the example of Austria," *N.A.A. Bulletin*, sec. 1, Aug. 1961, pp. 35-46.

LACEY, K., *Profit Measurement and Price Changes*. London: Isaac Pitman and Sons, Ltd. 1952.

LANHAM, JAMES S., "Financial statements converted into current dollars should be presented along with statement in historical dollars," *Journal of Accountancy*, June 1950, pp. 519-21.

LITTLETON, A. C., "The principle of irrelevant effects," *Illinois Certified Public Accountant*, Mar. 1954, pp. 21-24.

LITTLETON, A. C., *Structure of Accounting Theory*. American Accounting Association. 1953.

MACHINERY AND ALLIED PRODUCTS INSTITUTE. "Underdepreciation from inflation," *Capital Goods Review*, Apr. 1961, pp. 1-4.

MACNEAL, KENNETH, *Truth in Accounting*. University of Pennsylvania Press. 1939.

MACNEILL, JAMES H., "Accounting for inflation abroad; study of government—approved applications of price-level accounting in twelve different countries," *Journal of Accountancy*, Aug. 1961, pp. 67-73.

MANRARA, LUIS V., "We are dragging our anchor—the drift from historical cost," *N.A.C.A. Bulletin*, sec. 1, Nov. 1949, pp. 243-52.

MARRIS, ROBIN, *Economic Arithmetic*. London: Macmillan & Co., Ltd. 1958.

MASON, PERRY, *Price-Level Changes and Financial Statements—Basic Concepts and Methods*. American Accounting Association. 1956.

MAY, GEORGE O., "Business income and price levels—an accounting study," (unpublished manuscript).

MAY, GEORGE O., "Should the LIFO principle be considered in depreciation accounting when prices vary widely?" *Journal of Accountancy*, Dec. 1947, pp. 453-56.

MAY, GEORGE O., "Valuation or historical cost: some recent developments," *Journal of Accountancy*, Jan. 1940, pp. 14-21.

MATHEWS, RUSSELL, and GRANT, JOHN, McB., *Inflation and Company Finance*. Sydney: Law Book Co. of Australasia Pty. Ltd. 1958.

McANLY, HERBERT T., "LIFO for both inventory and plant assets," *N.A.A. Bulletin*, sec. 1, Aug. 1961, pp. 5-17.

McMULLEN, STEWART YARWOOD, "Depreciation and high costs: the emerging pattern," *Journal of Accountancy*, Oct. 1949, pp. 302-10.

McNICHOLS, THOMAS J., and BOYD, F. VIRGIL, "Adjustment of fixed assets to reflect price level changes," *Accounting Review*, Jan. 1954, pp. 106-13.

MITCHELL, WESLEY C., "The making and using of index numbers," *BLS Bulletin 284*, 1921.

MOONITZ, MAURICE, "Adaptations to price-level changes," *Accounting Review*, Apr. 1948, pp. 136-47.

261

Moonitz, Maurice, "The basic postulates of accounting," *Accounting Research Study No. 1*. American Institute of Certified Public Accountants. 1961.

Mudgett, Bruce D., *Index Numbers*. John Wiley & Sons, Inc. 1951.

Paton, William A., "Cost and value in accounting," *Journal of Accountancy*, Mar. 1946, pp. 192-99.

Paton, William A., "Depreciation, appreciation and productive capacity," *Journal of Accountancy*, July 1920, pp. 1-11.

Paton, William A., "Measuring profits under inflation conditions: a serious problem for accountants," *Journal of Accountancy*, Jan. 1950, pp. 16-27.

Paton, William A., "Replacement value theory," (corresp.), *Journal of Accountancy*, Sept. 1960, pp. 31-33.

Paton, William A., Jr., *Study in Liquidity; the Impact of Inflation on Monetary Accounts*. Michigan Business Studies, v. 14, No. 2. University of Michigan. 1958.

Peloubet, Maurice E., "Indictment of the accounting profession for failing to deal with effects of inflation," *Journal of Accountancy*, Dec. 1953, pp. 714-22; and *Accountants Journal* (Eng.), Feb. 1954, pp. 39-42.

Peloubet, Maurice E., "Replacement value theory," (corresp.), *Journal of Accountancy*, Aug. 1960, pp. 27-28.

Ray, Delmas D., *Accounting and Business Fluctuations*. University of Florida Press. 1960.

Replacement Costs and Depreciation Policy. Studies in Business Policy, No. 27. National Industrial Conference Board, Inc. 1948.

Rice, Stuart A., Hinrichs, A. Ford, Tolley, Howard R., and Hauser, Philip M., "Problems of integrating Federal statistics," *Journal of the American Statistical Association*, June 1945, pp. 237-44.

Robertson, D. H., *Money*. University of Chicago Press. 1957.

Sanders, Thomas H., "Inflation and accounting," *Harvard Business Review*, May-June 1952, pp. 50-58.

Schiff, Michael, "Application of the price index adjustment concept to depreciation charges," *N.A.C.A. Bulletin*, sec. 1, Apr. 15, 1949, pp. 927-36.

Schiff, Michael, "What happens to depreciation," *Journal of Accountancy*, Mar. 1959, pp. 37-41.

Searle, Allan D., "Weight revisions in the Wholesale Price Index, 1890-1960," *Monthly Labor Review*, Feb. 1962, pp. 175-82.

Siegel, Irving H., "Index-number differences: geometric means," *Journal of the American Statistical Association*, June 1942, pp. 271-74.

Sih, S. T., "My experience in price-level adjustments," *Accounting Review*, Apr. 1955, pp. 282-83.

Smith, Charles W., "What concept of depreciation for fixed assets is most useful today?" *Journal of Accountancy*, Aug. 1951, pp. 166-74.

Smith, Dan Throop, "Business profits during inflation," *Harvard Business Review*, Mar. 1948, pp. 216-29.

262

SOCIETY OF INCORPORATED ACCOUNTANTS AND AUDITORS. "Accounting implications of changing money values," *Journal of Accountancy*, Feb. 1954, pp. 248, 250, and 252-53; and *Accountancy* (Eng.), Jan. 1954, pp. 7-8.

SOLOMONS, DAVID, "Accounting for changing price levels: recent British views," *Journal of Accountancy*, June 1954, pp. 702-07.

SPACEK, LEONARD, "Can we define generally accepted accounting principles?" *Journal of Accountancy*, Dec. 1958, pp. 40-47.

SPACEK, LEONARD, "Inflation in business," *Controller*, Dec. 1957, pp. 578-81, and 597.

SPROUSE, ROBERT L. and MOONITZ, MAURICE, "A tentative set of broad accounting principles for business enterprises," *Accounting Research Study No. 3*, American Institute of Certified Public Accountants. 1962.

STANS, MAURICE H., "AAA proposals offer practical suggestions for dealing with price level changes in accounting," *Journal of Accountancy*, Jan. 1952, pp. 52-59.

STANS, MAURICE H., "Problem of accounting and financial reporting in an inflationary period." An address before Graduate Study Conference for Accountants. Harvard University. Sept. 15, 16, 17, 1948.

STUDY GROUP ON BUSINESS INCOME, *Changing Concepts of Business Income*. Macmillan Co. 1952.

STUDY GROUP ON BUSINESS INCOME. *Five Monographs on Business Income*. American Institute of Certified Public Accountants. July 1, 1950.

SWEENEY, HENRY W., "Effects of inflation on German accounting," *Journal of Accountancy*, Mar. 1927, pp. 180-91.

SWEENEY, HENRY W., "German inflation accounting," *Journal of Accountancy*, Feb. 1928, pp. 104-16. Also see *Journal of Accountancy*, (corresp.), Apr. 1928, pp. 310-11.

SWEENEY, HENRY W., "How inflation affects balance sheets," *Accounting Review*, Dec. 1934, pp. 275-99.

SWEENEY, HENRY W., *Stabilized Accounting*. Harper & Row. 1936.

SWEENEY, HENRY W., "Stabilized depreciation," *Accounting Review*, Sept. 1931, pp. 165-78.

THOMAS, R. D., "Accounting for price level changes; recent accounting developments," *Canadian Chartered Accountant*, Jan. 1961, pp. 65-70.

TRUMBULL, WENDELL, P., "Price-level depreciation and replacement cost," *Accounting Review*, Jan. 1958, pp. 26-34.

UNITED STATES DEPARTMENT OF COMMERCE, BUREAU OF THE CENSUS. *Historical Statistics of the United States, 1789-1945* (a supplement to the *Statistical Abstract of the United States*). 1949.

UNITED STATES DEPARTMENT OF COMMERCE, BUREAU OF THE CENSUS. *Historical Statistics of the United States, Colonial Times to 1957* (a supplement to the *Statistical Abstract of the United States*). 1960.

UNITED STATES DEPARTMENT OF COMMERCE, OFFICE OF BUSINESS ECONOMICS. *Business Statistics* (a supplement to the *Survey of Current Business*). 1959.

263

UNITED STATES DEPARTMENT OF COMMERCE, OFFICE OF BUSINESS ECONOMICS. *National Income* (a supplement to the *Survey of Current Business*). 1954.

UNITED STATES DEPARTMENT OF COMMERCE, OFFICE OF BUSINESS ECONOMICS. *U.S. Income and Output* (a supplement to the *Survey of Current Business*). 1959.

UNITED STATES DEPARTMENT OF LABOR, BUREAU OF LABOR STATISTICS. "Wholesale price index." Reprint of Chapter 10, *BLS Bulletin 1168*.

VATTER, WILLIAM J., "Fund-theory view of price-level adjustments," *Accounting Review*, Apr. 1962, pp. 189-207.

WALSH, FRANCIS J., JR., *Inflation and Corporate Accounting*. National Industrial Conference Board. Business Policy Study No. 104. 1962.

WARNER, GEORGE H., "Depreciation on a current basis," *Accounting Review*, Oct. 1954, pp. 628-33.

WASSERMAN, MAX J., "Accounting practice in France during the period of monetary inflation (1919-1927)," *Accounting Review*, Mar. 1931, pp. 1-32.

WEINER, JOSEPH L., "Balance-sheet valuation in German law," *Journal of Accountancy*, Sept. 1929, pp. 195-206.

WESTFALL, OTHEL D., *Balance Sheet Price Level Analysis*, (privately printed), 1950.

WESTFALL, OTHEL D., "Pro-forma economic balance sheet; a clarification of the changing price level problem with suggestions for solution," (unpublished manuscript, 1948).

WESTON, FRANK T., "Monetary inflation and financial statements," *The Arthur Young Journal*, October 1962, pp. 1-15.

WILCOX, EDWARD B., "Fluctuating price levels in relation to accounts," *Handbook of Modern Accounting Theory*, Morton Backer, editor, chapter 9. Prentice-Hall, Inc. 1955.

WILCOX, EDWARD B., and GREER, HOWARD C., "Case against price-level adjustments in income determination" (with comments by George O. May), *Journal of Accountancy*, Dec. 1950, pp. 492-505.

WILK, LIONEL A., *Accounting for Inflation*. London: Sweet and Maxwell. 1960.

Index

265

266

267

269

272

Moonitz, Maurice
  See also Sprouse, Robert T. and
    Moonitz, Maurice
  "Basic postulates of accounting," a
    monograph, 2, 83, 111
Monetary gains (losses)
  See also Profits and losses
  accrual accounting, 43
  adjustment technique, 126
  articulated statements completely
    adjusted, 137
  calculation, 126, 145
  cut-off date, resulting inaccuracy,
    112
  hedge, 142
  materiality, 144
  measurement, 126
  monetary items, 24, 42
  net income measure, 24
  new category, 12
  realization, 42
  reporting, 13, 126, 149
    differences of opinion, 149
Monetary items
  See also Foreign monetary items
    adjustment technique, 126,
    129
  asset examples, 138
  concept, 138
  gains or losses, realized or unreal-
    ized, 42
  holding-gains (losses), 126
  in current dollars, 138
  liabilities, 139
  nonmonetary items distinguished,
    138
  payable in foreign currencies, 148
  preferred stock, 141
Monetary units, calculation monetary
  gains (losses), 145
Money, by D. H. Robertson, 9
Money
  See also Dollar
  a commodity, 18
  common denominator, 111
  exchange value, 9, 20
  exchange value, direct measure, 9

exchange value, indirect measure,
  10
gold standard act of 1900, 11
"neutral," 21
standard of value, 18
"Money illusion," accounting prin-
  ciples, 14
Money illusion, by Irving Fisher, 62
Money supply, rate of growth, 80
Montecatini Mining and Chemical
  Company (Italy), 170, 202
Monthly labor review, 72, 90
  Statistical supplement, 72
Mudgett, Bruce D.
  Index numbers, 97
Muller, Wm. H. and Co. (The Nether-
  lands), 172, 218
McMullen, Stewart Y.
  See Kennedy, Ralph D. and
    McMullen, Stewart Y.
McNichols, Thomas J., and Boyd, F.
  Virgil
  "Adjustment of fixed assets to re-
    flect price level changes," an
    article, 245

National Bureau of Economic Research, 90, 108, 109, 113, 114
  national accounts review commit-
    tee, 109
  price statistics review committee,
    90, 108
National economic accounts of the
  United States, hearings before
  the subcommittee on economic
  statistics, 109
National income, supplement to the
  Survey of Current Business, U.S.
  Department of Commerce, 111
National income and product accounting
  consolidated earnings statements,
    83
  economic policy tool, 110
National Industrial Conference Board,
  33, 113
  Inflation and corporate accounting,
    a pamphlet, 33

275

277

278